hanley▲wood
HomePlanners

325
NEW HOME PLANS
FOR 2005

TOP DESIGNS FROM 1,000 TO 5,500 SQUARE FEET

325
NEW HOME PLANS
FOR 2005

Published by Home Planners, LLC
Wholly Owned by Hanley-Wood, LLC
One Thomas Circle, NW, Suite 600
Washington, DC 20005

DISTRIBUTION CENTER
29333 Lorie Lane
Wixom, Michigan 48393

Group Vice President, General Manager, Andrew Schultz
Vice President, Publishing, Jennifer Pearce
Executive Editor, Linda Bellamy
Managing Editor, Jason D. Vaughan
Editor, Nate Ewell
Associate Editor, Simon Hyoun
Lead Plan Merchandiser, Morenci C. Clark
Plan Merchandiser, Nicole Phipps
Proofreader/Copywriter, Dyana Weis
Graphic Artist, Joong Min
Plan Data Team Leader, Ryan Emge
Production Manager, Brenda McClary

Vice President, Retail Sales, Scott Hill
National Sales Manager, Bruce Holmes
Director, Plan Products, Matt Higgins

For direct sales, contact Retail Vision at (800) 381-1288 ext 6053

BIG DESIGNS, INC.
President, Creative Director, Anthony D'Elia
Vice President, Business Manager, Megan D'Elia
Vice President, Design Director, Chris Bonavita
Editorial Director, John Roach
Assistant Editor, Tricia Starkey
Senior Art Director, Stephen Reinfurt
Production Director, David Barbella
Photo Editor, Christine DiVuolo
Art Director, Jessica Hagenbuch
Graphic Designer, Mary Ellen Mulshine
Graphic Designer, Lindsey O'Neill-Myers
Graphic Designer, Jacque Young
Assistant Photo Editor, Brian Wilson
Assistant Production Manager, Rich Fuentes

PHOTO CREDITS
Front Cover Top and Title Page: Design HPK0100016 (p. 8) by Studer Residential Designs, photo by Exposures Unlimited, Ron & Donna Kolb
Front Cover Bottom Left: Design HPK0100010 (p. 9) by Donald A. Gardner Architects, Inc., photo by ©2003 Donald A. Gardner, Inc.
Front Cover Bottom Right and Facing Page Top: Design HPK0100005 (p. 6) by Studer Residential Designs, photo by Exposures Unlimited, Ron & Donna Kolb
Facing Page Bottom: Design HPK0100015 (p. 7) by Historical Replications, photo by Cecelia Reese-Bullock
Back Cover: Design HPK0100014 (p. 5) by Living Concepts Home Planning, Inc., photo by Living Concepts Home Planning

10 9 8 7 6 5 4 3 2 1

Library of Congress Catalog Control Number: 2004106183

ISBN: 1-931131-27-9

325
NEW HOME PLANS
FOR 2005

4	INTRODUCTION
5	NEW DESIGN SHOWCASE
17	SUMMER HOMES & COTTAGES
49	RUSTIC GETAWAYS & RETREATS
67	FARMHOUSES & RANCHES
111	URBAN DESIGNS & TRADITIONALS
155	COLONIALS & HISTORICAL HOUSES
195	ENGLISH & PROVENCAL MANORS
223	MEDITERRANEAN & SPANISH STYLES
249	HOW TO ORDER

ON THE COVER Clockwise from top: modern design with sun-loving windows and balconies, HPK0100016 (p. 8); charming gables for curbside appeal, HPK0100010 (p. 9); cottage with stone accents and European-style turret, HPK0100005 (p. 6).

Welcome

The book you're holding contains this year's best home designs, created by America's most celebrated and trusted architects. The plans are for homes ranging in size from under 900 to over 6,000 total square feet, in the styles most preferred by this year's home builders. In short, *325 New Home Plans for 2005* is your best bet for finding a design that fits your taste and respects your budget.

The book is divided into eight sections. The New Design showcase, which begins on the next page, highlights the hottest new plans available today. Summer Homes & Cottages offers an array of choices, from cozy bungalows to comfortable cottages, and you'll find plenty of Craftsman-style designs in Rustic Getaways & Retreats. And Farmhouses & Ranches features inviting designs of these very popular and versatile American homes.

Builders preferring more metropolitan architecture should consult Urban Designs & Traditionals, and admirers of classical designs will find inspiration in Colonials & Manors and in English & Provencal Manors. Finally, we offer Mediterranean & Spanish Styles for those living in warm climates—or just wish they were.

Once you find a plan you like, follow the instructions on page 248, which also offer tips, a price schedule, and other useful information. At this point, you may also want to consider a deck or landscape plans to complement your new home. Finally, go to page 254 and call 1-800-521-6797 to place your order! ∎

PHOTOGRAPHY BY EXPOSURES UNLIMITED, RON & DONNA KOLB

A mixture of exterior materials enhances the curb appeal of this hillside home, while a large deck, screened porch and patio promote outdoor living. See HPK0100010 on page 9 for details.

plan# HPK0100014

STYLE: FRENCH COUNTRY
MAIN LEVEL: 2,981 SQ. FT.
UPPER LEVEL: 1,017 SQ. FT.
LOWER LEVEL: 1,471 SQ. FT.
TOTAL: 5,469 SQ. FT.
BEDROOMS: 4
BATHROOMS: 4½ + ½
WIDTH: 79' - 4"
DEPTH: 91' - 0"
FOUNDATION: BASEMENT

SEARCH ONLINE @ EPLANS.COM

Majestic through and through, this stately home enjoys a stone exterior inspired by classical French architecture. In the center of the main floor the conservatory and elegant formal dining room reign. The massive country kitchen flows easily into the family room and the casual eating area. It also enjoys a butler's pantry leading to the dining room and a walk-in pantry. An exercise room and resplendent bath are found in the master suite, also on this level. Two more suites with private baths share a sitting room upstairs. The finished basement includes another bedroom suite, a recreation room, office, storage, and a book niche. Additional room is available for setting up a workshop.

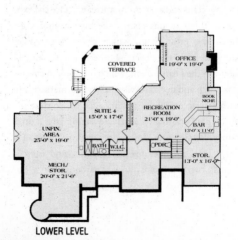

LOWER LEVEL

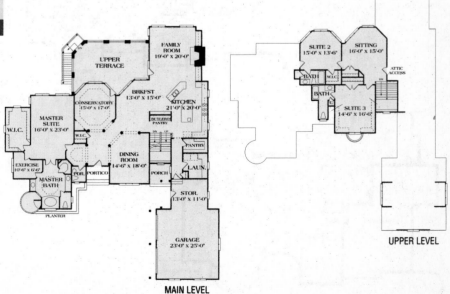

MAIN LEVEL

UPPER LEVEL

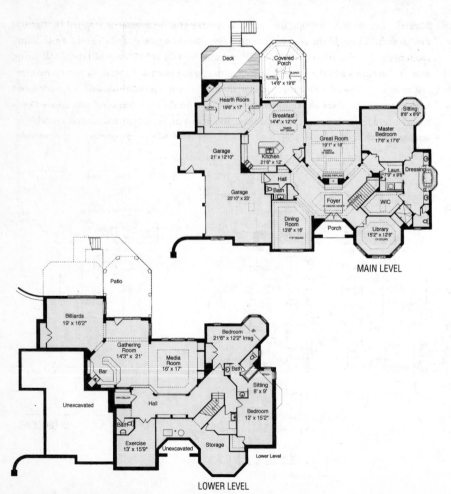

MAIN LEVEL

LOWER LEVEL

plan# HPK0100005

STYLE: EUROPEAN COTTAGE
MAIN LEVEL: 2,961 SQ. FT.
LOWER LEVEL: 2,416 SQ. FT.
TOTAL: 5,377 SQ. FT.
BEDROOMS: 3
BATHROOMS: 2½ + ½
WIDTH: 89' - 0"
DEPTH: 59' - 2"
FOUNDATION: BASEMENT

SEARCH ONLINE @ EPLANS.COM

Stone accents and a charming turret enhance the exterior of this spacious plan. A beamed ceiling highlights the great room, which shares a two-sided fireplace with the foyer; another fireplace can be found in the hearth room, which overlooks a covered rear porch and deck area. A resplendent master suite, with easy access to the laundry area, sits to the right of the plan and boasts a private sitting bay, a dual-vanity dressing area, and a large walk-in closet. The lower level includes media, billiards, and exercise rooms, two bedrooms, and a gathering area that opens to a patio.

plan# HPK0100015

STYLE: VICTORIAN
FIRST FLOOR: 1,266 SQ. FT.
SECOND FLOOR: 1,482 SQ. FT.
TOTAL: 2,748 SQ. FT.
BEDROOMS: 3
BATHROOMS: 2½
WIDTH: 42' - 6"
DEPTH: 50' - 6"
FOUNDATION: CRAWLSPACE

SEARCH ONLINE @ EPLANS.COM

If you've dreamed about living in a classic Victorian home with all the modern amenities, this is the house for you. Complete with a front tower, a captain's deck, and a wraparound porch this is an impressive plan. The two-story entry hallway leads into a comfortable living area that includes a great room with a fireplace flanked by windows. To the right, a kitchen that will delight any chef, if only for the ample counter space, is located between a dining room and breakfast area with a wall of windows. The upstairs master suite is regal in its grandeur. Most striking is the oversize tub located in the tower and surrounded by three windows. The master bedroom enjoys an array of windows including a bay window that illuminates the room. Two other bedrooms share a bath.

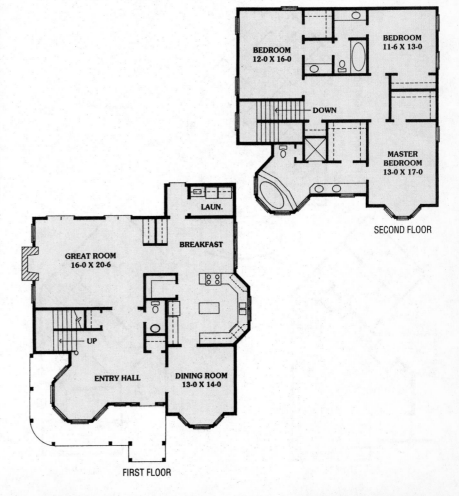

BEDROOM 12-0 X 16-0
BEDROOM 11-6 X 13-0
DOWN
MASTER BEDROOM 13-0 X 17-0
SECOND FLOOR

LAUN.
BREAKFAST
GREAT ROOM 16-0 X 20-6
UP
ENTRY HALL
DINING ROOM 13-0 X 14-0
FIRST FLOOR

UPPER LEVEL

LOWER LEVEL

MAIN LEVEL

plan # HPK0100016

STYLE: CONTEMPORARY
MAIN LEVEL: 1,227 SQ. FT.
UPPER LEVEL: 1,575 SQ. FT.
LOWER LEVEL: 1,069 SQ. FT.
TOTAL: 3,871 SQ. FT.
BEDROOMS: 3
BATHROOMS: 3
WIDTH: 41' - 10"
DEPTH: 73' - 0"
FOUNDATION: BASEMENT

SEARCH ONLINE @ EPLANS.COM

This beautiful home combines design, comfort, and luxury into an exquisite package. The entry at the side of the home introduces a foyer, library, and spectacular master bedroom suite with deluxe amenities. Split stairs adorned with wrought iron and wood trim directs you to the lower level where a fun game room, media area, and wet bar cluster around the wall of windows; or to the upper level where you will be dazzled by the beauty of the great room, dining room, and gourmet kitchen. An elevator is located at the rear for ease of movement between floors. An arts & crafts motif reflects clean lines reminiscent of turn of the century styling.

plan# HPK0100010

STYLE: CRAFTSMAN
MAIN LEVEL: 1,728 SQ. FT.
LOWER LEVEL: 915 SQ. FT.
TOTAL: 2,643 SQ. FT.
BEDROOMS: 3
BATHROOMS: 3
WIDTH: 70' - 6"
DEPTH: 59' - 6"

SEARCH ONLINE @ EPLANS.COM

A mixture of exterior materials enhances the curb appeal of this hillside home, while a large deck, screened porch and patio promote outdoor living. With the rear wall comprised of windows and French doors, both levels receive an abundance of natural light and take advantage of expansive views. A cathedral ceiling with exposed beams crowns the kitchen and great room, creating voluminous spaces. Built-in cabinetry, a versatile study/bedroom, sizable utility room, and home office all add convenience. The master suite is complete with a tray ceiling in the bedroom, French door leading to the screened porch, dual walk-in closets, and an exquisite bath.

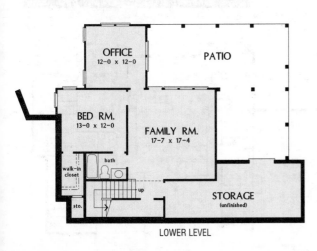

LOWER LEVEL

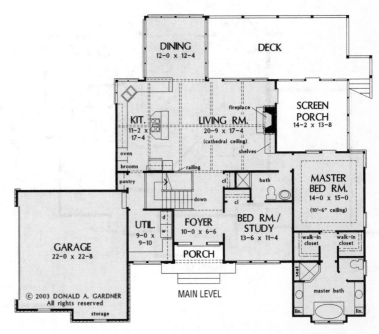

MAIN LEVEL

PHOTOGRAPHY BY EXPOSURES UNLIMITED. RON & DONNA KOLB
THIS HOME, AS SHOWN IN THE PHOTOGRAPH, MAY DIFFER FROM THE ACTUAL BLUEPRINTS.

A brick, stone, and shake-shingle facade makes this beautiful home a perfect choice for any neighborhood. A large great room, breakfast area, and kitchen create a comfortable and inviting atmosphere. Columns introduce the great room from the foyer, and 12-foot high ceilings top the great room, breakfast area, kitchen, dining room, and master bedroom. Formal dining is available for special occasions. A covered deck with fireplace and built-in grill offers stylish outdoor living. Angled stairs lead to a lower level where a large party room offers a bar, billiards area, recreation room, and media room. Additional bedrooms are available for the occasional overnight guest.

plan # HPK0100017

STYLE: CRAFTSMAN
MAIN LEVEL: 3,171 SQ. FT.
LOWER LEVEL: 1,897 SQ. FT.
TOTAL: 5,068 SQ. FT.
BEDROOMS: 5
BATHROOMS: 3½
WIDTH: 86' - 2"
DEPTH: 63' - 8"
FOUNDATION: BASEMENT

SEARCH ONLINE @ EPLANS.COM

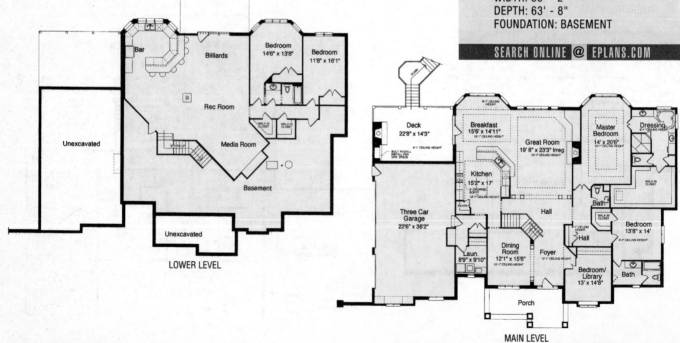

LOWER LEVEL

MAIN LEVEL

plan# HPK0100018

STYLE: CRAFTSMAN
FIRST FLOOR: 1,846 SQ. FT.
SECOND FLOOR: 1,309 SQ. FT.
TOTAL: 3,155 SQ. FT.
BONUS SPACE: 563 SQ. FT.
BEDROOMS: 4
BATHROOMS: 3½
WIDTH: 77' - 6"
DEPTH: 48' - 8"
FOUNDATION: CRAWLSPACE

Rustic Craftsman design meets luxury-size accommodations in this roomy rambler. Space abounds in the hearth-warmed vaulted great room, which flows into the huge kitchen and dining area. A bayed window nook with access to the rear property opens this area to the outdoors. For cozier times, retire to the front den that looks out to the wraparound porch. A huge laundry room and convenient spare bedroom round out the first floor. Upstairs, a deluxe master suite with a spa tub is joined by two family bedrooms, another bath, and a study. Bonus space on the left awaits your expansion plans.

SECOND FLOOR

FIRST FLOOR

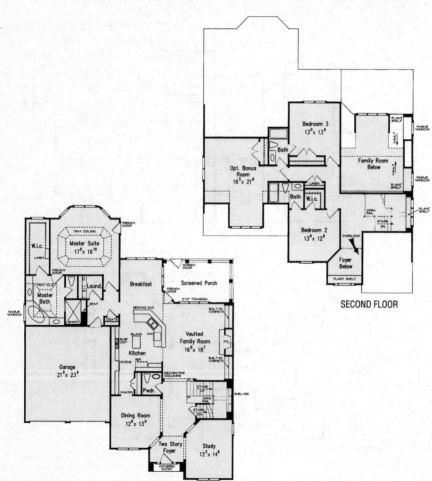

FIRST FLOOR

SECOND FLOOR

plan# HPK0100019

STYLE: COUNTRY COTTAGE
FIRST FLOOR: 2,101 SQ. FT.
SECOND FLOOR: 708 SQ. FT.
TOTAL: 2,809 SQ. FT.
BONUS SPACE: 347 SQ. FT.
BEDROOMS: 3
BATHROOMS: 3½
WIDTH: 54' - 0"
DEPTH: 68' - 0"
FOUNDATION: BASEMENT,
CRAWLSPACE, SLAB

SEARCH ONLINE @ EPLANS.COM

Colonial brick and country shingles combine for a unique family home that fits well on any street. An angled foyer makes a lovely entry; formal rooms on either side—a dining room and handsome study/living room—are perfect for entertaining. Continue past an open-rail staircase to the vaulted family room with a fireplace and access to the rear screened porch. The kitchen is long and open, equipped with an island, serving bar, and miles of counter space. Just past the breakfast nook, the master suite enjoys a private retreat with a grand bay window and pampering bath. Upper-level bedrooms are furnished with private baths and share an optional bonus space.

plan# HPK0100020

STYLE: CRAFTSMAN
FIRST FLOOR: 1,249 SQ. FT.
SECOND FLOOR: 1,458 SQ. FT.
TOTAL: 2,707 SQ. FT.
BEDROOMS: 4
BATHROOMS: 2½
WIDTH: 57' - 4"
DEPTH: 39' - 0"
FOUNDATION: BASEMENT, CRAWLSPACE

SEARCH ONLINE @ EPLANS.COM

Stylish windows and rooflines on the exterior and elegant arches inside reflect the designer's goal of giving you a good-looking, comfortable home. From the two-story foyer enter the formal living and dining rooms through wide arched entries. Straight ahead another arched entry takes you into the family room. The family room, breakfast area, and kitchen are a trio running along the entire rear of the plan; a classy arch marks the line between the family room and the others. Upstairs, the bright and airy master suite enjoys a vaulted sitting area and private access to a covered porch. Three more bedrooms, a bath, and a convenient laundry are also situated on this floor. The two-car garage can be accessed from either the kitchen or the dining room.

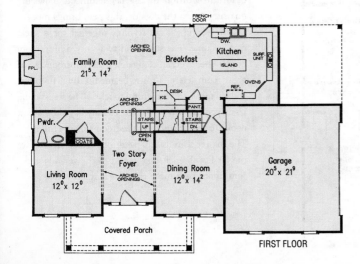

FIRST FLOOR

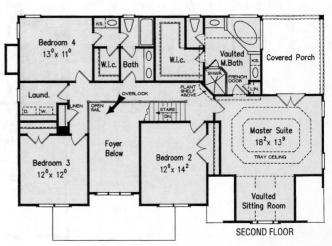

SECOND FLOOR

© The Sater Design Collection, Inc.

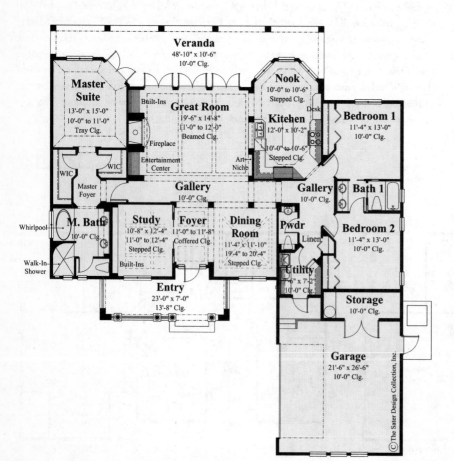

plan# HPK0100021

STYLE: ITALIANATE
SQUARE FOOTAGE: 2,191
BEDROOMS: 3
BATHROOMS: 2½
WIDTH: 62' - 10"
DEPTH: 73' - 6"
FOUNDATION: SLAB

SEARCH ONLINE @ EPLANS.COM

Perfect for a corner lot, this Mediterranean villa is a beautiful addition to any neighborhood. Low and unassuming on the outside, this plan brings modern amenities and classic stylings together for a great family home. The study and two-story dining room border the foyer; an elongated gallery introduces the great room. Here, a rustic beamed ceiling, fireplace, and art niche are thoughtful touches. The step-saving U-shaped kitchen flows into a sunny bayed breakfast nook. To the far right, two bedrooms share a full bath. The master suite is separated for privacy, situated to the far left. French-door access to the veranda and a sumptuous bath make this a pleasurable retreat.

plan # HPK0100022

STYLE: FLORIDIAN
FIRST FLOOR: 2,504 SQ. FT.
SECOND FLOOR: 640 SQ. FT.
TOTAL: 3,144 SQ. FT.
BEDROOMS: 4
BATHROOMS: 3
WIDTH: 77' - 6"
DEPTH: 70' - 0"
FOUNDATION: SLAB

SEARCH ONLINE @ EPLANS.COM

Textured stucco and tasteful brick accents announce a captivating home that was made for luxury living. The formal foyer opens on the right to a banquet-size dining room with patio access, expanding entertaining options. Both the living room and dining room feature arched entrances to the family gathering areas. The kitchen is well designed with an island counter with a double sink and a separate cooktop island. The light-filled family room capitalizes on a corner fireplace. Up three steps are two generous secondary bedrooms and a full bath. The master suite is secluded on the left, outfitted with patio access and a dazzling spa bath. A fourth bedroom and loft area join a patio on the upper level.

FIRST FLOOR

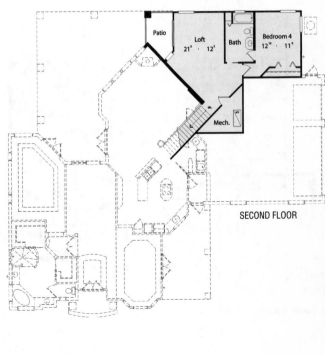

SECOND FLOOR

Colonial architecture, like this elegant home, lends a classic air to any neighborhood. The interior offers a completely modern arrangement with the dramatic foyer opening to the spectacular living room with its window wall, cathedral ceiling, and stunning fireplace. To the left, the kitchen is central to the more intimate family/sunroom and breakfast area. The formal dining room, to the left of the foyer, completes the living area. The sleeping quarters on the right include two bedrooms and a romantic master suite with its plush private bath.

plan# HPK0100023

STYLE: COLONIAL
SQUARE FOOTAGE: 2,639
BONUS SPACE: 396 SQ. FT.
BEDROOMS: 3
BATHROOMS: 2½
WIDTH: 73' - 8"
DEPTH: 58' - 6"
FOUNDATION: CRAWLSPACE

SEARCH ONLINE @ EPLANS.COM

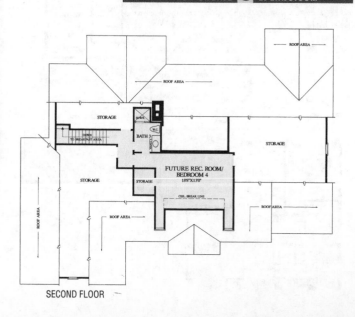

FIRST FLOOR

SECOND FLOOR

© 2001 Donald A. Gardner, Inc.

plan# HPK0100024

STYLE: EUROPEAN COTTAGE
FIRST FLOOR: 1,547 SQ. FT.
SECOND FLOOR: 684 SQ. FT.
TOTAL: 2,231 SQ. FT.
BONUS SPACE: 300 SQ. FT.
BEDROOMS: 3
BATHROOMS: 2½
WIDTH: 59' - 2"
DEPTH: 44' - 4"

SEARCH ONLINE @ EPLANS.COM

Stone and siding create a stunning exterior, especially when combined with a sloped roofline and a decorative wood bracket. A metal roof embellishes the garage's box-bay window, and arches are seen in and above windows as well as the front entrance. The great room is filled with light from its many windows and French doors, and a glimpse of the fireplace can be seen from every gathering room. The master bedroom is topped by a cathedral ceiling and has a large walk-in closet. The loft makes a perfect sitting or study area that receives a lot of light from the open, two-story great room. The second floor bathroom includes twin lavatories, and the versatile bonus room is easily accessible.

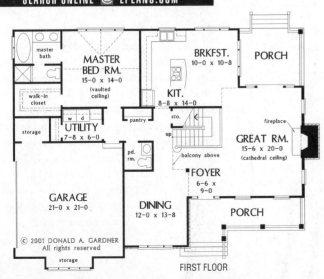

FIRST FLOOR

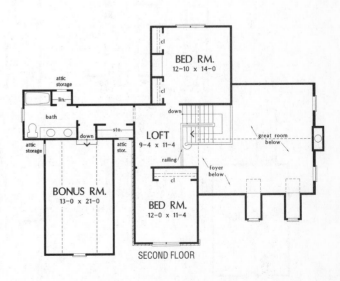

SECOND FLOOR

© 2003 Donald A. Gardner, Inc.

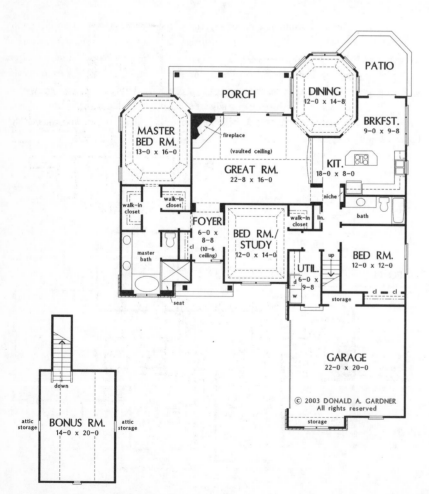

plan# HPK0100011

STYLE: CRAFTSMAN
SQUARE FOOTAGE: 1,929
BONUS SPACE: 335 SQ. FT.
BEDROOMS: 3
BATHROOMS: 2
WIDTH: 54' - 8"
DEPTH: 68' - 4"

SEARCH ONLINE @ EPLANS.COM

A hip-pitched roof, stone, and siding create cottage charm. Arches contrast with gables to provide architectural interest, and custom transoms usher in natural light. Tray ceilings crown the study/bedroom, dining room, and master bedroom; a vaulted ceiling tops the great room, which includes French doors and a corner fireplace. A cooktop island keeps the kitchen open and adds convenience, and a private patio is adjacent to the breakfast nook. Expanded by a bay, the master suite is positioned for privacy. With access to a rear porch and two walk-in closets, this luxurious retreat pampers with a double vanity, garden tub, shower with seat, and compartmented toilet.

© 2003 Donald A. Gardner, Inc.

plan# HPK0100025

STYLE: COUNTRY
FIRST FLOOR: 1,972 SQ. FT.
SECOND FLOOR: 721 SQ. FT.
TOTAL: 2,693 SQ. FT.
BONUS SPACE: 377 SQ. FT.
BEDROOMS: 4
BATHROOMS: 3
WIDTH: 77' - 4"
DEPTH: 50' - 8"

SEARCH ONLINE @ EPLANS.COM

This farmhouse has a touch of low-country flair. Columns and dormers accent a deep porch, and gables and half-circle transoms add angles and soft curves for architectural interest. Floor space is expanded by bay windows, which usher light into the home. Convenient features such as a central kitchen island, large utility room/mudroom, and two built-in desks in the secondary bedrooms make living easier for active families. The master suite includes a tray ceiling, dual walk-ins, and a private bath. A versatile study/bedroom and bonus room adapt as your family grows.

SECOND FLOOR

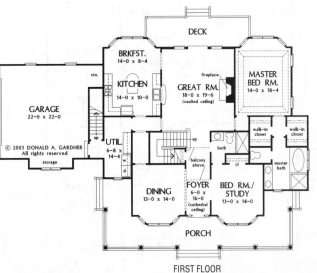

FIRST FLOOR

© 2003 Donald A. Gardner, Inc.

Brick and siding combine curb appeal with low maintenance. A Palladian window and bold columns add classic architectural interest. A sidelight and transom highlight the front door and allow natural light into the home. With tray ceilings in the dining room and master bedroom, along with a vaulted ceiling in the study/bedroom, this home showcases custom-styled elements. The family-efficient floor plan defines rooms without enclosing space. Note the savings on plumbing by having the kitchen, utility room, and master bath adjacent to each other; for future expansion purposes the bonus room staircase is located off the kitchen and garage, making the space perfect for a recreation room, home office, or gym.

plan# HPK0100026

STYLE: TRADITIONAL
SQUARE FOOTAGE: 1,486
BONUS SPACE: 341 SQ. FT.
BEDROOMS: 3
BATHROOMS: 2
WIDTH: 52' - 3"
DEPTH: 46' - 10"

SEARCH ONLINE @ EPLANS.COM

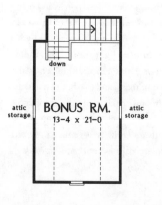

© 2002 Donald A. Gardner, Inc.

plan # HPK0100027

STYLE: TRADITIONAL
SQUARE FOOTAGE: 1,789
BONUS SPACE: 312 SQ. FT.
BEDROOMS: 3
BATHROOMS: 2
WIDTH: 39' - 0"
DEPTH: 79' - 4"

SEARCH ONLINE @ EPLANS.COM

Here's a narrow-lot home with a convenient front-entry garage. Columns make a statement outside and inside the home. A rear dormer above a set of French doors fill the great room with light, and the screened porch is perfectly positioned for outdoor entertaining. The bonus room can be easily entered from the common living areas and would make a great home theater, gym, or playroom for the kids. A cathedral ceiling in the great room and vaulted ceilings in the master bedroom and dining room add visual space as well as beauty. An angled counter keeps the cook in the heart of conversation and allows the kitchen to remain open to the great room.

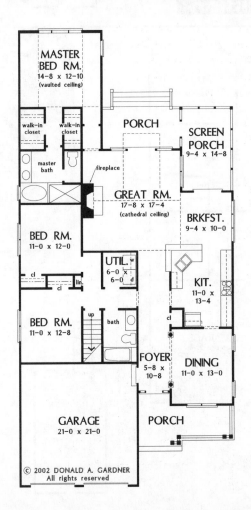

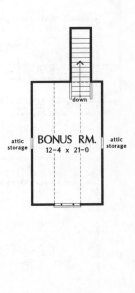

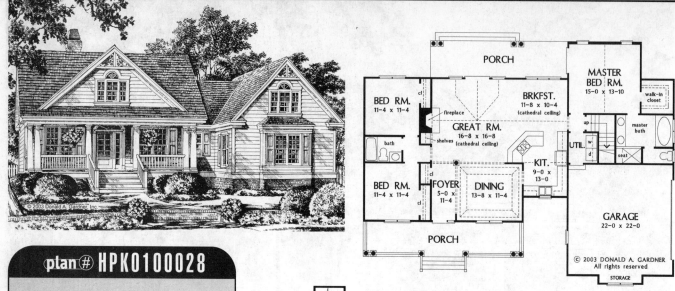

BED RM.
11-4 x 11-4

BED RM.
11-4 x 11-4

bath

cl

FOYER
5-0 x
11-4

DINING
13-8 x 11-4

PORCH

fireplace

shelves

GREAT RM.
16-8 x 16-8
(cathedral ceiling)

BRKFST.
11-8 x 10-4
(cathedral ceiling)

KIT.
9-0 x
13-0

UTIL.
w
d

seat

up

MASTER
BED RM.
15-0 x 13-10

walk-in
closet

master
bath

GARAGE
22-0 x 22-0

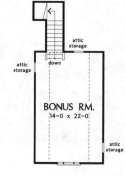

PORCH

STORAGE

plan # HPK0100028

STYLE: COUNTRY
SQUARE FOOTAGE: 1,660
BONUS SPACE: 374 SQ. FT.
BEDROOMS: 3
BATHROOMS: 2
WIDTH: 65' - 4"
DEPTH: 48' - 8"

SEARCH ONLINE @ EPLANS.COM

attic
storage

attic
storage

down

BONUS RM.
14-0 x 22-0

attic
storage

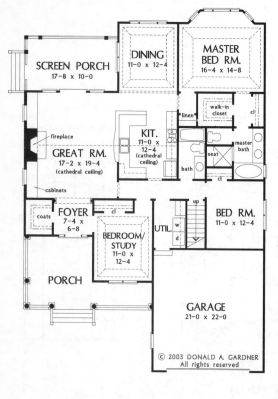

SCREEN PORCH
17-8 x 10-0

DINING
11-0 x 12-4

MASTER
BED RM.
16-4 x 14-8

fireplace

GREAT RM.
17-2 x 19-4
(cathedral ceiling)

cabinets

KIT.
11-0 x
12-4
(cathedral
ceiling)

linen

walk-in
closet

cl

bath

master
bath

seat

FOYER
7-4 x
6-8

coats

cl

BEDROOM/
STUDY
11-0 x
12-4

UTIL.
w
d

up

BED RM.
11-0 x 12-4

PORCH

GARAGE
21-0 x 22-0

down

attic
storage

attic
storage

BONUS RM.
13-4 x 22-0

plan # HPK0100029

STYLE: TRADITIONAL
SQUARE FOOTAGE: 1,727
BONUS SPACE: 346 SQ. FT.
BEDROOMS: 3
BATHROOMS: 2
WIDTH: 46' - 0"
DEPTH: 66' - 4"

SEARCH ONLINE @ EPLANS.COM

ORDER BLUEPRINTS 24 HOURS, 7 DAYS A WEEK, AT 1-800-521-6797

© 2002 Donald A. Gardner, Inc.

plan# HPK0100030

STYLE: CRAFTSMAN
SQUARE FOOTAGE: 1,952
BONUS SPACE: 339 SQ. FT.
BEDROOMS: 4
BATHROOMS: 3
WIDTH: 50' - 0"
DEPTH: 60' - 0"

SEARCH ONLINE @ EPLANS.COM

As at home in a development as it is in an orchard, this design combines country charm with Craftsman appeal. A Palladian-style window fills the study/bedroom with light, and a stone wall and cozy front porch recall times past. A sole column and tray ceiling distinguish the dining room that opens to a great room, which features French doors to the rear porch and a striking two-room fireplace. An angled counter separates the kitchen from the great room and breakfast nook. With a master bath, two full additional baths, an optional study/bedroom, and a bonus room, this home has plenty of space for growing families.

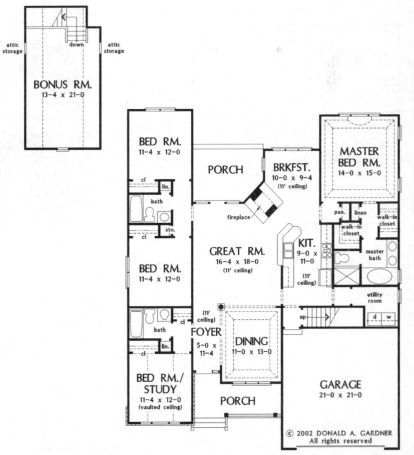

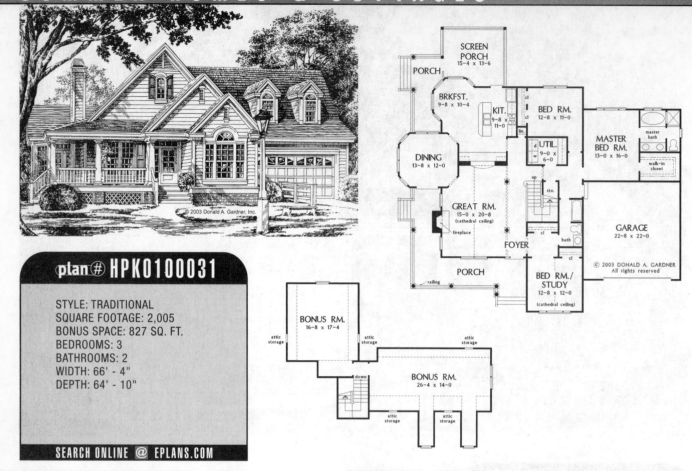

© 2003 Donald A. Gardner, Inc.

SCREEN PORCH
15-4 x 13-6

PORCH

BRKFST.
9-8 x 10-4

KIT.
9-8 x 11-0

BED RM.
12-8 x 11-0

UTIL.
9-0 x 6-0

MASTER BED RM.
13-0 x 16-0

master bath

walk-in closet

DINING
13-8 x 12-0

GREAT RM.
15-0 x 20-8
(cathedral ceiling)

fireplace

up

sto.

bath

GARAGE
22-8 x 22-0

© 2003 DONALD A. GARDNER
All rights reserved

FOYER

PORCH

railing

BED RM./ STUDY
12-8 x 12-0
(cathedral ceiling)

BONUS RM.
16-8 x 17-4

attic storage

attic storage

attic storage

down

BONUS RM.
26-4 x 14-0

attic storage

attic storage

plan ⊕ HPK0100031

STYLE: TRADITIONAL
SQUARE FOOTAGE: 2,005
BONUS SPACE: 827 SQ. FT.
BEDROOMS: 3
BATHROOMS: 2
WIDTH: 66' - 4"
DEPTH: 64' - 10"

SEARCH ONLINE @ EPLANS.COM

MASTER BED RM.
15-8 x 13-0
(cathedral ceiling)

walk-in closet

master bath

KIT.
11-0 x 13-4

PORCH

GREAT RM.
15-0 x 18-0
(cathedral ceiling)

fireplace

BED RM.
11-0 x 12-0

up

UTIL.
d 6-0
w 7-4

DINING
11-0 x 12-0

lin.

cl

bath

FOYER
5-0 x 5-0

GARAGE
21-0 x 22-0

PORCH

BED RM./ STUDY
11-0 x 12-0
(cathedral ceiling)

cl

© 2003 DONALD A. GARDNER
All rights reserved

down

BONUS RM.
13-0 x 22-0

attic storage

attic storage

© 2003 Donald A. Gardner, Inc.

plan ⊕ HPK0100032

STYLE: TRADITIONAL
SQUARE FOOTAGE: 1,535
BONUS SPACE: 355 SQ. FT.
BEDROOMS: 3
BATHROOMS: 2
WIDTH: 59' - 8"
DEPTH: 47' - 4"

SEARCH ONLINE @ EPLANS.COM

© 2003 Donald A. Gardner, Inc.

plan# HPK0100033

STYLE: TRADITIONAL
FIRST FLOOR: 1,408 SQ. FT.
SECOND FLOOR: 476 SQ. FT.
TOTAL: 1,884 SQ. FT.
BEDROOMS: 3
BATHROOMS: 2½
WIDTH: 41' - 8"
DEPTH: 56' - 4"

SEARCH ONLINE @ EPLANS.COM

If there's a narrow-lot home that provides a lot of living for its square footage, this is it. While a front-entry garage provides convenience, a spacious patio encourages outdoor relaxation. With a central hall dividing the common rooms from the sleeping quarters, the floor plan marries openness with privacy. Both the foyer and great room have two-story ceilings, which expand visual space; a bay window with a seat extends the breakfast nook. The dining room is topped by a cathedral ceiling. In the master suite, a tray ceiling crowns the bedroom. The master bath includes a double vanity, garden tub, shower with seat, and a compartmented toilet.

SECOND FLOOR

FIRST FLOOR

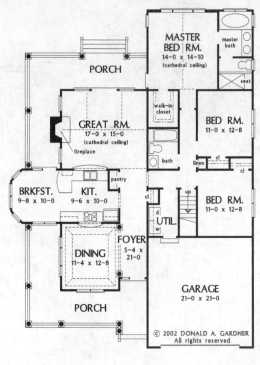

plan# HPK0100034

STYLE: TRADITIONAL
SQUARE FOOTAGE: 1,700
BONUS SPACE: 333 SQ. FT.
BEDROOMS: 3
BATHROOMS: 2
WIDTH: 49' - 0"
DEPTH: 65' - 4"

SEARCH ONLINE @ EPLANS.COM

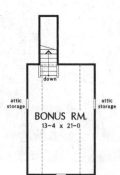
BONUS RM.
13-4 x 21-0

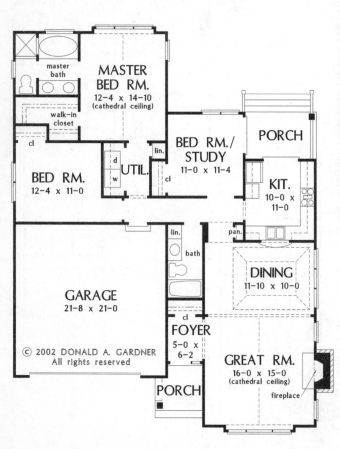

plan# HPK0100035

STYLE: CRAFTSMAN
SQUARE FOOTAGE: 1,472
BEDROOMS: 3
BATHROOMS: 2
WIDTH: 46' - 6"
DEPTH: 56' - 4"

SEARCH ONLINE @ EPLANS.COM

plan# HPK0100036

STYLE: CRAFTSMAN
SQUARE FOOTAGE: 2,818
BEDROOMS: 4
BATHROOMS: 3
WIDTH: 70' - 0"
DEPTH: 69' - 10"

SEARCH ONLINE @ EPLANS.COM

Promoting easy living, this home has plenty of Craftsman character with a low-maintenance exterior. Doubled columns and stone accents create architectural interest. Inside, columns and a tray ceiling distinguish the dining room, and beautiful double doors open into the study/bedroom. Art niches, fireplaces, and built-in cabinetry add beauty and convenience. The kitchen has a handy pass-through to the great room. The spacious deck accommodates outdoor living. The master suite has a bayed sitting area and French doors that lead to the deck. The master bath is equipped with a double vanity, garden tub, and shower with a shelf and seat.

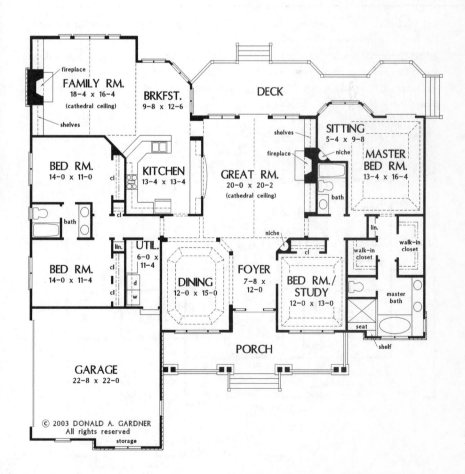

© 2002 Donald A. Gardner, Inc.

Elegant detail brings a sense of fresh refinement to this old-fashioned farmhouse. Gingerbread-style ornamentation on the gables combines with shutters and fanlight windows on the facade. Inside, the hearth-warmed great room—which accesses the rear porch—and open kitchen will be the center of family life. Dine in the bayed breakfast nook or the tray-ceilinged formal dining room. Two bedrooms share a bath on the left of the plan. A deluxe master suite, complete with a spacious bath and walk-in closet, takes up the right wing. A utility room and half-bath are convenient to both the kitchen and two-car garage. Bonus space upstairs awaits expansion.

plan# HPK0100037

STYLE: TRADITIONAL
SQUARE FOOTAGE: 2,037
BONUS SPACE: 361 SQ. FT.
BEDROOMS: 3
BATHROOMS: 2½
WIDTH: 62' - 4"
DEPTH: 61' - 8"

SEARCH ONLINE @ EPLANS.COM

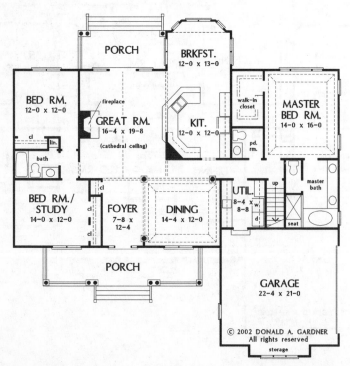

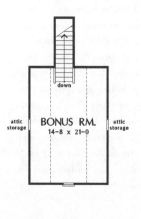

plan # HPK0100038

STYLE: TRADITIONAL
FIRST FLOOR: 1,569 SQ. FT.
SECOND FLOOR: 504 SQ. FT.
TOTAL: 2,073 SQ. FT.
BONUS SPACE: 320 SQ. FT.
BEDROOMS: 3
BATHROOMS: 2½
WIDTH: 47' - 0"
DEPTH: 55' - 0"

SEARCH ONLINE @ EPLANS.COM

Low-maintenance siding, a convenient front-entry garage, and architectural details such as gables and half-circle transoms make this narrow-lot charmer perfect for beginning families and empty-nesters. An abundance of windows and an open floor plan flood this home with natural light. Custom-styled features include a fireplace, two-story great room ceiling, kitchen pass-through, and French doors leading to the rear porch. The master suite is complete with a vaulted ceiling in the bedroom, walk-in and wardrobe closets, a double vanity, garden tub, and separate shower. Two secondary bedrooms share a full bath with the bonus room.

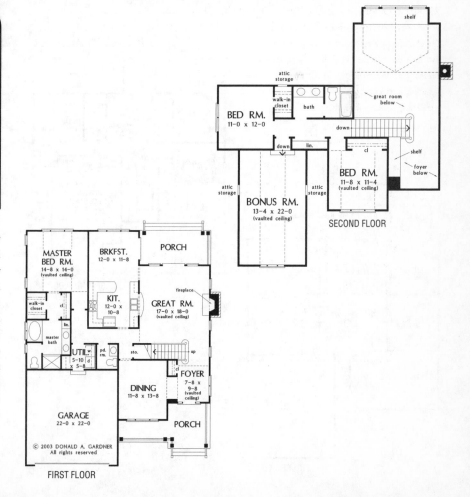

© William E. Poole Designs, Inc.

SECOND FLOOR

FIRST FLOOR

plan# HPK0100039

STYLE: CRAFTSMAN
FIRST FLOOR: 1,627 SQ. FT.
SECOND FLOOR: 783 SQ. FT.
TOTAL: 2,410 SQ. FT.
BONUS SPACE: 418 SQ. FT.
BEDROOMS: 4
BATHROOMS: 2½
WIDTH: 46' - 0"
DEPTH: 58' - 0"
FOUNDATION: CRAWLSPACE

SEARCH ONLINE @ EPLANS.COM

Graceful rooflines and front-porch columns speak to the elegance this wonderful home offers. A magnificent master suite with a gigantic walk-in closet and a private bath with shower and whirlpool tub ensures comfort. The main living areas on the main level are organized for both casual comfort and formal get-togethers. The island counter in the kitchen conveniently houses a sink, the dishwasher, and a serving bar. The two-story family room enjoys a media center, fireplace, and entry to the rear terrace (or make it a deck).

ALLEN

plan# HPK0100040

STYLE: TRADITIONAL
SQUARE FOOTAGE: 1,750
BONUS SPACE: 324 SQ. FT.
BEDROOMS: 3
BATHROOMS: 2
WIDTH: 54' - 0"
DEPTH: 61' - 6"
FOUNDATION: BASEMENT,
CRAWLSPACE

SEARCH ONLINE @ EPLANS.COM

This is a home earmarked for you...if you're looking for traditional, down-home styling on the outside and a roomy, modern layout inside. A decorative pillar helps demarcate the formal living room from the family room, yet allowing a sense of wide open space from the combined rooms. At the far end of the family room, a fireplace is flanked by radius windows; nearby, an angled serving bar pivots traffic into the breakfast alcove and the kitchen. The totally up-to-date bath highlights the pampering master suite, which enjoys privacy on the left side of the house. On the far right, two family bedrooms share a bath. A side-loading, two-car garage has inside access to the house through the laundry room.

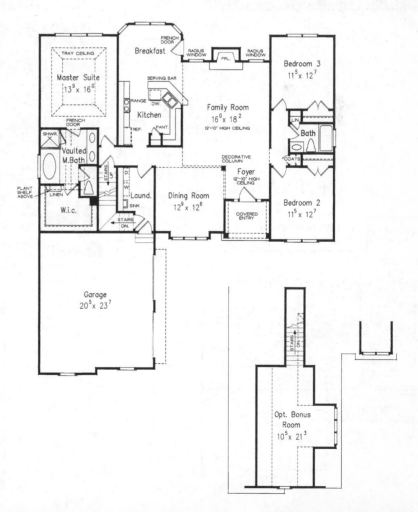

SECOND FLOOR

FIRST FLOOR

plan # HPK0100041

STYLE: CRAFTSMAN
FIRST FLOOR: 1,243 SQ. FT.
SECOND FLOOR: 1,474 SQ. FT.
TOTAL: 2,717 SQ. FT.
BEDROOMS: 4
BATHROOMS: 3½
WIDTH: 46' - 4"
DEPTH: 66' - 0"
FOUNDATION: BASEMENT,
CRAWLSPACE

SEARCH ONLINE @ EPLANS.COM

SECOND FLOOR

FIRST FLOOR

plan # HPK0100042

STYLE: CRAFTSMAN
FIRST FLOOR: 1,909 SQ. FT.
SECOND FLOOR: 835 SQ. FT.
TOTAL: 2,744 SQ. FT.
BEDROOMS: 4
BATHROOMS: 3½
WIDTH: 56' - 0"
DEPTH: 51' - 4"
FOUNDATION: BASEMENT,
CRAWLSPACE

SEARCH ONLINE @ EPLANS.COM

plan# HPK0100043

STYLE: CRAFTSMAN
FIRST FLOOR: 1,404 SQ. FT.
SECOND FLOOR: 959 SQ. FT.
TOTAL: 2,363 SQ. FT.
BONUS SPACE: 374 SQ. FT.
BEDROOMS: 4
BATHROOMS: 3
WIDTH: 56' - 10"
DEPTH: 45' - 6"
FOUNDATION: BASEMENT, CRAWLSPACE

SEARCH ONLINE @ EPLANS.COM

This traditional plan, with a hint of Craftsman style, enjoys many charms that will make it a home you'll long to come home to. The country kitchen, for example, is a real delight. It enjoys a handy island counter, a serving bar to the family room, and two pantries—one a butler's pantry, making service to the formal dining room especially efficient. Plant shelves in the upstairs master bath could help make this a semitropical retreat. A downstairs study—or make it a guest bedroom—has hall access to a full bath. Two more second-floor bedrooms with walk-in closets share a bath.

FIRST FLOOR

SECOND FLOOR

Brick pillars line the front porch of this vintage-style country home, as flower-box windows add undeniable charm. Inside, the two-story foyer opens on either side to formal rooms, adorned with columns. A touch of elegance graces the family room, where a coffered ceiling and built-in-framed fireplace create a welcoming atmosphere. Opening to the breakfast bay is the island kitchen, enjoying a plentiful pantry. Three secondary bedrooms on the upper level provide space for family and guests, including a generous suite. The master suite soothes with a vaulted sitting area and bath, and a walk-in closet with more than ample storage. A laundry room is located on this level for extra convenience.

plan# HPK0100044

STYLE: CRAFTSMAN
FIRST FLOOR: 1,335 SQ. FT.
SECOND FLOOR: 1,572 SQ. FT.
TOTAL: 2,907 SQ. FT.
BEDROOMS: 4
BATHROOMS: 3½
WIDTH: 55' - 0"
DEPTH: 45' - 0"
FOUNDATION: BASEMENT, CRAWLSPACE

SEARCH ONLINE @ EPLANS.COM

plan# HPK0100045

STYLE: CRAFTSMAN
SQUARE FOOTAGE: 1,724
BONUS SPACE: 375 SQ. FT.
BEDROOMS: 3
BATHROOMS: 2
WIDTH: 53' - 6"
DEPTH: 58' - 6"
FOUNDATION: BASEMENT,
CRAWLSPACE

SEARCH ONLINE @ EPLANS.COM

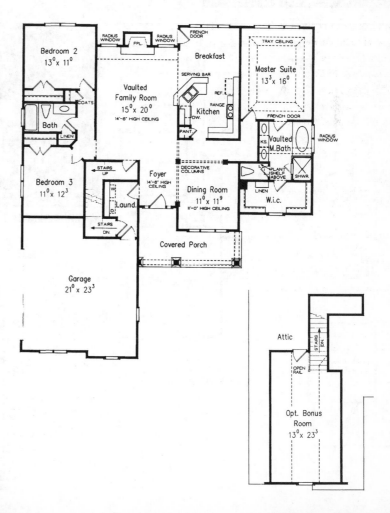

This down-home, one-story plan has all the comforts and necessities for solid family living. The vaulted family room, along with the adjoining country-style kitchen and breakfast nook, is at the center of the plan. The extended hearth fireplace flanked by radius windows will make this a cozy focus for family get-togethers and entertaining visitors. A formal dining room is marked off by decorative columns. The resplendent master suite assumes the entire right wing, where it is separated from two bedrooms located on the other side of the home. Built-in plant shelves in the master bath create a garden-like environment. Additional space is available for building another bedroom or study.

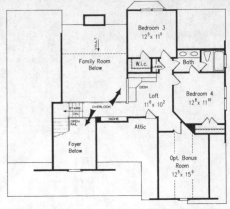

SECOND FLOOR

plan# HPK0100046

STYLE: TERRITORIAL
FIRST FLOOR: 1,663 SQ. FT.
SECOND FLOOR: 623 SQ. FT.
TOTAL: 2,286 SQ. FT.
BONUS SPACE: 211 SQ. FT.
BEDROOMS: 4
BATHROOMS: 3
WIDTH: 54' - 0"
DEPTH: 48' - 0"
FOUNDATION: BASEMENT,
CRAWLSPACE

SEARCH ONLINE @ EPLANS.COM

FIRST FLOOR

plan# HPK0100047

STYLE: COUNTRY COTTAGE
SQUARE FOOTAGE: 2,073
BONUS SPACE: 350 SQ. FT.
BEDROOMS: 3
BATHROOMS: 2½
WIDTH: 59' - 0"
DEPTH: 57' - 0"
FOUNDATION: BASEMENT,
CRAWLSPACE

SEARCH ONLINE @ EPLANS.COM

plan# HPK0100048

STYLE: CRAFTSMAN
FIRST FLOOR: 1,322 SQ. FT.
SECOND FLOOR: 1,262 SQ. FT.
TOTAL: 2,584 SQ. FT.
BEDROOMS: 4
BATHROOMS: 3
WIDTH: 48' - 0"
DEPTH: 50' - 0"
FOUNDATION: BASEMENT,
CRAWLSPACE

SEARCH ONLINE @ EPLANS.COM

With Craftsman detail and traditional charm, this four-bedroom home captures the comfort and style you've been searching for. From a wrapping porch, enter the two-story foyer with a decorative niche that displays special photos or treasures to all your guests. Continue to a beautiful family room, graced with a two-story ceiling and second-floor radius windows. The kitchen is open and spacious, leading to a breakfast area, hearth-warmed keeping room, and elegant dining room. A bedroom on this level also serves as an ideal den or home office. Upstairs, two secondary bedrooms share a full bath. The master suite is ready for relaxation with a sunny sitting room and soothing vaulted bath. A laundry room on this level makes wash day a breeze.

FIRST FLOOR

SECOND FLOOR

Craftsman-style pillars lend a country look to this Cape Cod-style home. An elegant entry opens to the vaulted family room, where a fireplace warms and bright windows illuminate. The kitchen is designed for the true chef, with step-saving orientation and a serving bar to the vaulted breakfast nook. A bedroom nearby is ideal for a home office or live-in help. The master suite is on the left, pampering with a vaulted bath and enormous walk-in closet. Two bedrooms upstairs share a full bath and an optional bonus room.

plan# HPK0100049

STYLE: CRAFTSMAN
FIRST FLOOR: 1,761 SQ. FT.
SECOND FLOOR: 577 SQ. FT.
TOTAL: 2,338 SQ. FT.
BONUS SPACE: 305 SQ. FT.
BEDROOMS: 4
BATHROOMS: 3
WIDTH: 56' - 0"
DEPTH: 48' - 0"
FOUNDATION: BASEMENT, CRAWLSPACE

SEARCH ONLINE @ EPLANS.COM

FIRST FLOOR

SECOND FLOOR

ORDER BLUEPRINTS 24 HOURS, 7 DAYS A WEEK, AT 1-800-521-6797

plan# HPK0100050

STYLE: CRAFTSMAN
FIRST FLOOR: 1,561 SQ. FT.
SECOND FLOOR: 578 SQ. FT.
TOTAL: 2,139 SQ. FT.
BONUS SPACE: 238 SQ. FT.
BEDROOMS: 3
BATHROOMS: 2½
WIDTH: 50' - 0"
DEPTH: 56' - 6"
FOUNDATION: BASEMENT,
CRAWLSPACE

SEARCH ONLINE @ EPLANS.COM

Come home to this delightful bungalow, created with you in mind. From the covered front porch, the foyer opens to the dining room on the left and vaulted family room ahead. An elongated island in the well-planned kitchen makes meal preparation a joy. A sunny breakfast nook is perfect for casual pursuits. Tucked to the rear, the master suite enjoys ultimate privacy and a luxurious break from the world with a vaulted bath and garden tub. Secondary bedrooms share a full bath upstairs; a bonus room is ready to expand as your needs change.

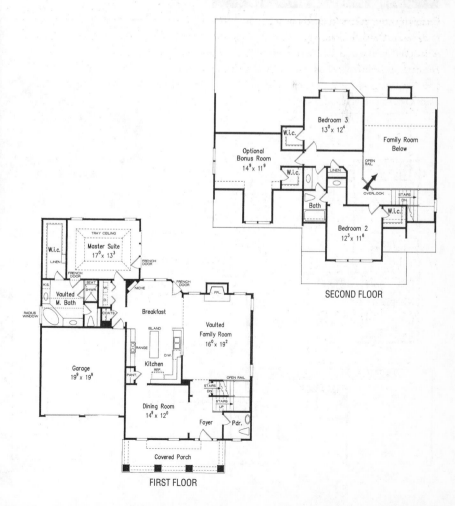

SECOND FLOOR

FIRST FLOOR

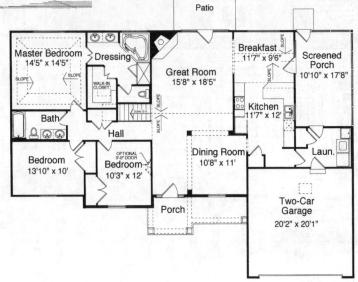

plan# HPK0100051

STYLE: CRAFTSMAN
SQUARE FOOTAGE: 1,798
BEDROOMS: 3
BATHROOMS: 2
WIDTH: 66' - 6"
DEPTH: 46' - 4"
FOUNDATION: BASEMENT

SEARCH ONLINE @ EPLANS.COM

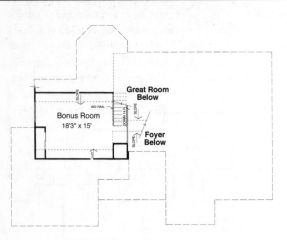

plan# HPK0100052

STYLE: COUNTRY COTTAGE
SQUARE FOOTAGE: 1,641
BONUS SPACE: 284 SQ. FT.
BEDROOMS: 3
BATHROOMS: 2
WIDTH: 62' - 4"
DEPTH: 46' - 4"
FOUNDATION: BASEMENT

SEARCH ONLINE @ EPLANS.COM

plan# HPK0100053

STYLE: CRAFTSMAN
FIRST FLOOR: 941 SQ. FT.
SECOND FLOOR: 786 SQ. FT.
TOTAL: 1,727 SQ. FT.
BEDROOMS: 3
BATHROOMS: 2½
WIDTH: 57' - 10"
DEPTH: 42' - 4"
FOUNDATION: BASEMENT

SEARCH ONLINE @ EPLANS.COM

A stone-and-siding exterior brings dimension and color to the exterior of this charming home. A two-story foyer greets you upon arrival, and the great room, with views to the rear and side yards, offers a 12-foot ceiling. The breakfast bay and entry to a covered porch creates a bright and cheery place to start the day. Counter space that wraps around from the kitchen provides additional storage and a convenient writing desk. A furniture alcove adds space to the formal dining room and a rear entry hall offers storage closets and a large laundry room. A second-floor master bedroom, with a ceiling that slopes to nine feet, keeps the parents close at hand to younger family members. This home has a full basement that can be developed for additional square footage.

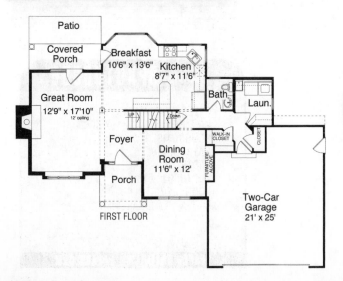

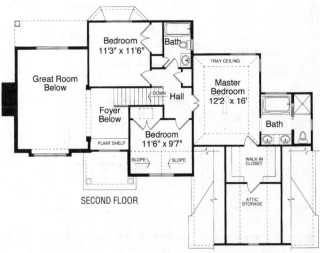

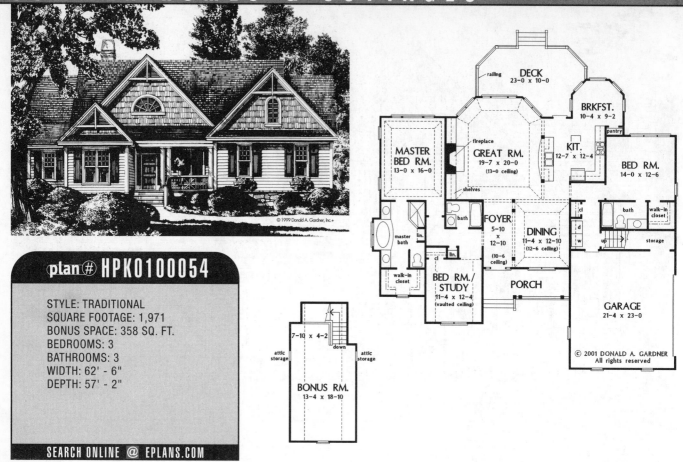

© 1999 Donald A. Gardner, Inc.+

© 2001 DONALD A. GARDNER
All rights reserved

plan # HPK0100054

STYLE: TRADITIONAL
SQUARE FOOTAGE: 1,971
BONUS SPACE: 358 SQ. FT.
BEDROOMS: 3
BATHROOMS: 3
WIDTH: 62' - 6"
DEPTH: 57' - 2"

SEARCH ONLINE @ EPLANS.COM

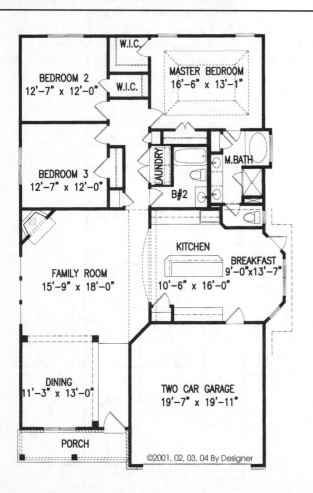

©2001, 02, 03, 04 By Designer

plan # HPK0100055

STYLE: BUNGALOW
SQUARE FOOTAGE: 1,768
BEDROOMS: 3
BATHROOMS: 2
WIDTH: 36' - 0"
DEPTH: 61' - 5"
FOUNDATION: SLAB

SEARCH ONLINE @ EPLANS.COM

ORDER BLUEPRINTS 24 HOURS, 7 DAYS A WEEK, AT 1-800-521-6797

plan # HPK0100056

STYLE: CAPE COD
SQUARE FOOTAGE: 1,093
BEDROOMS: 2
BATHROOMS: 2
WIDTH: 35' - 0"
DEPTH: 56' - 0"
FOUNDATION: SLAB

SEARCH ONLINE @ EPLANS.COM

This handsome bungalow offers many splendid features. A cozy fireplace in the family room, a rear covered porch, and a plant shelf in the laundry are some of the highlights. The plan includes two bedrooms, both with private baths, and a spacious dining room, off the well-equipped kitchen. A front-loading, two-car garage also comes with the plan.

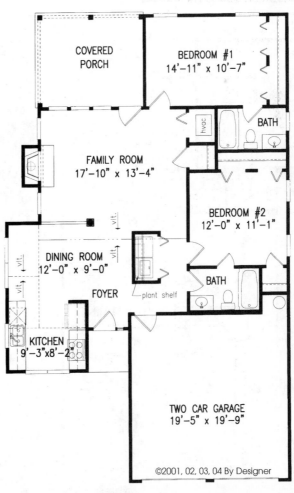

©2001, 02, 03, 04 By Designer

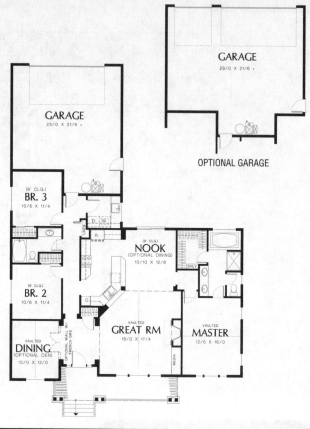

GARAGE
23/0 X 21/6

GARAGE
29/0 X 21/6

OPTIONAL GARAGE

BR. 3
[9' CLG.]
10/6 X 11/4

BR. 2
[9' CLG.]
10/6 X 11/4

NOOK
(OPTIONAL DINING)
[9' CLG.]
10/10 X 12/8

VAULTED
GREAT RM
18/0 X 17/4

VAULTED
MASTER
12/6 X 16/0

VAULTED
DINING
(OPTIONAL DEN)
10/0 X 12/0

plan # HPK0100057

STYLE: CRAFTSMAN
SQUARE FOOTAGE: 1,771
BEDROOMS: 3
BATHROOMS: 2
WIDTH: 50' - 0"
DEPTH: 70' - 0"
FOUNDATION: CRAWLSPACE

SEARCH ONLINE @ EPLANS.COM

GARAGE
26/0 X 22/0

OPTIONAL
DOOR

VAULTED
NOOK
10/0 X 10/0

BR. 3
[9' CLG.]
12/4 X 10/0

VAULTED
FAMILY
16/6 X 16/2

VAULTED

BR. 2
[9' CLG.]
12/4 X 10/0

PANTRY

DISPLAY

DINING
[9' CLG.]
12/0 X 10/4

VAULTED
MASTER
12/0 X 16/0+

DEN
[9' CLG.]
10/0 X 10/8

[9' CLG.]

VAULTED
LIVING
12/0 X 14/0

plan # HPK0100058

STYLE: CRAFTSMAN
SQUARE FOOTAGE: 2,218
BEDROOMS: 3
BATHROOMS: 2
WIDTH: 50' - 0"
DEPTH: 70' - 0"
FOUNDATION: CRAWLSPACE

SEARCH ONLINE @ EPLANS.COM

plan# HPK0100059

STYLE: CRAFTSMAN
FIRST FLOOR: 970 SQ. FT.
SECOND FLOOR: 988 SQ. FT.
TOTAL: 1,958 SQ. FT.
BEDROOMS: 3
BATHROOMS: 2½
WIDTH: 40' - 0"
DEPTH: 43' - 0"
FOUNDATION: CRAWLSPACE

SEARCH ONLINE @ EPLANS.COM

SECOND FLOOR

A sensible floor plan, with living spaces on the first floor and bedrooms on the second floor, is the highlight of this Craftsman home. Elegance reigns in the formal living room, with a vaulted ceiling and columned entry; this room is open to the dining room, which is brightened by natural light from two tall windows. Ideal for informal gatherings, the family room boasts a fireplace flanked by built-in shelves. The efficient kitchen includes a central island and double sink, and the nearby nook features easy access to the outdoors through sliding glass doors. The master suite includes a lavish bath with a corner spa tub and compartmented toilet; two additional bedrooms, one with a walk-in closet, share a full bath.

FIRST FLOOR

© 2001 Donald A. Gardner, Inc.

B. NATHAN

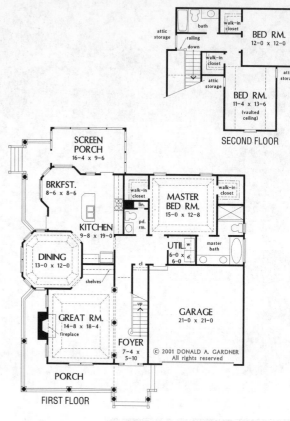

SECOND FLOOR

bath

attic storage

walk-in closet

railing

down

BED RM.
12-0 x 12-0

walk-in closet

attic storage

attic storage

BED RM.
11-4 x 13-6
(vaulted ceiling)

SCREEN PORCH
16-4 x 9-6

BRKFST.
8-6 x 8-6

walk-in closet

lin.

MASTER BED RM.
15-0 x 12-8

walk-in closet

KITCHEN
9-8 x 19-0

pd. rm.

DINING
13-0 x 12-0

UTIL.
6-0 x 6-0

master bath

w d

shelves

cl

GREAT RM.
14-8 x 18-4

fireplace

up

GARAGE
21-0 x 21-0

FOYER
7-4 x 5-10

PORCH

FIRST FLOOR

plan# HPK0100060

STYLE: COUNTRY
FIRST FLOOR: 1,459 SQ. FT.
SECOND FLOOR: 504 SQ. FT.
TOTAL: 1,963 SQ. FT.
BEDROOMS: 3
BATHROOMS: 2½
WIDTH: 50' - 0"
DEPTH: 58' - 10"

SEARCH ONLINE @ EPLANS.COM

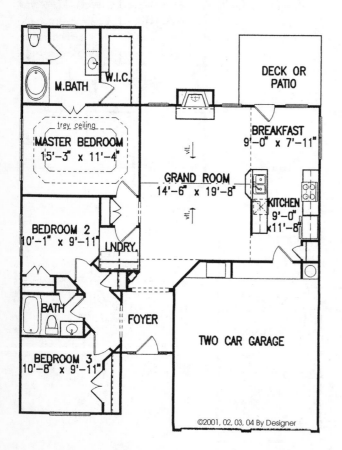

M.BATH

W.I.C.

DECK OR PATIO

trey ceiling

MASTER BEDROOM
15'-3" x 11'-4"

vlt.

BREAKFAST
9'-0" x 7'-11"

GRAND ROOM
14'-6" x 19'-8"

vlt.

KITCHEN
9'-0" x 11'-8"

BEDROOM 2
10'-1" x 9'-11"

LNDRY.

BATH

FOYER

TWO CAR GARAGE

BEDROOM 3
10'-8" x 9'-11"

Christine Canova 1/02

plan# HPK0100061

STYLE: COUNTRY COTTAGE
SQUARE FOOTAGE: 1,328
BEDROOMS: 3
BATHROOMS: 2
WIDTH: 40' - 0"
DEPTH: 52' - 0"
FOUNDATION: SLAB

SEARCH ONLINE @ EPLANS.COM

© William E. Poole Designs, Inc.

ptan# HPKO100062

STYLE: SOUTHERN COLONIAL
FIRST FLOOR: 1,542 SQ. FT.
SECOND FLOOR: 755 SQ. FT.
TOTAL: 2,297 SQ. FT.
BEDROOMS: 3
BATHROOMS: 2½
WIDTH: 48' - 4"
DEPTH: 39' - 6"
FOUNDATION: BASEMENT

SEARCH ONLINE @ EPLANS.COM

The raised front porch, reached by twin staircases and enhanced by graceful pillars, dominates the exterior of this wonderful Southern Colonial home. A front dining room is perfect for formal dinner parties, and the spacious great room will host many memorable get-togethers. The kitchen enjoys ample counter space and easily serves the sunlit breakfast alcove. Soothing comfort is guaranteed in the master suite, with a walk-in closet, whirlpool tub, and shower with a seat. Upstairs, two bedrooms share a bath.

BASEMENT

FIRST FLOOR

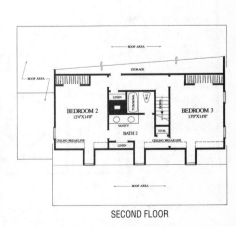

SECOND FLOOR

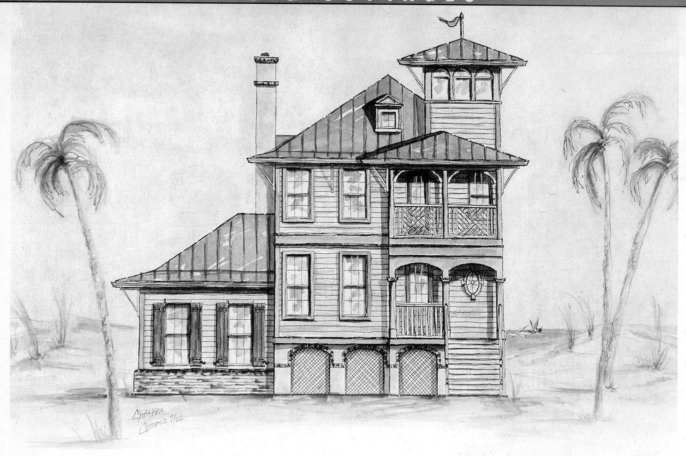

COVERED PORCH

BATH
MBR
11'-2"x12'-0"

SITTING ROOM
6'-8"x7'-6"

BATH

W.I.C.

DOWN

BDRM#2
13'-9" x 11'-3"

SECOND FLOOR

PORCH

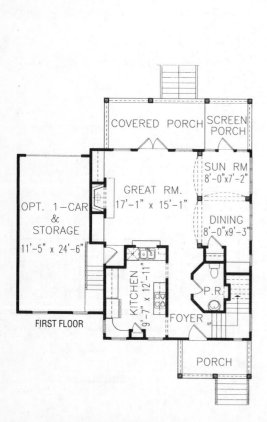

COVERED PORCH

SCREEN PORCH

SUN RM
8'-0"x7'-2"

GREAT RM.
17'-1" x 15'-1"

OPT. 1-CAR & STORAGE
11'-5" x 24'-6"

DINING
8'-0"x9'-3"

KITCHEN
9'-7" x 12'-11"

P.R.

FOYER

UP

FIRST FLOOR

PORCH

plan# HPK0100063

STYLE: FLORIDIAN
FIRST FLOOR: 754 SQ. FT.
SECOND FLOOR: 662 SQ. FT.
TOTAL: 1,416 SQ. FT.
BEDROOMS: 2
BATHROOMS: 2½
WIDTH: 38' - 0"
DEPTH: 44' - 0"
FOUNDATION: CRAWLSPACE

SEARCH ONLINE @ EPLANS.COM

For families that enjoy lots of sun and ocean breezes, this dazzling Sun Country home is made for you. Rear and front covered porches and a rear screened porch extend the living space outdoors. A sunroom, perfect for your favorite plants, opens to the dining area and grand room. The kitchen and a half-bath are also located on the main floor. Two bedrooms, each with private baths, are found upstairs. The plan comes with an optional one-car garage with room for storage.

plan# HPK0100003

STYLE: CRAFTSMAN
FIRST FLOOR: 1,640 SQ. FT.
SECOND FLOOR: 1,083 SQ. FT.
TOTAL: 2,723 SQ. FT.
BONUS SPACE: 350 SQ. FT.
BEDROOMS: 3
BATHROOMS: 3
WIDTH: 62' - 0"
DEPTH: 65' - 6"
FOUNDATION: BASEMENT

SEARCH ONLINE @ EPLANS.COM

If you're looking for a spacious vacation home, big enough for the entire family and guests, this plan is worth taking a close look at. You will be astounded by the kitchen...easy to work in and miles of counter space. One counter serves both as a divider and a connector to the dining room, and double French doors open to the rear porch. The two-story grand room warmed by a fireplace opens to another porch. A downstairs bedroom enjoys a private bath, and two more bedrooms on the upper level, one of them a resplendent master suite, also include private baths. Also, you get a bonus upstairs...extra space that can be turned into a fourth bedroom or a hobby area. Don't overlook the laundry room that opens to the three-car garage.

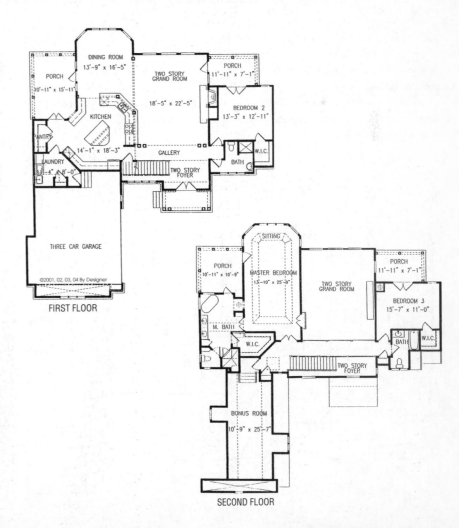

FIRST FLOOR

SECOND FLOOR

© 2002 Donald A. Gardner, Inc.

Full of charm, this home combines stone, cedar shake, and siding for outstanding curb appeal. Ushering light into an upstairs bedroom and the two-story foyer, triple dormers lie above a cozy front porch. Columns in the dining room and a tray ceiling in the master suite add architectural interest; built-in cabinetry, a kitchen island, and butler's pantry add convenience. A screened porch awaits outdoor entertaining, and two upstairs bonus rooms anticipate expansion opportunities. A curved balcony overlooks the great room, and French doors lead outside from the great room and master suite.

plan# HPK0100064

STYLE: CRAFTSMAN
FIRST FLOOR: 1,856 SQ. FT.
SECOND FLOOR: 610 SQ. FT.
TOTAL: 2,466 SQ. FT.
BONUS SPACE: 322 SQ. FT.
BEDROOMS: 3
BATHROOMS: 2½
WIDTH: 59' - 0"
DEPTH: 47' - 8"

SEARCH ONLINE @ EPLANS.COM

FIRST FLOOR

DECK

SCREEN PORCH
12-8 x 14-4

BRKFST.
14-0 x 9-0

seat

(two story ceiling)

fireplace

GREAT RM.
17-0 x 18-2

MASTER BED RM.
14-0 x 16-0

UTILITY
8-8 x 8-0

KITCHEN
14-0 x 10-8

shelves

balcony above

butler's pantry

pd. rm.

cl

walk-in closet

linen

seat

master bath

GARAGE
21-0 x 22-0

DINING
13-4 x 11-8

up

FOYER
7-0 x 4-10

PORCH

STUDY
12-0 x 13-0
(vaulted ceiling)

FIRST FLOOR

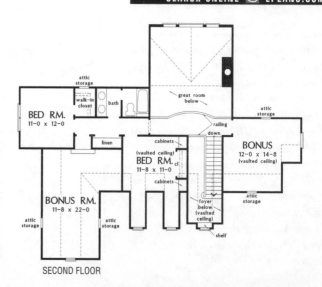

SECOND FLOOR

attic storage

walk-in closet

bath

great room below

attic storage

BED RM.
11-0 x 12-0

linen

railing

down

cabinets

BONUS
12-0 x 14-8
(vaulted ceiling)

(vaulted ceiling)
BED RM.
11-8 x 11-0

cl

cabinets

attic storage

BONUS RM.
11-8 x 22-0

foyer below
(vaulted ceiling)

shelf

attic storage

attic storage

SECOND FLOOR

© 2002 Donald A. Gardner, Inc.

plan # HPK0100065

STYLE: CRAFTSMAN
FIRST FLOOR: 1,496 SQ. FT.
SECOND FLOOR: 615 SQ. FT.
TOTAL: 2,111 SQ. FT.
BONUS SPACE: 277 SQ. FT.
BEDROOMS: 3
BATHROOMS: 2½
WIDTH: 40' - 4"
DEPTH: 70' - 0"

SEARCH ONLINE @ EPLANS.COM

Stone, siding, and jack-arch details create a traditional Craftsman plan you will love to come home to. Thoughtful details, including built-in cabinets, a fireplace, and a snack bar to the kitchen, will make the great room a family favorite. Porches off the great room and breakfast nook, one screened and one open, invite outdoor living. The master suite is located at the rear of the plan for quiet and privacy. Here, His and Hers closets and a lavish bath are sure to delight. Two upstairs bedrooms and a bonus room round out this home.

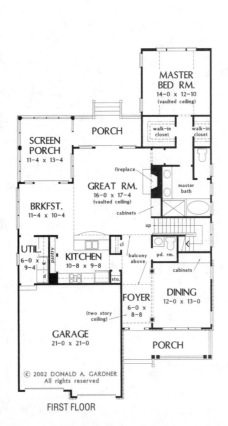

FIRST FLOOR

SECOND FLOOR

plan# HPK0100066

STYLE: FARMHOUSE
FIRST FLOOR: 1,080 SQ. FT.
SECOND FLOOR: 928 SQ. FT.
TOTAL: 2,008 SQ. FT.
BONUS SPACE: 249 SQ. FT.
BEDROOMS: 3
BATHROOMS: 2½
WIDTH: 40' - 8"
DEPTH: 51' - 0"
FOUNDATION: BASEMENT

SEARCH ONLINE @ EPLANS.COM

SECOND FLOOR

FIRST FLOOR

SECOND FLOOR

FIRST FLOOR

plan# HPK0100067

STYLE: FARMHOUSE
FIRST FLOOR: 1,244 SQ. FT.
SECOND FLOOR: 987 SQ. FT.
TOTAL: 2,231 SQ. FT.
BEDROOMS: 3
BATHROOMS: 3½
WIDTH: 67' - 0"
DEPTH: 40' - 0"
FOUNDATION: BASEMENT

SEARCH ONLINE @ EPLANS.COM

plan # HPK0100068

STYLE: FARMHOUSE
FIRST FLOOR: 1,618 SQ. FT.
SECOND FLOOR: 586 SQ. FT.
TOTAL: 2,204 SQ. FT.
BONUS SPACE: 334 SQ. FT.
BEDROOMS: 3
BATHROOMS: 2½
WIDTH: 65' - 0"
DEPTH: 44' - 0"
FOUNDATION: BASEMENT

SEARCH ONLINE @ EPLANS.COM

The stone-and-siding facade and arched front windows give this two-story home an impressive distinction matched by the charm and comfort found inside. Built-in cabinets flank the living-room fireplace; the spacious dining area is separated from the kitchen by an island counter, convenient for light meals and snacks. A double-bowl vanity, shower, and huge corner tub mark the resplendent bath in the first-floor master suite. Upstairs, two family bedrooms are separated by a bath, and additional to-be-developed space is nearby. Off the kitchen, a full laundry with a wash tub adjoins a half-bath and opens to the two-car garage. A wraparound front porch and rear deck complete this plan.

FIRST FLOOR

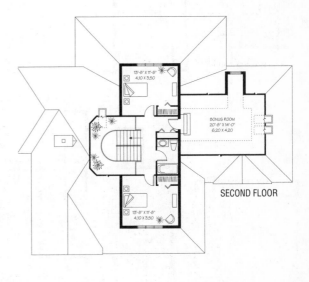

SECOND FLOOR

UPPER LEVEL

MAIN LEVEL

LOWER LEVEL

plan# HPK0100069

STYLE: CONTEMPORARY
MAIN LEVEL: 891 SQ. FT.
UPPER LEVEL: 323 SQ. FT.
LOWER LEVEL: 891 SQ. FT.
TOTAL: 2,105 SQ. FT.
BEDROOMS: 4
BATHROOMS: 2
WIDTH: 34' - 4"
DEPTH: 27' - 4"
FOUNDATION: BASEMENT

SEARCH ONLINE @ EPLANS.COM

SECOND FLOOR

FIRST FLOOR

plan# HPK0100070

STYLE: COUNTRY COTTAGE
FIRST FLOOR: 853 SQ. FT.
SECOND FLOOR: 645 SQ. FT.
TOTAL: 1,498 SQ. FT.
BEDROOMS: 3
BATHROOMS: 2
WIDTH: 32' - 0"
DEPTH: 34' - 0"
FOUNDATION: BASEMENT

SEARCH ONLINE @ EPLANS.COM

ORDER BLUEPRINTS 24 HOURS, 7 DAYS A WEEK, AT 1-800-521-6797

plan# HPK0100071

STYLE: FARMHOUSE
FIRST FLOOR: 1,299 SQ. FT.
SECOND FLOOR: 1,030 SQ. FT.
TOTAL: 2,329 SQ. FT.
BONUS SPACE: 468 SQ. FT.
BEDROOMS: 3
BATHROOMS: 2½
WIDTH: 54' - 8"
DEPTH: 42' - 0"
FOUNDATION: BASEMENT

SEARCH ONLINE @ EPLANS.COM

An inviting covered porch welcomes family and friends to this comfortable country home. Inside, peace and quiet are assured in the living room/den. The gathering room is spacious and bright, opening into a sitting area and the dining room. The kitchen cooks up gourmet meals and easily serves both formal and casual areas. The romantic master suite is located upstairs, featuring a fireplace and pampering bath. Two additional bedrooms share a full bath and hall linen closet. A two-car garage with a service entrance completes the plan.

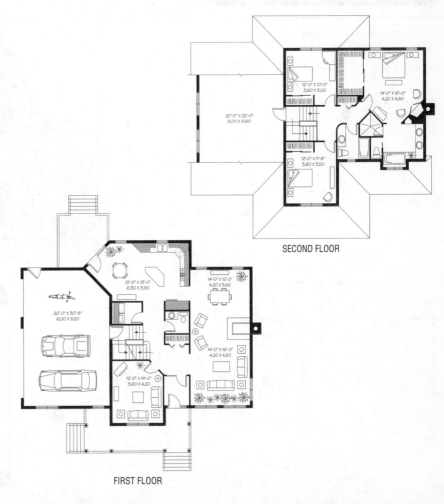

SECOND FLOOR

FIRST FLOOR

SECOND FLOOR

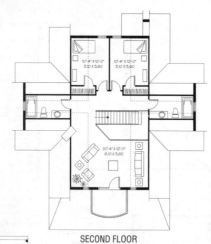

FIRST FLOOR

plan # HPK0100072

STYLE: LAKEFRONT
FIRST FLOOR: 1,519 SQ. FT.
SECOND FLOOR: 705 SQ. FT.
TOTAL: 2,224 SQ. FT.
BEDROOMS: 3
BATHROOMS: 2½
WIDTH: 54' - 0"
DEPTH: 50' - 0"
FOUNDATION: BASEMENT

SEARCH ONLINE @ EPLANS.COM

SECOND FLOOR

FIRST FLOOR

plan # HPK0100073

STYLE: TRADITIONAL
FIRST FLOOR: 1,416 SQ. FT.
SECOND FLOOR: 977 SQ. FT.
TOTAL: 2,393 SQ. FT.
BEDROOMS: 3
BATHROOMS: 3
WIDTH: 46' - 0"
DEPTH: 39' - 0"
FOUNDATION: BASEMENT

SEARCH ONLINE @ EPLANS.COM

plan# HPK0100074

STYLE: TRADITIONAL
FIRST FLOOR: 918 SQ. FT.
SECOND FLOOR: 908 SQ. FT.
TOTAL: 1,826 SQ. FT.
BEDROOMS: 3
BATHROOMS: 2
WIDTH: 48' - 0"
DEPTH: 35' - 4"
FOUNDATION: BASEMENT

SEARCH ONLINE @ EPLANS.COM

Rich with a brick facade, floods of natural light, and a comfortable, warm interior, this home may just be perfect. Enter to a foyer with a separate interior door, creating a mudroom-style entry. The family room is on the right, warmed by a cozy hearth and lit by a tall Palladian window. In the kitchen, an island snack bar is great for casual meals, or dine in luxury in the bright, bayed dining room. Three generous bedrooms are located upstairs, the master boasting dual walk-in closets. A shared bath will pamper and soothe with a corner whirlpool tub and twin sinks.

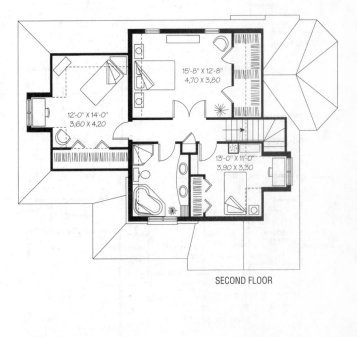

SECOND FLOOR

FIRST FLOOR

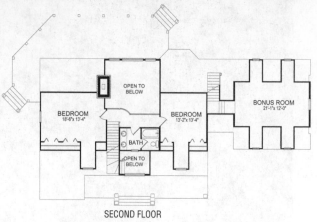

SECOND FLOOR

plan# HPK0100075

STYLE: CRAFTSMAN
FIRST FLOOR: 1,799 SQ. FT.
SECOND FLOOR: 709 SQ. FT.
TOTAL: 2,508 SQ. FT.
BONUS SPACE: 384 SQ. FT.
BEDROOMS: 3
BATHROOMS: 2½
WIDTH: 77' - 4"
DEPTH: 41' - 4"
FOUNDATION: BASEMENT

SEARCH ONLINE @ EPLANS.COM

FIRST FLOOR

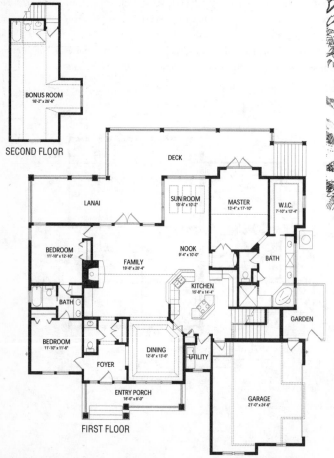

plan# HPK0100076

STYLE: CRAFTSMAN
SQUARE FOOTAGE: 2,326
BONUS SPACE: 358 SQ. FT.
BEDROOMS: 3
BATHROOMS: 2½
WIDTH: 64' - 0"
DEPTH: 72' - 4"
FOUNDATION: BASEMENT

SEARCH ONLINE @ EPLANS.COM

plan# HPK0100077

STYLE: CRAFTSMAN
FIRST FLOOR: 1,799 SQ. FT.
SECOND FLOOR: 709 SQ. FT.
TOTAL: 2,508 SQ. FT.
BONUS SPACE: 384 SQ. FT.
BEDROOMS: 3
BATHROOMS: 2½
WIDTH: 77' - 4"
DEPTH: 41' - 4"
FOUNDATION: BASEMENT

SEARCH ONLINE @ EPLANS.COM

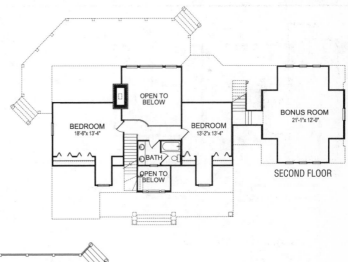

An oversized dormer above the entryway and a steep, side-gabled roof produce an interesting front perspective to this Craftsman-style vacation home. Inside, a wood-burning fireplace warms the family room, overlooked by the second-floor walkway. To the left, the master suite is attended by a large walk-in closet and double vanities in the bathroom. Owners will also appreciate the private access to the deck. The full-sized garage at the right of the plan features a bonus room on the upper floor.

REAR EXTERIOR

UPPER LEVEL

LOWER LEVEL

MAIN LEVEL

plan # HPK0100078

STYLE: TRADITIONAL
MAIN LEVEL: 1,434 SQ. FT.
UPPER LEVEL: 524 SQ. FT.
LOWER LEVEL: 1,434 SQ. FT.
TOTAL: 3,392 SQ. FT.
BEDROOMS: 4
BATHROOMS: 3½
WIDTH: 72' - 0"
DEPTH: 42' - 0"
FOUNDATION: BASEMENT

SEARCH ONLINE @ EPLANS.COM

MAIN LEVEL

LOWER LEVEL

REAR EXTERIOR

plan # HPK0100079

STYLE: TRADITIONAL
MAIN LEVEL: 1,406 SQ. FT.
LOWER LEVEL: 1,406 SQ. FT.
TOTAL: 2,812 SQ. FT.
BEDROOMS: 4
BATHROOMS: 3
WIDTH: 58' - 0"
DEPTH: 41' - 4"
FOUNDATION: BASEMENT

SEARCH ONLINE @ EPLANS.COM

plan# HPK0100080

STYLE: COUNTRY COTTAGE
FIRST FLOOR: 2,589 SQ. FT.
SECOND FLOOR: 981 SQ. FT.
TOTAL: 3,570 SQ. FT.
BEDROOMS: 4
BATHROOMS: 3½
WIDTH: 70' - 8"
DEPTH: 61' - 10"
FOUNDATION: CRAWLSPACE

SEARCH ONLINE @ EPLANS.COM

You can get away from it all in this woodsy cottage—but you won't have to rough it! A formal dining room and spacious study set the tone for fine living as you enter the grand foyer. Straight ahead, the hearth-warmed living room opens to a huge rear deck. To the right, a deluxe-size gourmet kitchen, complete with island counter, utility room, and office space adjoins a cozy family room with a fireplace. The left side of the first floor is taken up by the stunning master suite, which enjoys a stepped ceiling, two walk-in closets, and a relaxing bath. Upstairs, three bedrooms and two baths surround a dramatic balcony overlook.

SECOND FLOOR

FIRST FLOOR

SECOND FLOOR

plan# HPK0100081

STYLE: FARMHOUSE
FIRST FLOOR: 2,589 SQ. FT.
SECOND FLOOR: 981 SQ. FT.
TOTAL: 3,570 SQ. FT.
BEDROOMS: 4
BATHROOMS: 3½
WIDTH: 70' - 8"
DEPTH: 61' - 10"
FOUNDATION: CRAWLSPACE

SEARCH ONLINE @ EPLANS.COM

FIRST FLOOR

SECOND FLOOR

FIRST FLOOR

plan# HPK0100082

STYLE: COUNTRY COTTAGE
FIRST FLOOR: 2,589 SQ. FT.
SECOND FLOOR: 981 SQ. FT.
TOTAL: 3,570 SQ. FT.
BEDROOMS: 4
BATHROOMS: 3½
WIDTH: 70' - 8"
DEPTH: 61' - 10"
FOUNDATION: CRAWLSPACE

SEARCH ONLINE @ EPLANS.COM

This uniquely designed home, which will win applause from your neighbors, very effectively breaks down the boundary between indoors and outdoors. Walls of windows facing the expansive rear deck not only bring superb views from all the living areas; they also bring in cascades of sunlight. From the living room a bumped-out sunroom extends onto the deck; a perfect place for your favorite plants. The master suite is large enough for a sitting area and enjoys a resplendent bath with all the comforts designed to please. An island snack counter and open space to the dining area make serving meals a breeze. The upstairs bath with a dual-sink vanity serves two bedrooms with a hallway entry. Both rooms share access to a cozy sitting room. A laundry and nearby half-bath are located on the first floor.

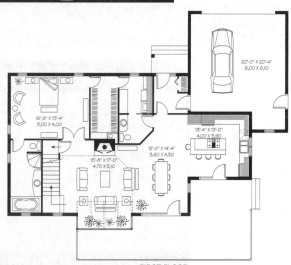

FIRST FLOOR

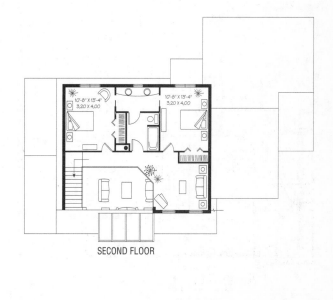

SECOND FLOOR

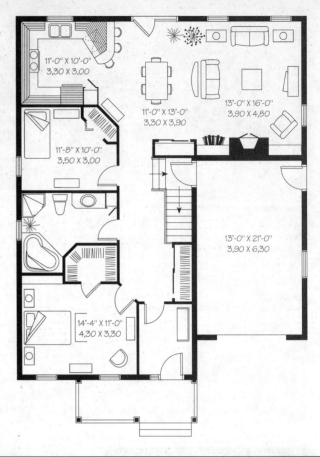

plan # HPK0100084

STYLE: TRADITIONAL
SQUARE FOOTAGE: 1,220
BEDROOMS: 2
BATHROOMS: 1
WIDTH: 36' - 0"
DEPTH: 44' - 0"
FOUNDATION: BASEMENT

SEARCH ONLINE @ EPLANS.COM

plan # HPK0100085

STYLE: BUNGALOW
SQUARE FOOTAGE: 1,026
BEDROOMS: 2
BATHROOMS: 1
WIDTH: 30' - 0"
DEPTH: 36' - 0"
FOUNDATION: BASEMENT

SEARCH ONLINE @ EPLANS.COM

plan# HPK0100086

STYLE: COUNTRY COTTAGE
SQUARE FOOTAGE: 1,456
BEDROOMS: 3
BATHROOMS: 2
WIDTH: 54' - 0"
DEPTH: 45' - 6"
FOUNDATION: CRAWLSPACE

SEARCH ONLINE @ EPLANS.COM

For the family that likes to spend time outdoors this home is sure to please. Expansive rear and front porches extend living space outward, and the master suite enjoys private access to a deck. A cozy fireplace is tucked into the corner of the main living room, which is separated from the front dining room by classy columns. The center island in the kitchen eases meal preparation. The sleeping arrangements are separated from each other; the deluxe master suite, with a walk-in closet and a private bath, is on the left, and two more bedrooms are on the right side of the home. A laundry room is close-by.

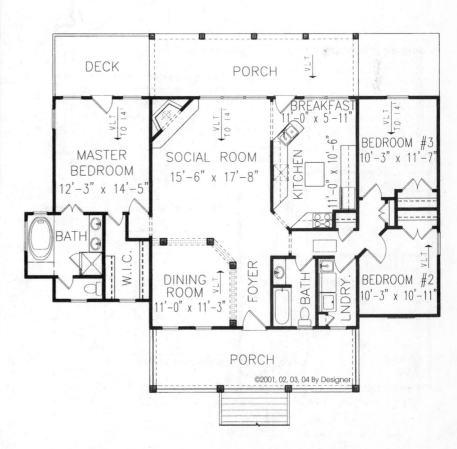

©2001, 02, 03, 04 By Designer

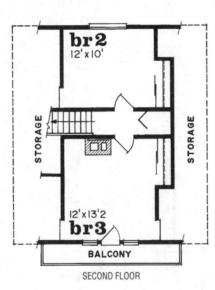

SECOND FLOOR

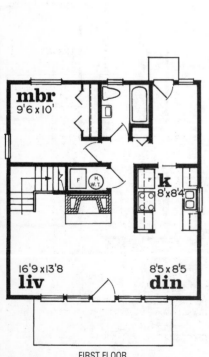

FIRST FLOOR

plan# HPK0100008

STYLE: COUNTRY COTTAGE
FIRST FLOOR: 728 SQ. FT.
SECOND FLOOR: 350 SQ. FT.
TOTAL: 1,078 SQ. FT.
BEDROOMS: 3
BATHROOMS: 1
WIDTH: 26' - 0"
DEPTH: 28' - 0"
FOUNDATION: CRAWLSPACE

SEARCH ONLINE @ EPLANS.COM

Alpine style sets the tone for this mountain cabin. Warm up in front of the fireplace in the living room while enjoying the scenery from the ribbon of windows at the front of the plan. A galley-style kitchen opens to a convenient dining area as well as flex space that accesses the rear property. The master bedroom is secluded at the back left and boasts another set of gorgeous views. Two additional bedrooms, one with balcony access, are upstairs along with storage space.

© 2002 Donald A. Gardner, Inc.

plan # HPK0100087

STYLE: TRADITIONAL
FIRST FLOOR: 1,687 SQ. FT.
SECOND FLOOR: 807 SQ. FT.
TOTAL: 2,494 SQ. FT.
BEDROOMS: 4
BATHROOMS: 2½
WIDTH: 52' - 8"
DEPTH: 67' - 0"

SEARCH ONLINE @ EPLANS.COM

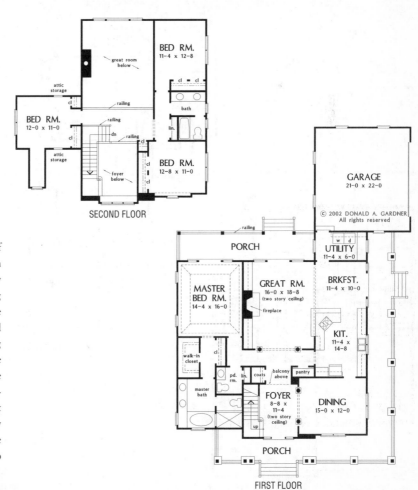

This glorious farmhouse was designed with the best of family living in mind. The beautiful wraparound porch is accented with stone and columns, and varying window detail adds a custom look to the facade. Inside, a soaring two-story foyer opens to a gallery hall that opens to the great room through columns. A fireplace, built-ins, and rear-porch access make this room perfect for entertaining or just hanging out. The swanky master suite takes up the entire left wing of the plan with its enormous private bath and double closets. To the right of the plan, the spacious kitchen is bookended by a formal dining room at the front and a cozy breakfast nook to the rear. A utility room opens to the garage. Upstairs, three bedrooms share a bath as well as attic storage. A balcony looks down into the foyer and great room.

© William E. Poole Designs, Inc.

FIRST FLOOR

SECOND FLOOR

plan # HPK0100001

STYLE: TIDEWATER
FIRST FLOOR: 1,314 SQ. FT.
SECOND FLOOR: 552 SQ. FT.
TOTAL: 1,866 SQ. FT.
BONUS SPACE: 398 SQ. FT.
BEDROOMS: 3
BATHROOMS: 2½
WIDTH: 44' - 2"
DEPTH: 62' - 0"
FOUNDATION: CRAWLSPACE

SEARCH ONLINE @ EPLANS.COM

Tall gables and dormers offer warm greetings to visitors of this rustic beach home. The sensible interior features a brief foyer leading to the dining room and great room, with a wood-burning fireplace. To the left, the master suite is attended by a large master bath with dual vanities, private toilet, and a walk-in closet. Two bedrooms upstairs share a similar bath. Above the garage, a future rec room would enjoy plenty of space and views of the beach.

© William E. Poole Designs, Inc.

plan# HPK0100088

STYLE: GREEK REVIVAL
FIRST FLOOR: 1,688 SQ. FT.
SECOND FLOOR: 630 SQ. FT.
TOTAL: 2,318 SQ. FT.
BONUS SPACE: 506 SQ. FT.
BEDROOMS: 3
BATHROOMS: 3½
WIDTH: 44' - 4"
DEPTH: 62' - 4"
FOUNDATION: BASEMENT,
CRAWLSPACE

SEARCH ONLINE @ EPLANS.COM

Truth, as we have always been told, is stranger than fiction—and so we begin. Years ago two elderly sisters lived in the Easton. Kindly and scatterbrained, they invited neighbors for Thanksgiving dinner. The turkey was delivered and the sisters decided (after a toddie or two) to administer chloroform so the defrocking would be painless. When the turkey waked, the sisters, not being able to "do the deed," put a belt around the naked turkey's neck and walked him to the butcher shop. That Thanksgiving celebration has yet to be equaled.

SECOND FLOOR

FIRST FLOOR

© 2003 Donald A. Gardner, Inc.

plan# HPK0100089

STYLE: CRAFTSMAN
FIRST FLOOR: 1,648 SQ. FT.
SECOND FLOOR: 777 SQ. FT.
TOTAL: 2,425 SQ. FT.
BONUS SPACE: 353 SQ. FT.
BEDROOMS: 4
BATHROOMS: 2½
WIDTH: 48' - 8"
DEPTH: 57' - 8"

SEARCH ONLINE @ EPLANS.COM

SECOND FLOOR

FIRST FLOOR

© 2003 DONALD A. GARDNER
All rights reserved

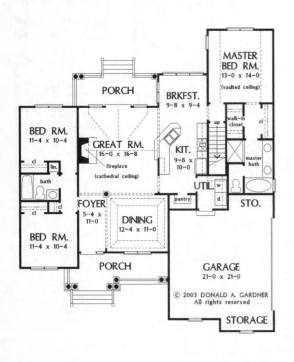

© 2003 Donald A. Gardner
All rights reserved

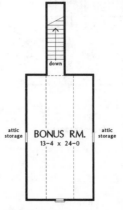

© 2003 Donald A. Gardner, Inc.

plan# HPK0100090

STYLE: TRADITIONAL
SQUARE FOOTAGE: 1,547
BONUS SPACE: 391 SQ. FT.
BEDROOMS: 3
BATHROOMS: 2
WIDTH: 51' - 8"
DEPTH: 59' - 0"

SEARCH ONLINE @ EPLANS.COM

© 2003 Donald A. Gardner, Inc.

plan# HPK0100091

STYLE: FARMHOUSE
FIRST FLOOR: 1,562 SQ. FT.
SECOND FLOOR: 502 SQ. FT.
TOTAL: 2,064 SQ. FT.
BONUS SPACE: 416 SQ. FT.
BEDROOMS: 3
BATHROOMS: 2½
WIDTH: 54' - 0"
DEPTH: 55' - 10"

SEARCH ONLINE @ EPLANS.COM

Capturing the Heartland feel, this farmhouse is designed to make an impression. A welcoming front porch guides family and friends inside, where they're greeted by a two-story foyer. Columns mark the entry to the dining room. The great room features numerous windows, French doors, and a stunning fireplace. The kitchen is the hub of the home, servicing the great room through a pass-through. A cathedral ceiling visually expands the master suite, and a French door leads to the rear porch. The master bath features a double vanity, garden tub, shower with seat, and a compartmented toilet. Secondary bedrooms share a full bath with the bonus room.

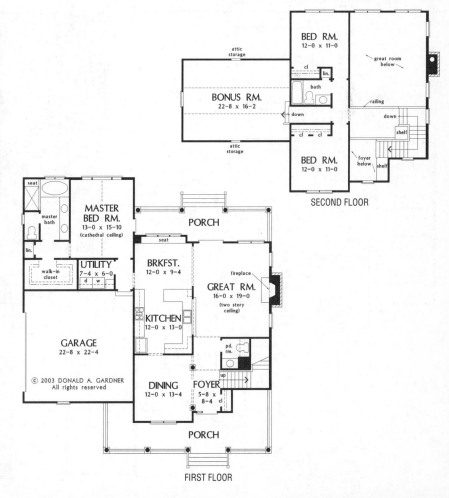

BED #3
12'-8" x 14'-6"
8' Ceiling

Attic

BED #5
12'-4" x 12'-6"
8' Ceiling

STUDY LOFT
Rail

BED #4
12'-4" x 12'
8' Ceiling

Open to Below

Down

GAME ROOM
16' x 14'-6"
8' Ceiling

Attic

Optional Bonus Room
12' x 15'

4' 8' 8' 4'

SECOND FLOOR

plan# HPK0100092

STYLE: TRADITIONAL
FIRST FLOOR: 2,185 SQ. FT.
SECOND FLOOR: 1,197 SQ. FT.
TOTAL: 3,382 SQ. FT.
BONUS SPACE: 180 SQ. FT.
BEDROOMS: 5
BATHROOMS: 4½
WIDTH: 68' - 0"
DEPTH: 62' - 0"

SEARCH ONLINE @ EPLANS.COM

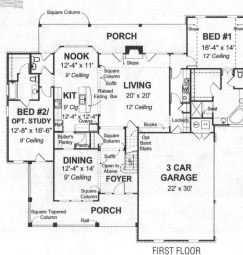

Square Column

PORCH

NOOK
12'-4" x 11'
9' Ceiling

BED #1
16'-4" x 14'
12' Ceiling

Slope

KIT
9' Clg
12'-4" x 12'-4"

Square Column
Soffit
Raised Eating Bar

LIVING
20' x 20'
12' Ceiling

BED #2/ OPT. STUDY
12'-8" x 16'-6"
9' Ceiling

Ovens

Ref

Butler's Pantry

Pantry

Square Column

Books

Seat

Lockers

DINING
12'-4" x 14'
9' Ceiling

Soffit
Open to Above

Opt Bsmt Stairs

FOYER

3 CAR GARAGE
22' x 30'

Square Column

Square Tapered Column

Rail

PORCH

FIRST FLOOR

BED #2
11' x 12'-6"
8' Ceiling

Down

OPT GAME RM
14' x 19'
(Adds 292 Sq Ft)

Attic
Slope

BED #3
10'-8" x 12'
8' Ceiling

SECOND FLOOR

plan# HPK0100093

STYLE: FARMHOUSE
FIRST FLOOR: 1,529 SQ. FT.
SECOND FLOOR: 448 SQ. FT.
TOTAL: 1,977 SQ. FT.
BONUS SPACE: 292 SQ. FT.
BEDROOMS: 3
BATHROOMS: 2½
WIDTH: 49' - 0"
DEPTH: 59' - 0"

SEARCH ONLINE @ EPLANS.COM

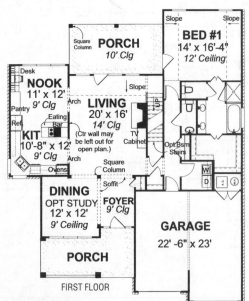

Desk

NOOK
11' x 12'
9' Clg

Pantry
Ref

PORCH
10' Clg

Square Column

Slope

BED #1
14' x 16'-4"
12' Ceiling

Slope

LIVING
20' x 16'
14' Clg
(Ctr wall may be left out for open plan.)

Eating Bar

KIT
10'-8" x 12'
9' Clg

Ovens

Arch

Arch

TV Cabinet

Opt Bsmt Stairs

Square Column

Soffit

DINING OPT STUDY
12' x 12'
9' Ceiling

FOYER
9' Clg

GARAGE
22'-6" x 23'

PORCH

FIRST FLOOR

© 2003 Donald A. Gardner, Inc.

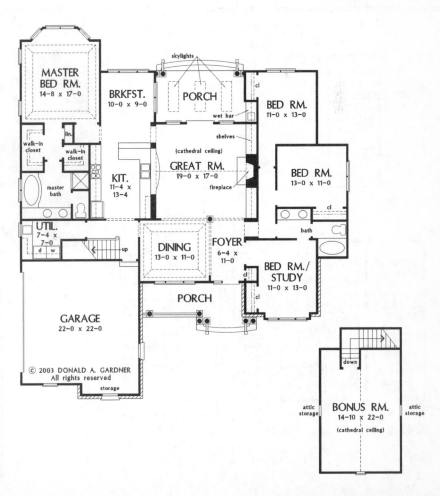

plan# HPK0100094

STYLE: BUNGALOW
SQUARE FOOTAGE: 2,243
BONUS SPACE: 332 SQ. FT.
BEDROOMS: 4
BATHROOMS: 2
WIDTH: 62' - 0"
DEPTH: 67' - 2"

SEARCH ONLINE @ EPLANS.COM

Twin dormers, multiple gables, and bold columns create a lovely exterior; inside, the floor plan provides a natural traffic flow. A tray ceiling and column distinguish the dining room, and double doors grace the flexible study/bedroom and master suite. A pass-through with a breakfast bar connects the kitchen to the great room, and built-ins flank the fireplace. The master suite also features a bay window, which provides a sitting area. Perfect for outdoor entertaining and relaxation, the rear porch includes a wet bar, skylights, and French doors that lead into the great room. The bonus room could also provide additional recreation space.

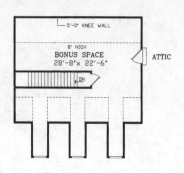

5'-0" KNEE WALL

8' HIGH
BONUS SPACE
28'-8" x 22'-6"

ATTIC

plan# HPK0100095

STYLE: NEOCLASSIC
SQUARE FOOTAGE: 1,994
BONUS SPACE: 770 SQ. FT.
BEDROOMS: 4
BATHROOMS: 2
WIDTH: 77' - 41"
DEPTH: 54' - 0"
FOUNDATION: BASEMENT,
CRAWLSPACE, SLAB

SEARCH ONLINE @ EPLANS.COM

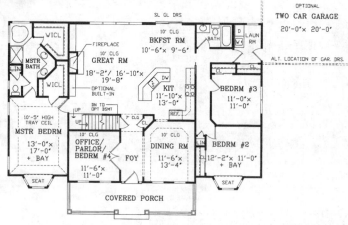

ALT. LOCATION OF GAR. DRS.

OPTIONAL
TWO CAR GARAGE
20'-0" x 20'-0"

ALT. LOCATION OF GAR. DRS.

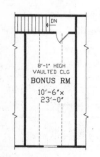

8'-1" HIGH
VAULTED CLG
BONUS RM
10'-6" x
23'-0"

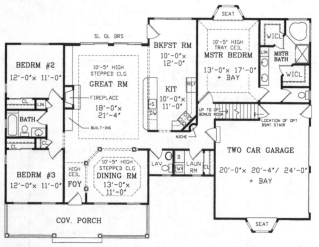

plan# HPK0100096

STYLE: COUNTRY COTTAGE
SQUARE FOOTAGE: 1,892
BONUS SPACE: 285 SQ. FT.
BEDROOMS: 3
BATHROOMS: 2½
WIDTH: 65' - 4"
DEPTH: 45' - 10"
FOUNDATION: BASEMENT,
CRAWLSPACE, SLAB

SEARCH ONLINE @ EPLANS.COM

br 3
11 x 10

BATH

BATH

HALL

future game rm
22 x 12

mbr
18 x 12

br 2
14 x 11

CLO.

© Breland & Farmer Designers

CLO.

SECOND FLOOR

plan# HPK0100097

STYLE: VICTORIAN
FIRST FLOOR: 767 SQ. FT.
SECOND FLOOR: 776 SQ. FT.
TOTAL: 1,543 SQ. FT.
BEDROOMS: 3
BATHROOMS: 2½
WIDTH: 54' - 0"
DEPTH: 32' - 0"
FOUNDATION: BASEMENT,
CRAWLSPACE, SLAB

SEARCH ONLINE @ EPLANS.COM

patio

storage   24 x 4

porch

bath

eating
10 x 8

© Breland & Farmer Designers

garage
24 x 20

living
18 x 14

kit
12 x 10

DISHWASHER

RANGE

REF

foy

dining
12 x 12

por

FIRST FLOOR

Dormer for Opt
Bed #5
w/ Window

ATTIC/
OPT
BED #5

Attic

GAME
ROOM
17'-6" x 20'
8' Ceiling

Down

Slope

BED #3
16' x 14'
8' Ceiling

BED #4
16' x 14'
8' Ceiling

SECOND FLOOR

plan# HPK0100098

STYLE: TRADITIONAL
FIRST FLOOR: 3,249 SQ. FT.
SECOND FLOOR: 1,202 SQ. FT.
TOTAL: 4,451 SQ. FT.
BONUS SPACE: 240 SQ. FT.
BEDROOMS: 4
BATHROOMS: 4½
WIDTH: 89' - 0"
DEPTH: 65' - 0"

SEARCH ONLINE @ EPLANS.COM

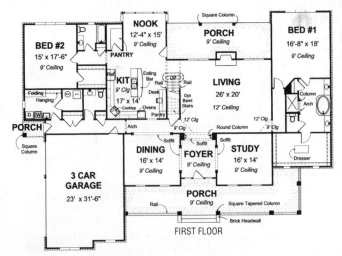

NOOK
12'-4" x 15'
9' Ceiling

PORCH
9' Ceiling

BED #1
16'-8" x 18'
9' Ceiling

BED #2
15' x 17'-6"
9' Ceiling

PANTRY

KIT
9' Clg
17' x 14'

Eating
Bar
Rail

LIVING
26' x 20'
12' Ceiling

Square Column

Opt
Bsmt
Stairs

Desk

Cooktop

Ovens

Pantry

12' Clg

9' Clg

Folding
Hanging

Round Column

Column
Arch

Arch

9' Clg

Soffit

Soffit

Soffit

12' Clg

9' Clg

Dresser

PORCH

Square
Column

3 CAR
GARAGE
23' x 31'-6"

DINING
16' x 14'
9' Ceiling

FOYER
9' Ceiling

STUDY
16' x 14'
9' Ceiling

PORCH
9' Ceiling

Rail

Square Tapered Column

Brick Headwall

FIRST FLOOR

This engaging country home offers classic details and quaint charm in a sprawling floor plan designed for today's family. A wide front porch opens through double doors directly into the welcoming great room. Natural light fills the home through rear windows, and the fireplace can be viewed from the efficient kitchen and breakfast nook. Both the dining room and front-facing bedroom enjoy bayed window seats. The master suite stands out with a massive walk-in closet and soothing bath. A two-car garage with extra storage completes the picture.

plan# HPK0100099

STYLE: COUNTRY COTTAGE
SQUARE FOOTAGE: 1,823
BONUS SPACE: 323 SQ. FT.
BEDROOMS: 3
BATHROOMS: 2
WIDTH: 75' - 0"
DEPTH: 43' - 4"
FOUNDATION: BASEMENT, CRAWLSPACE, SLAB

SEARCH ONLINE @ EPLANS.COM

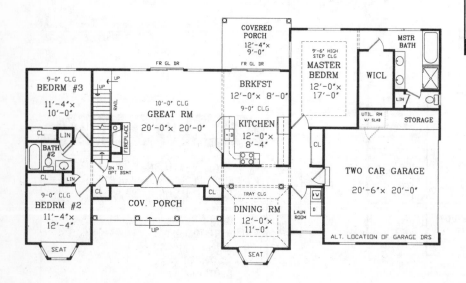

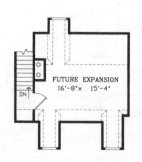

plan # HPK0100100

STYLE: TRADITIONAL
FIRST FLOOR: 1,986 SQ. FT.
SECOND FLOOR: 986 SQ. FT.
TOTAL: 2,972 SQ. FT.
BONUS SPACE: 396 SQ. FT.
BEDROOMS: 4
BATHROOMS: 3½
WIDTH: 55' - 8"
DEPTH: 49' - 2"
FOUNDATION: BASEMENT

SEARCH ONLINE @ EPLANS.COM

What immediately strikes you about this spacious, rustic retreat is the connection between interior living areas and outside space. An inviting wraparound porch with columns will surely be a family gathering place on warm summer evenings. In the rear, an expansive deck offers plenty of room for barbecues or simply basking in the sun, and a screened porch provides a congenial place outdoors for reading or conversation, even when mosquitoes are thick. Inside, the breakfast nook opens to the screened porch and to the breezeway that connects the three-car garage to the house. A huge kitchen with an island counter will make meal preparation a delight. The two-story family room with a fireplace radiates cozy comfort, and the palatial master suite will make all your fantasies come true. Living and dining rooms near the entry will hospitably welcome guests to your home. Upstairs are three family bedrooms and two baths.

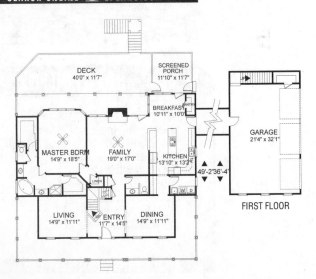

FIRST FLOOR

SECOND FLOOR

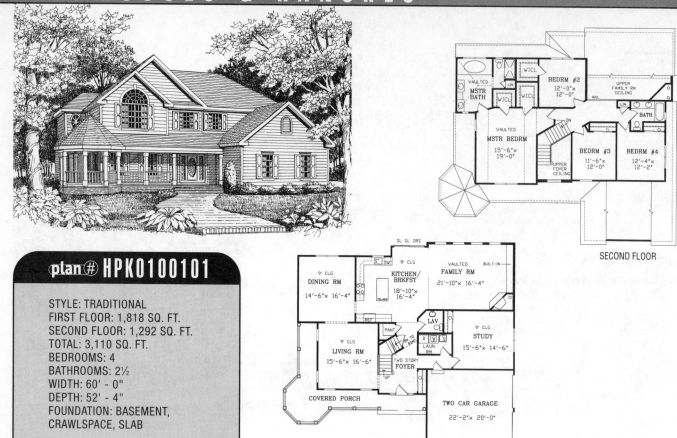

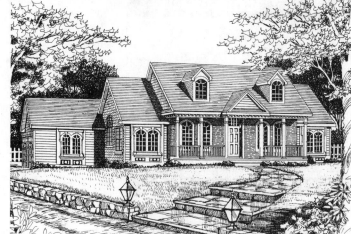

SECOND FLOOR

plan# HPK0100101

STYLE: TRADITIONAL
FIRST FLOOR: 1,818 SQ. FT.
SECOND FLOOR: 1,292 SQ. FT.
TOTAL: 3,110 SQ. FT.
BEDROOMS: 4
BATHROOMS: 2½
WIDTH: 60' - 0"
DEPTH: 52' - 4"
FOUNDATION: BASEMENT,
CRAWLSPACE, SLAB

SEARCH ONLINE @ EPLANS.COM

FIRST FLOOR

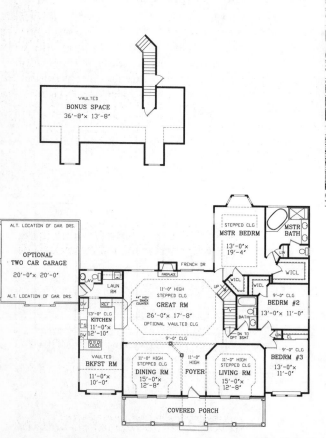

plan# HPK0100102

STYLE: SOUTHERN COLONIAL
SQUARE FOOTAGE: 2,282
BONUS SPACE: 576 SQ. FT.
BEDROOMS: 3
BATHROOMS: 2½
WIDTH: 80' - 4"
DEPTH: 57' - 4"
FOUNDATION: BASEMENT,
CRAWLSPACE, SLAB

SEARCH ONLINE @ EPLANS.COM

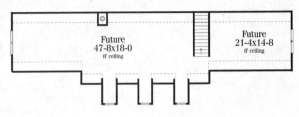

Future
47-8x18-0
8' ceiling

Future
21-4x14-8
8' ceiling

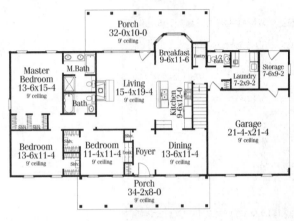

Porch
32-0x10-0
9' ceiling

Master
Bedroom
13-6x15-4
9' ceiling

M.Bath

Breakfast
9-6x11-6

Pantry

1/2
Bath

Bath

Living
15-4x19-4
9' ceiling

Kitchen
9-6x12-0

Laundry
7-2x9-2

Storage
7-6x9-2

Bedroom
13-6x11-4
9' ceiling

Bedroom
11-4x11-4
9' ceiling

Desk

Foyer

Dining
13-6x11-4
9' ceiling

Garage
21-4-x21-4
9' ceiling

Porch
34-2x8-0
9' ceiling

plan# HPK0100103

STYLE: COUNTRY COTTAGE
SQUARE FOOTAGE: 1,916
BONUS SPACE: 1,245 SQ. FT.
BEDROOMS: 3
BATHROOMS: 2½
WIDTH: 74' - 0"
DEPTH: 49' - 8"
FOUNDATION: BASEMENT,
CRAWLSPACE, SLAB

SEARCH ONLINE @ EPLANS.COM

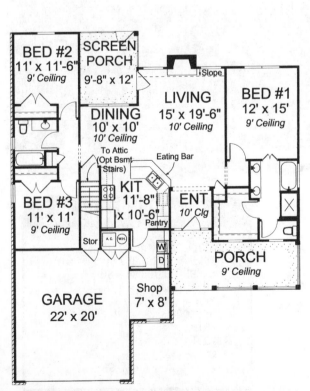

BED #2
11' x 11'-6"
9' Ceiling

SCREEN
PORCH
9'-8" x 12'

DINING
10' x 10'
10' Ceiling

Slope

LIVING
15' x 19'-6"
10' Ceiling

BED #1
12' x 15'
9' Ceiling

To Attic
(Opt Bsmt
Stairs)

Eating Bar

BED #3
11' x 11'
9' Ceiling

KIT
11'-8"
x 10'-6"

Pantry

ENT
10' Clg

Stor

A.C.

W.H.

W
D

PORCH
9' Ceiling

GARAGE
22' x 20'

Shop
7' x 8'

plan# HPK0100104

STYLE: TRADITIONAL
SQUARE FOOTAGE: 1,416
BEDROOMS: 3
BATHROOMS: 2
WIDTH: 49' - 0"
DEPTH: 58' - 0"

SEARCH ONLINE @ EPLANS.COM

SECOND FLOOR

FIRST FLOOR

plan# HPK0100105

STYLE: COUNTRY COTTAGE
FIRST FLOOR: 1,921 SQ. FT.
SECOND FLOOR: 921 SQ. FT.
TOTAL: 2,842 SQ. FT.
BONUS SPACE: 454 SQ. FT.
BEDROOMS: 4
BATHROOMS: 3½
WIDTH: 62' - 2"
DEPTH: 71' - 0"
FOUNDATION: BASEMENT,
CRAWLSPACE

SEARCH ONLINE @ EPLANS.COM

SECOND FLOOR

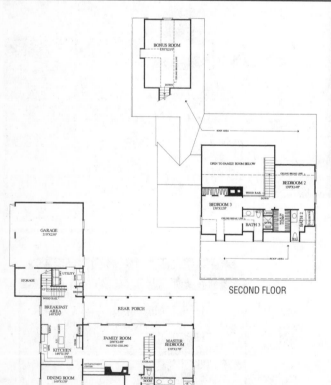

FIRST FLOOR

plan# HPK0100106

STYLE: COUNTRY COTTAGE
FIRST FLOOR: 1,892 SQ. FT.
SECOND FLOOR: 608 SQ. FT.
TOTAL: 2,500 SQ. FT.
BONUS SPACE: 370 SQ. FT.
BEDROOMS: 3
BATHROOMS: 3½
WIDTH: 61' - 4"
DEPTH: 82' - 6"
FOUNDATION: CRAWLSPACE

SEARCH ONLINE @ EPLANS.COM

© William E. Poole Designs, Inc.

plan# HPK0100107

STYLE: FARMHOUSE
FIRST FLOOR: 1,291 SQ. FT.
SECOND FLOOR: 1,087 SQ. FT.
TOTAL: 2,378 SQ. FT.
BONUS SPACE: 366 SQ. FT.
BEDROOMS: 3
BATHROOMS: 2½
WIDTH: 65' - 4"
DEPTH: 40' - 0"
FOUNDATION: CRAWLSPACE

SEARCH ONLINE @ EPLANS.COM

No gimmicks, just the real thing—Texarkana is a farmhouse of such handsome proportions that, once you see it for the first time, you know for certain that it is meant to be your home. Simple, solid and secure in its place in the scheme of things, the Texarkana is a favorite place for neighbors to gather in the early evening hours for a friendly game of baseball and, hopefully, a special treat of homemade ice cream.

SECOND FLOOR

FIRST FLOOR

Dining

Laundry
10-4x5-6

Storage
4-6x9-4

Garage
Optional
Basement
Stairs

plan# HPK0100108

STYLE: COUNTRY COTTAGE
SQUARE FOOTAGE: 1,670
BEDROOMS: 3
BATHROOMS: 2
WIDTH: 70' - 0"
DEPTH: 46' - 0"
FOUNDATION: BASEMENT,
CRAWLSPACE, SLAB

SEARCH ONLINE @ EPLANS.COM

Porch
31-8x9-0

M.Bath
10-2x18-0

Master
Bedroom
14-8x13-0

Greatroom
17-0x18-0

Dining
10-10x17-6

Laundry
10-4x5-6

Storage
4-6x9-4

Shelves

Bedroom
12-6x12-0

Bath
5-8x12-0

Bedroom
10-8x12-0

Foyer

Ref.

Kitchen
12-0x14-3

D.W.

Pantry

Range

Garage
19-6x19-6

Pantry

Porch
32-0x7-0

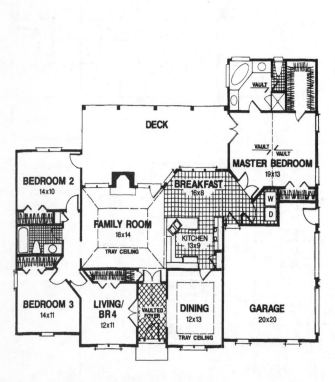

DECK

BEDROOM 2
14x10

VAULT

VAULT

VAULT

MASTER BEDROOM
19x13

BREAKFAST
16x8

FAMILY ROOM
18x14

KITCHEN
13x9

W
D

TRAY CEILING

BEDROOM 3
14x11

LIVING/
BR 4
12x11

VAULTED
FOYER

DINING
12x13

GARAGE
20x20

TRAY CEILING

plan# HPK0100109

STYLE: TRADITIONAL
SQUARE FOOTAGE: 1,886
BEDROOMS: 4
BATHROOMS: 2
WIDTH: 66' - 0"
DEPTH: 49' - 0"
FOUNDATION: BASEMENT,
CRAWLSPACE, SLAB

SEARCH ONLINE @ EPLANS.COM

ORDER BLUEPRINTS 24 HOURS, 7 DAYS A WEEK, AT 1-800-521-6797

© 2002 Donald A. Gardner, Inc.

plan# HPK0100110

STYLE: TRADITIONAL
FIRST FLOOR: 1,420 SQ. FT.
SECOND FLOOR: 1,065 SQ. FT.
TOTAL: 2,485 SQ. FT.
BONUS SPACE: 411 SQ. FT.
BEDROOMS: 4
BATHROOMS: 3
WIDTH: 57' - 8"
DEPTH: 49' - 0"

SEARCH ONLINE @ EPLANS.COM

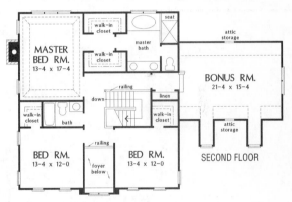

SECOND FLOOR

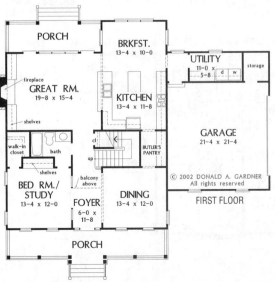

FIRST FLOOR

Looking every bit like the big country homes of yesteryear, this plan's traditional facade belies the up-to-date floor plan inside. The two-story foyer—lit by a glorious Palladian window on top—opens to flex space on the left. This room can be a bedroom or a study, depending on your needs. On the other side of the foyer lies the dining room, which accesses the kitchen through a convenient butler's pantry. The roomy island kitchen flows into a sunny breakfast room, which in turn accesses the hearth-warmed great room. The rear porch can be accessed by the great room and the breakfast room. Upstairs, two family bedrooms share a hall bath and the deluxe master suite boasts two walk-in closets and a twin-vanity bath with a garden tub. To the right is bonus space, which you can define any way you wish.

plan# HPK0100111

STYLE: TRADITIONAL
SQUARE FOOTAGE: 2,358
BEDROOMS: 3
BATHROOMS: 2½
WIDTH: 80' - 0"
DEPTH: 62' - 0"
FOUNDATION: CRAWLSPACE, SLAB

SEARCH ONLINE @ EPLANS.COM

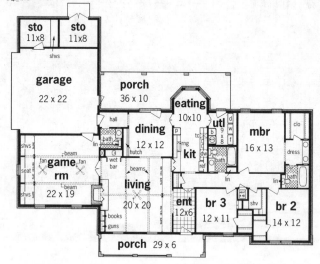

sto 11x8
sto 11x8
garage 22 x 22
porch 36 x 10
eating 10x10
utl
mbr 16 x 13
clo
dress
hall
dining 12 x 12
kit
bath
game rm 22 x 19
living 20 x 20
ent 12x6
br 3 12 x 11
br 2 14 x 12
books guns
porch 29 x 6

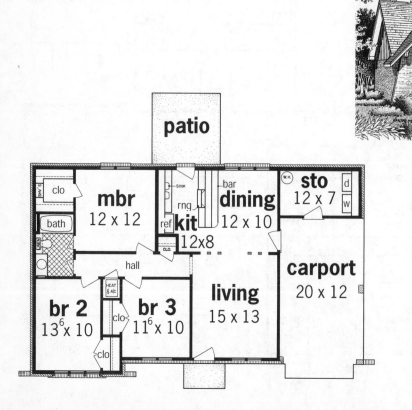

patio

mbr 12 x 12
dining 12 x 10
sto 12 x 7
bath
kit 12x8
carport 20 x 12
hall
br 2 13⁶ x 10
br 3 11⁶ x 10
living 15 x 13
clo

plan# HPK0100112

STYLE: TRADITIONAL
SQUARE FOOTAGE: 998
BEDROOMS: 3
BATHROOMS: 1
WIDTH: 48' - 0"
DEPTH: 29' - 0"
FOUNDATION: CRAWLSPACE, SLAB

SEARCH ONLINE @ EPLANS.COM

plan# HPK0100113

STYLE: TRADITIONAL
SQUARE FOOTAGE: 3,408
BONUS SPACE: 560 SQ. FT.
BEDROOMS: 4
BATHROOMS: 4
WIDTH: 95' - 0"
DEPTH: 63' - 0"

SEARCH ONLINE @ EPLANS.COM

The simple exterior of this home belies the luxury within. A formal dining room and high-ceilinged study flank the foyer, which opens to a spacious hearth-warmed living room. To the left, the island kitchen and dining nook access the screen porch through French doors. The master suite on the right enjoys a sitting area and its own bath, as well as a huge walk-in closet. Three more bedrooms share two baths at the front left of the plan. Upstairs, a game room and small study can be used as flex space or additional guest accommodations.

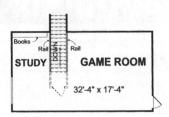

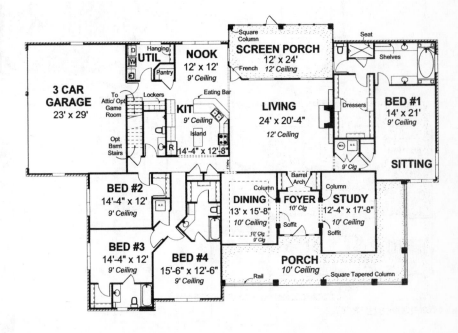

SECOND FLOOR

BED RM.
12-4 x 15-0

LOFT
12-8 x 8-8

BED RM.
12-4 x 12-8

BONUS RM.
20-8 x 15-0

great room below

walk-in closet

lin.

bath

shelf

railing

down

foyer below

shelf

bath

shelf

down

cl

attic storage

attic storage

plan# HPK0100114

STYLE: FARMHOUSE
FIRST FLOOR: 1,633 SQ. FT.
SECOND FLOOR: 751 SQ. FT.
TOTAL: 2,384 SQ. FT.
BONUS SPACE: 359 SQ. FT.
BEDROOMS: 3
BATHROOMS: 3½
WIDTH: 69' - 8"
DEPTH: 44' - 0"

SEARCH ONLINE @ EPLANS.COM

FIRST FLOOR

DECK

MASTER BED RM.
13-0 x 18-0

GREAT RM.
18-4 x 15-10
(vaulted ceiling)

BRKFST.
10-0 x 9-8

UTILITY
7-8 x 7-4

w | d

shelves

fireplace

balcony above

KITCHEN
12-4 x 12-0

GARAGE
20-8 x 23-4

walk-in closet

walk-in closet

cl

pd. rm.

DINING
12-4 x 15-0

master bath

balcony above

FOYER
11-8 x 8-8
(two story ceiling)

up

PORCH

BONUS RM.
13-4 x 21-0

attic storage

attic storage

down

PORCH

BRKFST.
10-0 x 7-4

BED RM.
12-0 x 11-4

shelves

fireplace

GREAT RM.
18-4 x 19-0
(cathedral ceiling)

KITCHEN
12-4 x 15-4

MASTER BED RM.
14-0 x 15-4

master bath

cl

lin.

bath

walk-in closet

shelves

BED RM.
12-0 x 11-4

cl

cl

FOYER
6-4 x 11-4

DINING
14-4 x 11-4

cl

pd. rm.

lin.

util. rm.

w

d

up

storage

GARAGE
21-0 x 21-0

PORCH

storage

plan# HPK0100115

STYLE: TRADITIONAL
SQUARE FOOTAGE: 1,925
BONUS SPACE: 343 SQ. FT.
BEDROOMS: 3
BATHROOMS: 2½
WIDTH: 70' - 0"
DEPTH: 49' - 8"

SEARCH ONLINE @ EPLANS.COM

ORDER BLUEPRINTS 24 HOURS, 7 DAYS A WEEK, AT 1-800-521-6797

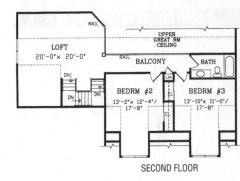

SECOND FLOOR

FIRST FLOOR

plan# HPK0100116

STYLE: TRADITIONAL
FIRST FLOOR: 2,196 SQ. FT.
SECOND FLOOR: 1,008 SQ. FT.
TOTAL: 3,204 SQ. FT.
BEDROOMS: 4
BATHROOMS: 4
WIDTH: 62' - 4"
DEPTH: 65' - 10"
FOUNDATION: BASEMENT,
CRAWLSPACE, SLAB

SEARCH ONLINE @ EPLANS.COM

This country favorite rambles over 3,000 square feet, yet retains a sense of cozy comfort. Inside, the foyer opens on the left to a formal dining room and on the right to a home office or guest suite. A vaulted great room beckons just ahead; the vault continues to the sunny breakfast room. Equipped for professional chefs, the kitchen pleases with an island cooktop and walk-in pantry. Situated for privacy, the master suite features a bumped-out sitting area and lavish bath with a corner whirlpool tub. Generous upper-level bedrooms share a full bath and loft area.

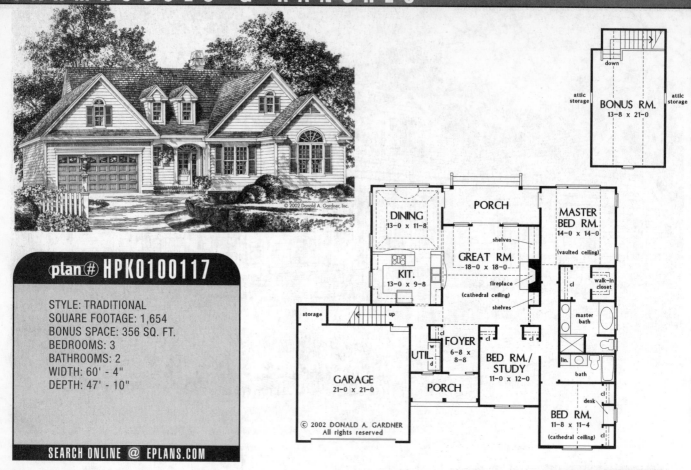

© 2002 Donald A. Gardner, Inc.

BONUS RM.
13-8 x 21-0

attic storage / attic storage

down

DINING
13-0 x 11-8

PORCH

MASTER BED RM.
14-0 x 14-0
(vaulted ceiling)

shelves

GREAT RM.
18-0 x 18-0

KIT.
13-0 x 9-8

fireplace
(cathedral ceiling)

shelves

walk-in closet

cl

master bath

storage

up

lin.

bath

FOYER
6-8 x 8-8

UTIL.

w / d

BED RM./ STUDY
11-0 x 12-0

GARAGE
21-0 x 21-0

PORCH

desk

BED RM.
11-8 x 11-4
(cathedral ceiling)

cl

plan# HPK0100117

STYLE: TRADITIONAL
SQUARE FOOTAGE: 1,654
BONUS SPACE: 356 SQ. FT.
BEDROOMS: 3
BATHROOMS: 2
WIDTH: 60' - 4"
DEPTH: 47' - 10"

SEARCH ONLINE @ EPLANS.COM

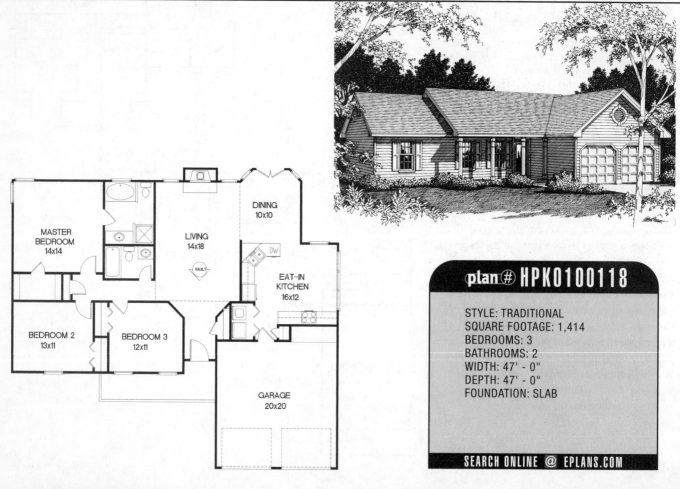

MASTER BEDROOM
14x14

LIVING
14x18

VAULT

DINING
10x10

EAT-IN KITCHEN
16x12

DW

BEDROOM 2
13x11

BEDROOM 3
12x11

GARAGE
20x20

plan# HPK0100118

STYLE: TRADITIONAL
SQUARE FOOTAGE: 1,414
BEDROOMS: 3
BATHROOMS: 2
WIDTH: 47' - 0"
DEPTH: 47' - 0"
FOUNDATION: SLAB

SEARCH ONLINE @ EPLANS.COM

ORDER BLUEPRINTS 24 HOURS, 7 DAYS A WEEK, AT 1-800-521-6797

plan# HPK0100119

STYLE: CRAFTSMAN
SQUARE FOOTAGE: 2,017
BONUS SPACE: 319 SQ. FT.
BEDROOMS: 3
BATHROOMS: 2½
WIDTH: 54' - 0"
DEPTH: 74' - 0"

SEARCH ONLINE @ EPLANS.COM

This beautiful Arts and Crafts cottage combines stone and siding to create stunning curb appeal. A pair of columns and an arch make a dramatic entrance to an open floor plan. A tray ceiling crowns the great room that features built-in cabinetry, French-door access to the rear porch, a fireplace, and a convenient pass-through to the kitchen. The dining room and break-fast nook are surrounded by windows and open space for an airy feeling. The master suite, located in the quiet wing includes a sitting area, porch access, twin walk-ins, and a master bath. Note the optional study/bedroom and flexible bonus room.

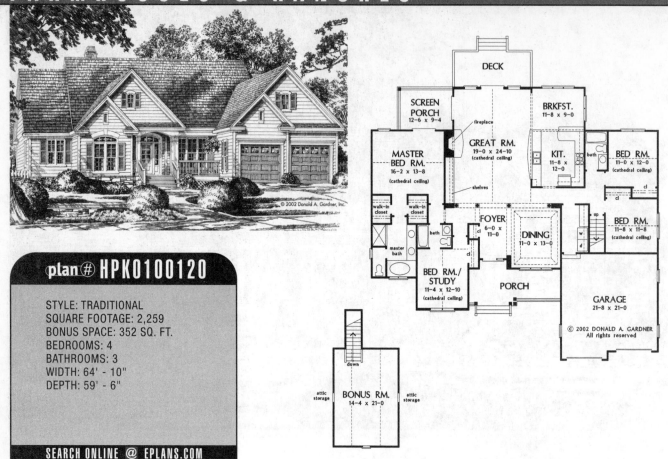

plan# HPK0100120

STYLE: TRADITIONAL
SQUARE FOOTAGE: 2,259
BONUS SPACE: 352 SQ. FT.
BEDROOMS: 4
BATHROOMS: 3
WIDTH: 64' - 10"
DEPTH: 59' - 6"

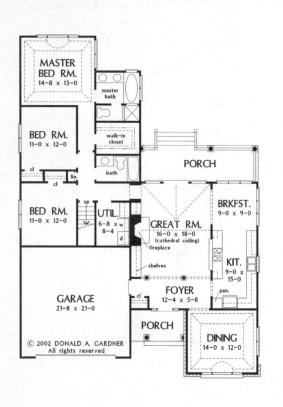

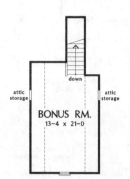

plan# HPK0100121

STYLE: TRADITIONAL
SQUARE FOOTAGE: 1,707
BONUS SPACE: 323 SQ. FT.
BEDROOMS: 3
BATHROOMS: 2
WIDTH: 48' - 6"
DEPTH: 65' - 6"

plan# HPK0100122

STYLE: TRADITIONAL
SQUARE FOOTAGE: 1,457
BONUS SPACE: 341 SQ. FT.
BEDROOMS: 3
BATHROOMS: 2
WIDTH: 50' - 4"
DEPTH: 46' - 4"

SEARCH ONLINE @ EPLANS.COM

Poised and cozy, this traditional home features a split-bedroom plan, along with half-circle transoms and tall gables on the front exterior. Above the convenient front-entry garage is a versatile bonus room for expansion. Economical and builder-friendly, the floor plan is family efficient and has a variety of custom-styled touches, such as tray ceilings in the dining room and master bedroom. The cathedral kitchen is convenient to the great room, which is highlighted by a cathedral ceiling, fireplace and French doors that lead to the rear porch. The master suite is complete with a walk-in closet and master bath; an additional bedroom and study/bedroom are located on the opposite side of the house and are separated by a full bath.

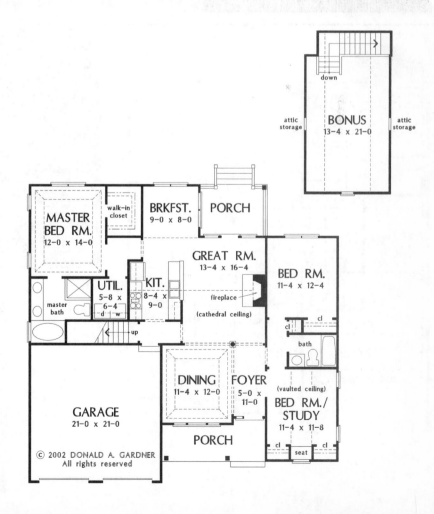

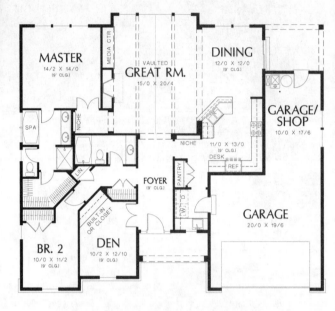

plan# HPK0100123

STYLE: CRAFTSMAN
SQUARE FOOTAGE: 1,728
BEDROOMS: 2
BATHROOMS: 2
WIDTH: 55' - 0"
DEPTH: 48' - 0"
FOUNDATION: CRAWLSPACE

SEARCH ONLINE @ EPLANS.COM

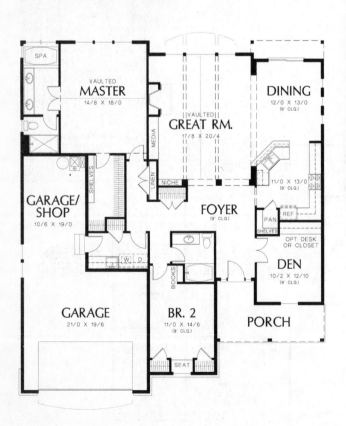

plan# HPK0100124

STYLE: COUNTRY COTTAGE
SQUARE FOOTAGE: 1,975
BEDROOMS: 2
BATHROOMS: 2
WIDTH: 52' - 0"
DEPTH: 58' - 0"
FOUNDATION: CRAWLSPACE

SEARCH ONLINE @ EPLANS.COM

plan # HPK0100125

STYLE: COUNTRY COTTAGE
SQUARE FOOTAGE: 2,367
BEDROOMS: 3
BATHROOMS: 2½
WIDTH: 72' - 0"
DEPTH: 62' - 0"
FOUNDATION: CRAWLSPACE

SEARCH ONLINE @ EPLANS.COM

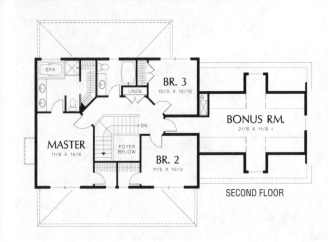

SECOND FLOOR

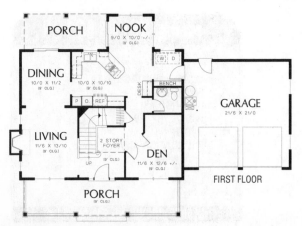

FIRST FLOOR

plan # HPK0100126

STYLE: FARMHOUSE
FIRST FLOOR: 954 SQ. FT.
SECOND FLOOR: 783 SQ. FT.
TOTAL: 1,737 SQ. FT.
BONUS SPACE: 327 SQ. FT.
BEDROOMS: 3
BATHROOMS: 2½
WIDTH: 56' - 0"
DEPTH: 40' - 0"
FOUNDATION: CRAWLSPACE

SEARCH ONLINE @ EPLANS.COM

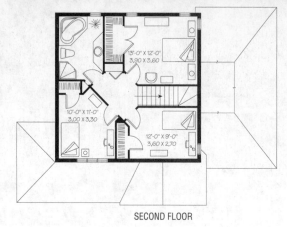

SECOND FLOOR

plan# HPK0100127

STYLE: TRADITIONAL
FIRST FLOOR: 756 SQ. FT.
SECOND FLOOR: 676 SQ. FT.
TOTAL: 1,432 SQ. FT.
BEDROOMS: 3
BATHROOMS: 2
WIDTH: 38' - 8"
DEPTH: 32' - 0"
FOUNDATION: BASEMENT

SEARCH ONLINE @ EPLANS.COM

FIRST FLOOR

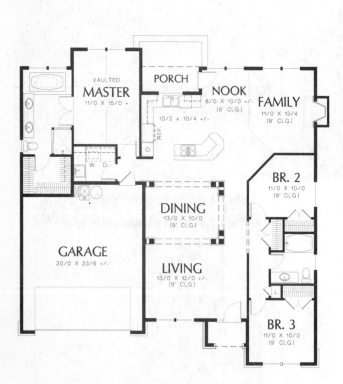

plan# HPK0100128

STYLE: TRADITIONAL
SQUARE FOOTAGE: 1,699
BEDROOMS: 3
BATHROOMS: 2
WIDTH: 50' - 0"
DEPTH: 51' - 0"
FOUNDATION: CRAWLSPACE

SEARCH ONLINE @ EPLANS.COM

ORDER BLUEPRINTS 24 HOURS, 7 DAYS A WEEK, AT 1-800-521-6797

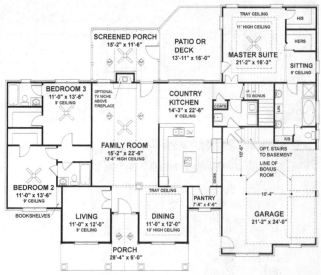

plan# HPK0100129

STYLE: COUNTRY COTTAGE
SQUARE FOOTAGE: 2,184
BONUS SPACE: 379 SQ. FT.
BEDROOMS: 3
BATHROOMS: 3
WIDTH: 71' - 2"
DEPTH: 58' - 1"
FOUNDATION: BASEMENT, SLAB

SEARCH ONLINE @ EPLANS.COM

plan# HPK0100130

STYLE: TRADITIONAL
SQUARE FOOTAGE: 2,097
BONUS SPACE: 452 SQ. FT.
BEDROOMS: 3
BATHROOMS: 3
WIDTH: 70' - 2"
DEPTH: 59' - 0"
FOUNDATION: SLAB

SEARCH ONLINE @ EPLANS.COM

SECOND FLOOR

FIRST FLOOR

plan# HPK0100131

STYLE: FARMHOUSE
FIRST FLOOR: 1,670 SQ. FT.
SECOND FLOOR: 763 SQ. FT.
TOTAL: 2,433 SQ. FT.
BEDROOMS: 3
BATHROOMS: 2½
WIDTH: 53' - 0"
DEPTH: 54' - 0"
FOUNDATION: CRAWLSPACE

SEARCH ONLINE @ EPLANS.COM

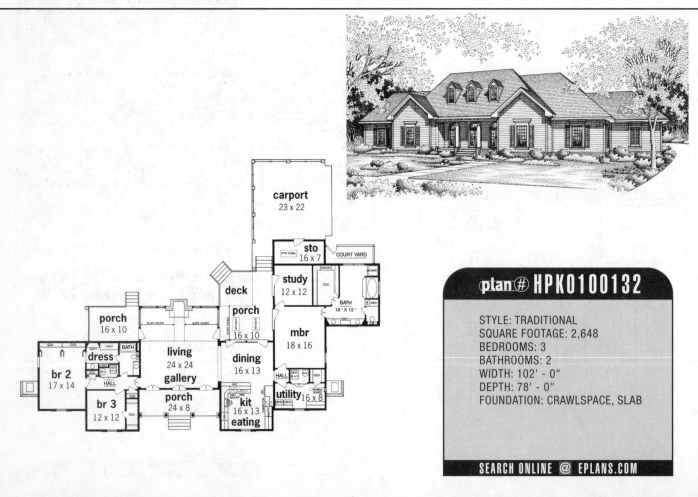

plan# HPK0100132

STYLE: TRADITIONAL
SQUARE FOOTAGE: 2,648
BEDROOMS: 3
BATHROOMS: 2
WIDTH: 102' - 0"
DEPTH: 78' - 0"
FOUNDATION: CRAWLSPACE, SLAB

SEARCH ONLINE @ EPLANS.COM

plan# HPK0100133

STYLE: NEOCOLONIAL
FIRST FLOOR: 1,907 SQ. FT.
SECOND FLOOR: 908 SQ. FT.
TOTAL: 2,815 SQ. FT.
BONUS SPACE: 183 SQ. FT.
BEDROOMS: 4
BATHROOMS: 3½
WIDTH: 64' - 8"
DEPTH: 51' - 0"

SEARCH ONLINE @ EPLANS.COM

Dormers and transom windows lend charm to this Colonial design. Inside, columns define the formal dining room to the right of the foyer, and the study to the left of the foyer is accessed by double doors. The vaulted family room offers a corner fireplace. A bay window, large closet, and spacious private bath highlight the first-floor master suite; a bay window also decorates the breakfast area. Upstairs are three family bedrooms, all with walk-in closets, and two full baths.

SECOND FLOOR

FIRST FLOOR

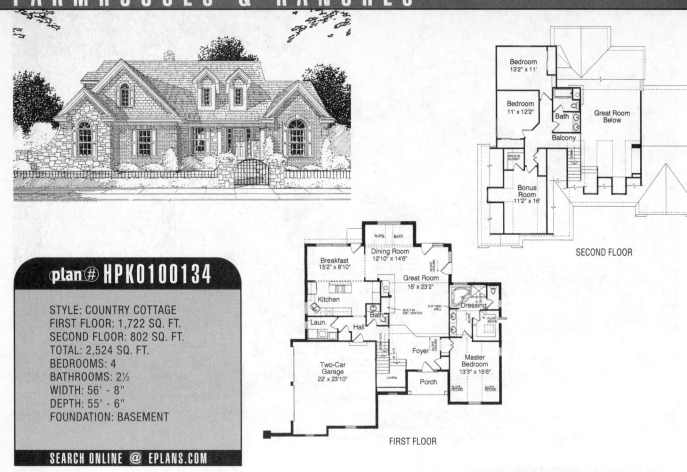

SECOND FLOOR

Bedroom
13'2" x 11'

Bedroom
11' x 12'2"

Bath

Great Room
Below

Balcony

WALK-IN CLOSET

Bonus Room
11'2" x 16'

FIRST FLOOR

Breakfast
15'2" x 8'10"

Dining Room
12'10" x 14'6"

Kitchen

Great Room
16' x 23'2"

Laun.

Bath

Dressing

Hall

BUILT-IN ENT. CENTER

8'-0" HIGH WALL

PLANT LEDGE ABOVE

Two-Car Garage
22' x 23'10"

Foyer

Master Bedroom
13'3" x 16'6"

Landing

Porch

plan # HPK0100134

STYLE: COUNTRY COTTAGE
FIRST FLOOR: 1,722 SQ. FT.
SECOND FLOOR: 802 SQ. FT.
TOTAL: 2,524 SQ. FT.
BEDROOMS: 4
BATHROOMS: 2½
WIDTH: 56' - 8"
DEPTH: 55' - 6"
FOUNDATION: BASEMENT

SEARCH ONLINE @ EPLANS.COM

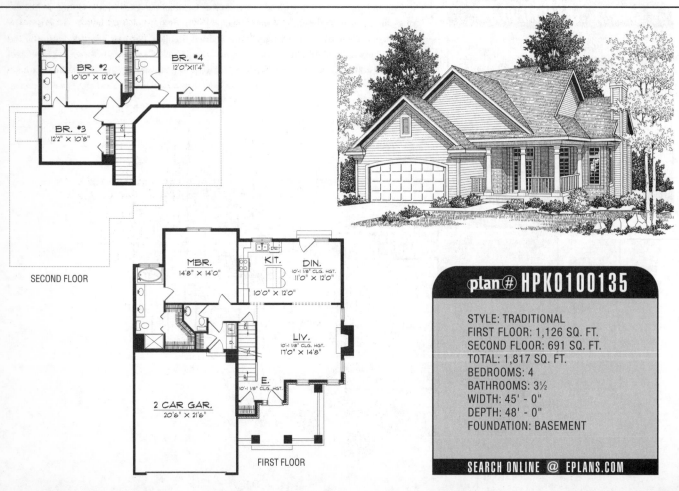

SECOND FLOOR

BR. #2
10'10" x 12'0"

BR. #4
12'0" X 11'4"

BR. #3
12'2" x 10'8"

FIRST FLOOR

MBR.
14'8" x 14'0"

KIT.
10'0" x 12'0"

DIN.
11'-1 1/8" CLG. HGT.
11'0" X 12'0"

LIV.
10'-1 1/8" CLG. HGT.
17'0" X 14'8"

E.
10'-1 1/8" CLG.

2 CAR GAR.
20'6" x 21'6"

plan # HPK0100135

STYLE: TRADITIONAL
FIRST FLOOR: 1,126 SQ. FT.
SECOND FLOOR: 691 SQ. FT.
TOTAL: 1,817 SQ. FT.
BEDROOMS: 4
BATHROOMS: 3½
WIDTH: 45' - 0"
DEPTH: 48' - 0"
FOUNDATION: BASEMENT

SEARCH ONLINE @ EPLANS.COM

ORDER BLUEPRINTS 24 HOURS, 7 DAYS A WEEK, AT 1-800-521-6797

plan# HPK0100136

STYLE: TRADITIONAL
FIRST FLOOR: 2,074 SQ. FT.
SECOND FLOOR: 600 SQ. FT.
TOTAL: 2,674 SQ. FT.
BONUS SPACE: 520 SQ. FT.
BEDROOMS: 4
BATHROOMS: 3
WIDTH: 88' - 0"
DEPTH: 36' - 10"
FOUNDATION: SLAB

SEARCH ONLINE @ EPLANS.COM

A sweeping front porch and a rear covered patio that leads to an inviting swimming pool mark this outstanding plan as the right home for an active, outward-looking family. An impressive entrance brings you to a spacious gallery that opens to a study, the formal dining room, and to a living room designed for gracious entertaining. The kitchen boasts an island counter that will put most tasks within an arm's reach. An absolutely lavish master suite is also found on the main floor, and two other bedrooms, a full bath, and lots of room for expansion are located upstairs. The house comes with a three-car garage.

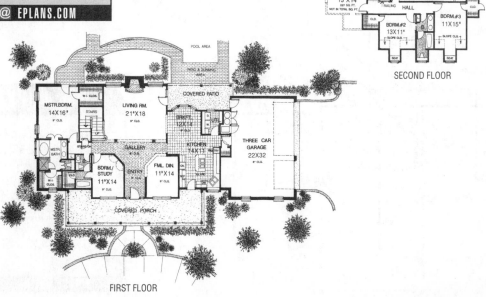

SECOND FLOOR

FIRST FLOOR

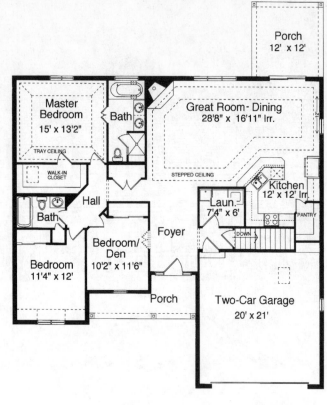

plan# HPK0100137

STYLE: COUNTRY COTTAGE
SQUARE FOOTAGE: 1,698
BEDROOMS: 3
BATHROOMS: 2
WIDTH: 51' - 8"
DEPTH: 49' - 8"
FOUNDATION: BASEMENT

SEARCH ONLINE @ EPLANS.COM

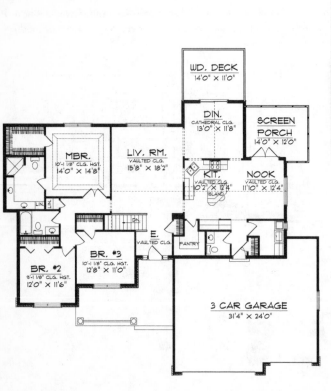

plan# HPK0100138

STYLE: BUNGALOW
SQUARE FOOTAGE: 1,922
BEDROOMS: 3
BATHROOMS: 2½
WIDTH: 69' - 0"
DEPTH: 57' - 4"
FOUNDATION: BASEMENT

SEARCH ONLINE @ EPLANS.COM

plan# HPK0100139

STYLE: TRADITIONAL
FIRST FLOOR: 1,101 SQ. FT.
SECOND FLOOR: 734 SQ. FT.
TOTAL: 1,835 SQ. FT.
BEDROOMS: 3
BATHROOMS: 3
WIDTH: 63' - 2"
DEPTH: 41' - 2"

SEARCH ONLINE @ EPLANS.COM

With farmhouse flair and colonial sensibilities, this three-bedroom home creates a compelling presence. The entry leads to a two-story family room with bright windows and a warming fireplace. From here, the kitchen opens to the left and easily serves the breakfast bay and dining room. Completing this level, a bedroom (or make it a den or home office) accesses a full bath. At the top of the stairs, a bedroom suite is lit by a Palladian window. The master suite is graced with a cathedral ceiling and lovely spa bath. A balcony just outside the master bedroom door overlooks the family room below.

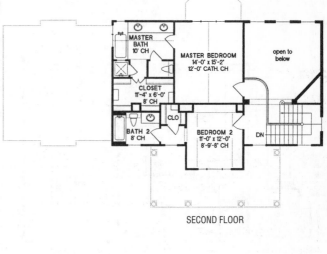

SECOND FLOOR

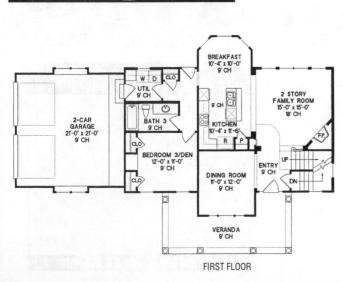

FIRST FLOOR

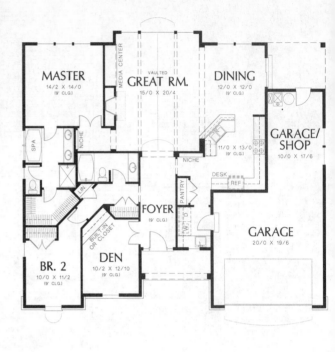

plan# HPK0100140

STYLE: COUNTRY COTTAGE
SQUARE FOOTAGE: 1,728
BEDROOMS: 2
BATHROOMS: 2
WIDTH: 55' - 0"
DEPTH: 48' - 0"
FOUNDATION: CRAWLSPACE

SEARCH ONLINE @ EPLANS.COM

plan# HPK0100141

STYLE: TRADITIONAL
SQUARE FOOTAGE: 1,873
BEDROOMS: 3
BATHROOMS: 2
WIDTH: 70' - 0"
DEPTH: 51' - 6"
FOUNDATION: CRAWLSPACE

SEARCH ONLINE @ EPLANS.COM

plan# HPK0100142

STYLE: COUNTRY COTTAGE
MAIN LEVEL: 2,213 SQ. FT.
LOWER LEVEL: 1,333 SQ. FT.
TOTAL: 3,546 SQ. FT.
BONUS SPACE: 430 SQ. FT.
BEDROOMS: 4
BATHROOMS: 3½
WIDTH: 67' - 2"
DEPTH: 93' - 1"
FOUNDATION: BASEMENT

SEARCH ONLINE @ EPLANS.COM

Interesting window treatments highlight this stone-and-shake facade, but don't overlook the columned porch to the left of the portico. Arches outline the formal dining room and the family room, both of which are convenient to the island kitchen. Household chores are made easier by the placement of a pantry, powder room, laundry room, and office between the kitchen and the entrances to the side porch and garage. If your goal is relaxation, the breakfast room, screened porch, and covered deck are also nearby. The master suite features a beautiful bay, and three secondary bedrooms and a recreation room are on the lower level.

LOWER LEVEL

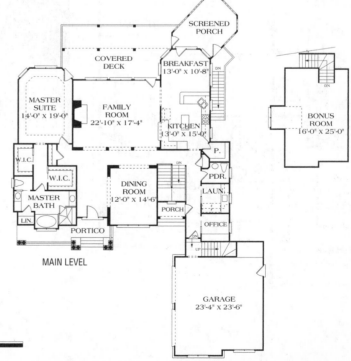

MAIN LEVEL

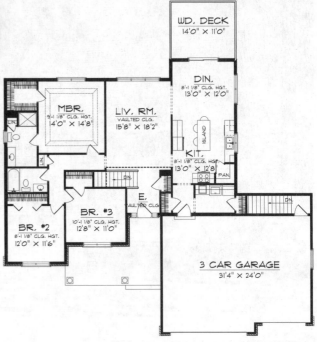

plan# HPK0100143

STYLE: BUNGALOW
SQUARE FOOTAGE: 1,636
BEDROOMS: 3
BATHROOMS: 2
WIDTH: 65' - 0"
DEPTH: 56' - 4"
FOUNDATION: BASEMENT

SEARCH ONLINE @ EPLANS.COM

plan# HPK0100144

STYLE: TRADITIONAL
SQUARE FOOTAGE: 1,296
BEDROOMS: 3
BATHROOMS: 2
WIDTH: 46' - 0"
DEPTH: 42' - 0"
FOUNDATION: BASEMENT,
CRAWLSPACE, SLAB

SEARCH ONLINE @ EPLANS.COM

plan# HPK0100145

STYLE: TRADITIONAL
SQUARE FOOTAGE: 2,040
BONUS SPACE: 627 SQ. FT.
BEDROOMS: 4
BATHROOMS: 3
WIDTH: 69' - 5"
DEPTH: 63' - 6"

SEARCH ONLINE @ EPLANS.COM

This European country home boasts a master bedroom and bath that will bring a warm smile to any homeowner. Three other bedrooms—make one a study—offer ample sleeping space in this one-story plan. An island kitchen easily services the formal dining room and sunlit breakfast nook. It flows easily into the family room, which enjoys a fireplace and vault ceiling. A utility room conveniently opens to the two-car garage. An optional attic adds 627 square feet of space that can be developed at a later date.

SECOND FLOOR

FIRST FLOOR

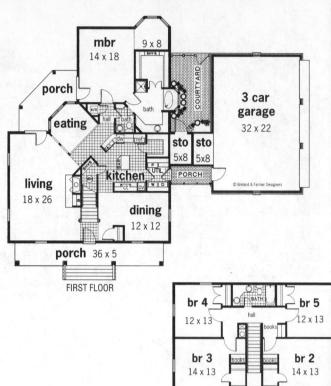

FIRST FLOOR

- mbr 14 x 18
- 9 x 8
- porch
- eating
- 3 car garage 32 x 22
- COURTYARD
- bath
- living 18 x 26
- sto 5x8
- sto 5x8
- kitchen
- PORCH
- dining 12 x 12
- porch 36 x 5
- © Breland & Farmer Designers

plan# HPK0100146

STYLE: TIDEWATER
FIRST FLOOR: 1,671 SQ. FT.
SECOND FLOOR: 980 SQ. FT.
TOTAL: 2,651 SQ. FT.
BEDROOMS: 5
BATHROOMS: 2
WIDTH: 72' - 0"
DEPTH: 58' - 0"
FOUNDATION: BASEMENT,
CRAWLSPACE, SLAB

SEARCH ONLINE @ EPLANS.COM

SECOND FLOOR

- br 4 12 x 13
- br 5 12 x 13
- hall
- br 3 14 x 13
- br 2 14 x 13
- © Breland & Farmer Designers

SECOND FLOOR

- Bedroom 11'4" x 14'5"
- Bedroom 12'8" x 12'2"
- Hall
- STAIRS DOWN
- Bedroom/ Study 10' x 11'10"
- Bath

FIRST FLOOR

- Porch 11' x 7'
- Dining 12' X 12'4"
- Master Bedroom 13' x 13'6"
- Great Room 15'10" x 16'10"
- Kitchen 9'10" x 16'10"
- Garage 20'2" x 24'4"
- Dressing
- WALK-IN CLOSET
- STAIRS UP
- STAIRS DOWN
- Hall
- Foyer
- Bath
- Laun.
- Porch 25'4" x 7'

plan# HPK0100147

STYLE: FARMHOUSE
FIRST FLOOR: 1,310 SQ. FT.
SECOND FLOOR: 741 SQ. FT.
TOTAL: 2,051 SQ. FT.
BEDROOMS: 4
BATHROOMS: 2½
WIDTH: 62' - 6"
DEPTH: 49' - 7"
FOUNDATION: BASEMENT

SEARCH ONLINE @ EPLANS.COM

ptan# HPK0100148

STYLE: TRADITIONAL
FIRST FLOOR: 1,729 SQ. FT.
SECOND FLOOR: 847 SQ. FT.
TOTAL: 2,576 SQ. FT.
BEDROOMS: 4
BATHROOMS: 3½
WIDTH: 84' - 8"
DEPTH: 51' - 9"

SEARCH ONLINE @ EPLANS.COM

This alluring country manor is sure to catch the eye of every passerby. The entry expands into a central foyer that opens to the main living areas. The study and dining room (or use one as a formal living room) are set in bay windows to bring in tons of natural light. An octagonal family room is to the rear, surrounded by windows and open to the island kitchen and breakfast nook. The master suite is bathed in light and delights in the posh spa bath. Upstairs, three bedrooms (one a full suite) may overlook the family room from an elegant balcony.

FIRST FLOOR

SECOND FLOOR

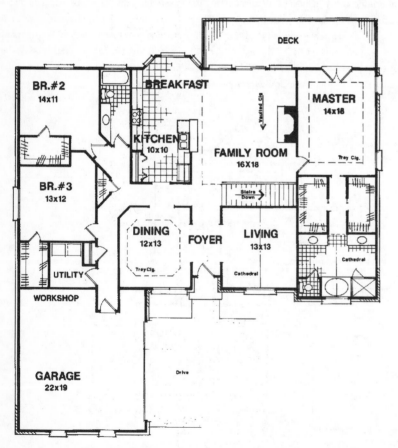

Tall arched windows and a brick facade mark this trim one-story home. Inside, the plan is designed to accommodate both congenial formal gatherings and laid-back family comfort. Guests entering through the foyer will either come into the living room with an impressive cathedral ceiling on the right or the tray-ceilinged dining area on the left. A spacious family room that opens into a sunlit breakfast bay and well-laid-out kitchen will be where family members gather for conversation, games, reading, or snacks. The master suite enjoys His and Hers walk-in closets and vanities and a glorious cathedral ceiling above the tub and shower. Double French doors from the bedroom lead out onto the rear deck. Two more bedrooms with walk-in closets share a bath. A convenient laundry area and a workshop at the rear of the garage round out this plan.

plan # HPK0100150

STYLE: TRADITIONAL
FIRST FLOOR: 1,429 SQ. FT.
SECOND FLOOR: 545 SQ. FT.
TOTAL: 1,974 SQ. FT.
BEDROOMS: 3
BATHROOMS: 3
WIDTH: 63' - 0"
DEPTH: 54' - 0"
FOUNDATION: CRAWLSPACE, SLAB

SEARCH ONLINE @ EPLANS.COM

This unique home masterfully blends the old with the new for a modern design with antiquated roots. Cool, crisp siding introduces the plan, as traditional brick adorns the sides. The entry opens on the right to a sloped-ceiling living room, warmed by a hearth and lit by a bay window. The U-shaped kitchen is ahead, facing a turret-style dining room, surrounded by windows. Two bedrooms on this level are situated for ultimate privacy; the master suite has a generous bedroom and lavish bath with a garden tub. The secondary bedroom enjoys a semiprivate bath. The upper level contains a dormer-lit bedroom with a semiprivate bath and a game room with overlooks to the living areas below.

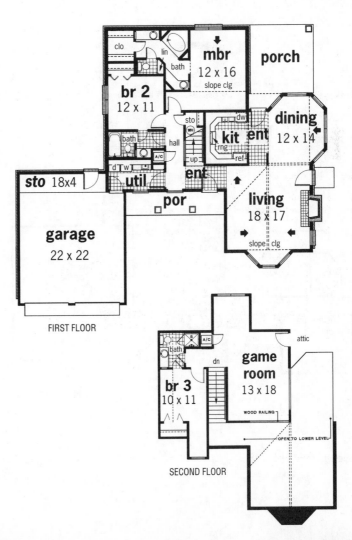

FIRST FLOOR

SECOND FLOOR

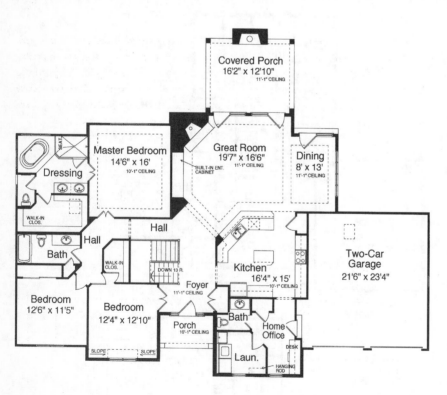

Covered Porch
16'2" x 12'10"
11'-1" CEILING

Master Bedroom
14'6" x 16'
10'-1" CEILING

Great Room
19'7" x 16'6"
11'-1" CEILING

BUILT-IN ENT. CABINET

Dining
8' x 13'
11'-1" CEILING

Dressing

WALK-IN CLOS.

Hall

Hall

Bath

WALK-IN CLOS.

DOWN 13 R.

Bedroom
12'6" x 11'5"

Bedroom
12'4" x 12'10"

Foyer
11'-1" CEILING

Kitchen
16'4" x 15'
10'-1" CEILING

Two-Car Garage
21'6" x 23'4"

Porch
10'-1" CEILING

SLOPE   SLOPE

Bath

Home Office

DESK

Laun.

HANGING ROD

---

plan # HPK0100151

STYLE: CRAFTSMAN
SQUARE FOOTAGE: 2,199
BEDROOMS: 3
BATHROOMS: 2½
WIDTH: 74' - 8"
DEPTH: 60' - 7"
FOUNDATION: BASEMENT

SEARCH ONLINE @ EPLANS.COM

Multiple gables, a stone-and-siding exterior, and a covered entry create a beautiful facade on this one-level home. The great room, dining area, and spacious kitchen combine to offer a large family gathering place. The placement of the entertainment alcove and fireplace provide a view from all three locations. An 11-foot ceiling tops the great room and dining area. Generous counter space, cabinetry, an island, and pantry in the kitchen, in addition to the adjacent laundry room and a small home office form an efficient work area. For privacy, the master suite is separated from the secondary bedrooms. A spectacular covered rear porch with fireplace extends the outdoor enjoyment to cooler weather. Split stairs lead to a full basement for storage or additional square footage.

plan# HPK0100152

STYLE: EUROPEAN COTTAGE
FIRST FLOOR: 1,685 SQ. FT.
SECOND FLOOR: 1,123 SQ. FT.
TOTAL: 2,808 SQ. FT.
BONUS SPACE: 385 SQ. FT.
BEDROOMS: 3
BATHROOMS: 2½
WIDTH: 53' - 0"
DEPTH: 55' - 6"
FOUNDATION: CRAWLSPACE

SEARCH ONLINE @ EPLANS.COM

A traditional home with Victorian elements, this three-bedroom home is designed to suit your needs. From the covered front porch, a two-story foyer leads you to a sunny dining room with a bay window. The angled kitchen looks out to the breakfast nook, bathed in light. The gathering room features a fireplace with surrounding built-ins and access to the rear patio. The master suite enjoys an octagonal tray ceiling, elongated walk-in closet, and a lavish bath. Upstairs, twin bedrooms share a bath and a bonus room. Future space is ready to grow as your family does.

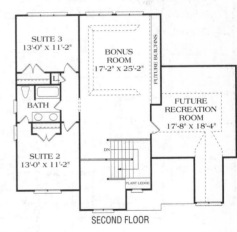

SECOND FLOOR

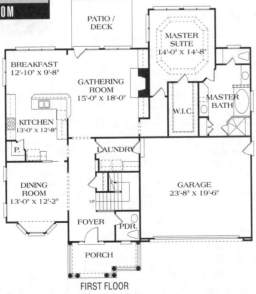

FIRST FLOOR

Diverse rooflines and window styles blend to project a sense of splendor, which is continued throughout the interior of this Southern-style home. With a soaring two-story vault ceiling and an extended-hearth fireplace, the family room assumes center stage in this design. The island kitchen, located between the formal dining room and breakfast corner, is well suited to serve both. A fully furnished master suite, with French doors separating the bath from the sleeping area, occupies the entire left wing. Upstairs, a similar-size suite offers posh quarters for overnight guests. A third bedroom, and space for a fourth, also are on this floor. All the upstairs bedrooms share access to a balcony overlooking the family room.

plan# HPK0100153

STYLE: COUNTRY COTTAGE
FIRST FLOOR: 1,390 SQ. FT.
SECOND FLOOR: 764 SQ. FT.
TOTAL: 2,154 SQ. FT.
BONUS SPACE: 282 SQ. FT.
BEDROOMS: 3
BATHROOMS: 3½
WIDTH: 42' - 0"
DEPTH: 57' - 4"
FOUNDATION: BASEMENT, CRAWLSPACE

SEARCH ONLINE @ EPLANS.COM

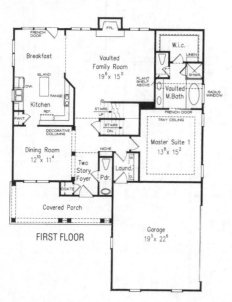

FIRST FLOOR

SECOND FLOOR

plan# HPK0100154

STYLE: SOUTHERN COLONIAL
FIRST FLOOR: 2,262 SQ. FT.
SECOND FLOOR: 638 SQ. FT.
TOTAL: 2,900 SQ. FT.
BONUS SPACE: 252 SQ. FT.
BEDROOMS: 4
BATHROOMS: 4
WIDTH: 64' - 0"
DEPTH: 56' - 4"
FOUNDATION: BASEMENT,
CRAWLSPACE, SLAB

SEARCH ONLINE @ EPLANS.COM

Brick, siding, and shutters spell country classic for this four-bedroom plan. A two-story ceiling begins in the foyer and becomes a graceful vault in the cozy family room. On the left, the kitchen is positioned to best serve the bright breakfast nook and elegant dining room, complete with a furniture niche. A vaulted keeping room at the rear makes a wonderful spot to curl up with a good book. On the left side of the plan, the stunning master suite is joined by a versatile bedroom, perfect as a nursery or home office when outfitted with optional French doors. Two upstairs bedroom suites share a loft with a family-room overlook, and a bonus room.

FIRST FLOOR

SECOND FLOOR

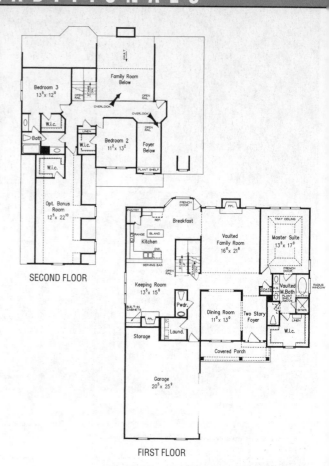

SECOND FLOOR

FIRST FLOOR

plan# HPK0100155

STYLE: COUNTRY COTTAGE
FIRST FLOOR: 1,816 SQ. FT.
SECOND FLOOR: 684 SQ. FT.
TOTAL: 2,500 SQ. FT.
BONUS SPACE: 422 SQ. FT.
BEDROOMS: 3
BATHROOMS: 2½
WIDTH: 51' - 0"
DEPTH: 64' - 0"
FOUNDATION: BASEMENT, CRAWLSPACE

SEARCH ONLINE @ EPLANS.COM

SECOND FLOOR

FIRST FLOOR

ALTERNATE GARAGE
DOOR LOCATION

plan# HPK0100007

STYLE: FARMHOUSE
FIRST FLOOR: 1,317 SQ. FT.
SECOND FLOOR: 1,208 SQ. FT.
TOTAL: 2,525 SQ. FT.
BONUS SPACE: 235 SQ. FT.
BEDROOMS: 4
BATHROOMS: 2½
WIDTH: 55' - 0"
DEPTH: 39' - 0"
FOUNDATION: CRAWLSPACE

SEARCH ONLINE @ EPLANS.COM

ORDER BLUEPRINTS 24 HOURS, 7 DAYS A WEEK, AT 1-800-521-6797

plan # HPK0100156

STYLE: COLONIAL
SQUARE FOOTAGE: 1,675
BONUS SPACE: 528 SQ. FT.
BEDROOMS: 3
BATHROOMS: 2
WIDTH: 54' - 6"
DEPTH: 62' - 10"
FOUNDATION: BASEMENT,
CRAWLSPACE, SLAB

SEARCH ONLINE @ EPLANS.COM

With farmhouse qualities and a traditional layout, this design is a true slice of Americana. From the covered entry, vaulted ceilings grace the foyer and hearth-warmed great room. The kitchen is situated for efficiency and easy meal preparations. A convenient serving bar overlooking the breakfast nook is great for meals on the go, and a columned dining room with a box-bay window will wow your guests. Bedrooms on the right share a full bath with a compartmented vanity for privacy. The master suite is on the left, highlighted by a tray ceiling, vaulted bath, and walk-in closet. Completing the plan is a two-car garage, reminiscent of a country barn. A bonus room may be added as your family grows.

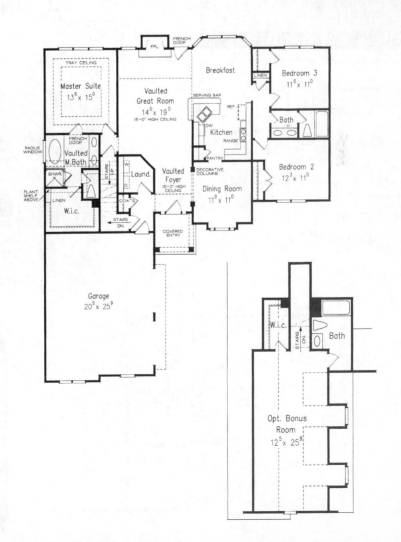

SECOND FLOOR

plan # HPK0100157

STYLE: CRAFTSMAN
FIRST FLOOR: 1,634 SQ. FT.
SECOND FLOOR: 2,207 SQ. FT.
TOTAL: 3,841 SQ. FT.
BEDROOMS: 4
BATHROOMS: 3½
WIDTH: 64' - 0"
DEPTH: 50' - 0"
FOUNDATION: CRAWLSPACE

SEARCH ONLINE @ EPLANS.COM

FIRST FLOOR

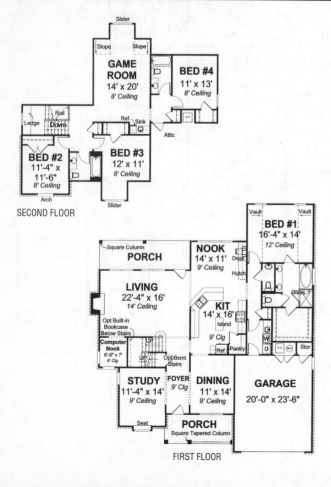

SECOND FLOOR

FIRST FLOOR

plan # HPK0100158

STYLE: FARMHOUSE
FIRST FLOOR: 1,923 SQ. FT.
SECOND FLOOR: 1,150 SQ. FT.
TOTAL: 3,073 SQ. FT.
BEDROOMS: 4
BATHROOMS: 3½
WIDTH: 54' - 0"
DEPTH: 60' - 0"

SEARCH ONLINE @ EPLANS.COM

ORDER BLUEPRINTS 24 HOURS, 7 DAYS A WEEK, AT 1-800-521-6797

plan# HPK0100009

STYLE: COUNTRY COTTAGE
FIRST FLOOR: 1,502 SQ. FT.
SECOND FLOOR: 1,073 SQ. FT.
TOTAL: 2,575 SQ. FT.
BONUS SPACE: 373 SQ. FT.
BEDROOMS: 3
BATHROOMS: 2½
WIDTH: 60' - 0"
DEPTH: 44' - 0"
FOUNDATION: CRAWLSPACE

SEARCH ONLINE @ EPLANS.COM

Charm abounds in this smart yet cozy traditional. Craftsman detailing adds interest to tried-and-true shutters, siding, and welcoming front porch. Inside, the living space goes on and on with a den and formal living room to the front of the plan, and a dining room, spacious kitchen, and family room to the back. The kitchen features a cooktop island and access to the rear property. Upstairs, a vaulted master suite with a luxurious bath is joined by two additional bedrooms, another bath, and a huge bonus room.

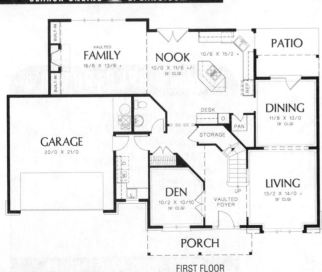

FIRST FLOOR

SECOND FLOOR

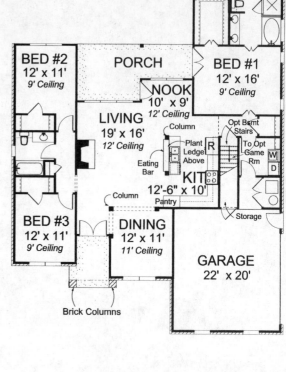

BED #2
12' x 11'
9' Ceiling

PORCH

BED #1
12' x 16'
9' Ceiling

NOOK
10' x 9'
12' Ceiling

LIVING
19' x 16'
12' Ceiling

Column

Plant Ledge Above

Opt Bsmt Stairs

To Opt Game Rm

W
D

Eating Bar

KIT
12'-6" x 10'

R

BED #3
12' x 11'
9' Ceiling

Column

Pantry

DINING
12' x 11'
11' Ceiling

Storage

GARAGE
22' x 20'

Brick Columns

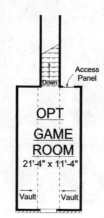

Access Panel

Down

OPT GAME ROOM
21'-4" x 11'-4"

Vault   Vault

plan# HPK0100159

STYLE: EUROPEAN COTTAGE
SQUARE FOOTAGE: 1,595
BONUS SPACE: 312 SQ. FT.
BEDROOMS: 3
BATHROOMS: 2
WIDTH: 49' - 0"
DEPTH: 60' - 0"

SEARCH ONLINE @ EPLANS.COM

BED #1
20' x 15'
12' Ceiling

Slope

SCREEN PORCH
19' x 20'
12' Ceiling

Square Column

French

Atrium

10' Ceiling

NOOK
10' x 12'-4"
10' Ceiling

LIVING
19' x 22'-8"
12' Ceiling

BED #2
14' x 12'
10' Ceiling

BED #3
14' x 12'
10' Ceiling

MEDIA ROOM
19' x 16'
12' Ceiling

Pantry

Eating Bar

KIT
15'-4" x 16'-4"

Island

Cook top

Desk

Ovens

10' Clg

Pocket

BED #4
14' x 12'
10' Ceiling

Walk-in Shower

Glass Block

Dresser

EMERALD FOYER
14' Ceiling
Round Column

Soffit

Slope

Opti Bsmt Stairs

W
D

EXERCISE ROOM
13' x 13'
12' Clg

STUDY
14' x 16'
12' Ceiling

FOYER
12' Ceiling

DINING
14' x 16'
12' Ceiling

PORCH
14' Clg

4 CAR GARAGE
26' x 38'

Arch

plan# HPK0100160

STYLE: TRADITIONAL
SQUARE FOOTAGE: 4,121
BEDROOMS: 4
BATHROOMS: 4½
WIDTH: 99' - 10"
DEPTH: 81' - 0"

SEARCH ONLINE @ EPLANS.COM

plan# HPK0100161

STYLE: TRADITIONAL
FIRST FLOOR: 766 SQ. FT.
SECOND FLOOR: 812 SQ. FT.
TOTAL: 1,578 SQ. FT.
BONUS SPACE: 291 SQ. FT.
BEDROOMS: 3
BATHROOMS: 2½
WIDTH: 34' - 0"
DEPTH: 38' - 0"
FOUNDATION: BASEMENT

SEARCH ONLINE @ EPLANS.COM

Snappy rooflines with stylish shuttered windows preview the family comforts offered inside this two-story contemporary home. A master bedroom with a private bath that enjoys a shower is separated from two other family bedrooms. All three rooms have hallway access to a swanky bath with a shower and a huge corner tub. The spacious island kitchen has plenty of room for more than one cook (the walk-in pantry is especially attractive) and easily serves the adjoining dining area. A laundry opens from the kitchen and a half-bath is located down the hall. The front living room can be entered through the foyer, which comes with a roomy coat closet.

Dramatic high arches on the facade of this home are a fitting welcome to the grand accommodations inside. The spacious foyer opens to a vaulted, hearth-warmed living room on the left and a bayed dining room on the right. Ahead, a cozy den opens through French doors, and a family room with a fireplace awaits at the back. The enormous island kitchen features a pantry and miles of counter space. A three-car garage to the right accesses the home through a mudroom area and utility/laundry room. The second floor houses three family bedrooms that share a twin-sink bath, as well as a mini library and a deluxe master suite. The master bath enjoys a garden tub and a walk-in closet that never ends.

plan # HPK0100162

STYLE: EUROPEAN COTTAGE
FIRST FLOOR: 1,821 SQ. FT.
SECOND FLOOR: 1,577 SQ. FT.
TOTAL: 3,398 SQ. FT.
BEDROOMS: 4
BATHROOMS: 2½
WIDTH: 60' - 0"
DEPTH: 50' - 0"
FOUNDATION: CRAWLSPACE

SEARCH ONLINE @ EPLANS.COM

FIRST FLOOR

SECOND FLOOR

plan# HPK0100163

STYLE: CONTEMPORARY
FIRST FLOOR: 1,554 SQ. FT.
SECOND FLOOR: 1,414 SQ. FT.
TOTAL: 2,968 SQ. FT.
BEDROOMS: 3
BATHROOMS: 2½
WIDTH: 50' - 0"
DEPTH: 43' - 0"
FOUNDATION: BASEMENT

SEARCH ONLINE @ EPLANS.COM

You are sure to be amazed at what lies behind this traditional stone facade. A luxurious floor plan from top to bottom, this home is a dream come true for anyone who loves to entertain or just enjoys the finer things. A living room with a bay window resides on the left, defined by a two-way fireplace that also warms the dining room. The kitchen is wide and inviting with a bumped-out window over the sink. Family areas include a two-story main gathering room—with space for an indoor spa—and a closed off entertainment room. A U-shaped staircase reveals four bedrooms, each with beautiful bay windows. The master suite will pamper and soothe.

SECOND FLOOR

FIRST FLOOR

plan # HPK0100164

STYLE: RANCH
SQUARE FOOTAGE: 2,695
BEDROOMS: 4
BATHROOMS: 3½
WIDTH: 74' - 0"
DEPTH: 57' - 0"

SEARCH ONLINE @ EPLANS.COM

SCREEN PORCH
18'-6" x 12'
12' Ceiling

PORCH

BED #1
13'-4" x 17'-4"
10' Ceiling

LIVING
18' x 21'-6"
12' Ceiling

NOOK
13'-8" x 12'
9' Clg

Desk

BED #2
11' x 12'-6"
9' Ceiling

BED #3
11'-6" x 12'
9' Ceiling

Pantry

Eating Bar

Pantry

Up to Attic
Opt Bonus Rm

BED #4
12'-6" x 12'-8"
9' Ceiling

KIT
13'-8" x 12'

Island

Ref

Ovens

Opt Bsmt
Stairs

W D

A.C.

Appliance
Garage

Walk-In
Shower

STUDY
11' x 14'
10' Ceiling

Barrel
Arch

FOYER
10' Clg

DINING
11' x 14'
10' Ceiling

3 CAR GARAGE
30' x 23'

Dresser

Seat

PORCH
10' Ceiling

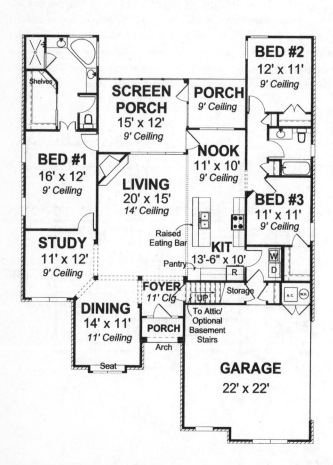

Shelves

SCREEN PORCH
15' x 12'
9' Ceiling

PORCH
9' Ceiling

BED #2
12' x 11'
9' Ceiling

BED #1
16' x 12'
9' Ceiling

NOOK
11' x 10'
9' Ceiling

LIVING
20' x 15'
14' Ceiling

BED #3
11' x 11'
9' Ceiling

Raised
Eating Bar

KIT
13'-6" x 10'

Pantry

W
D

R

STUDY
11' x 12'
9' Ceiling

FOYER
11' Clg

Storage

A.C.

W.H.

UP

To Attic/
Optional
Basement
Stairs

DINING
14' x 11'
11' Ceiling

PORCH
Arch

Seat

GARAGE
22' x 22'

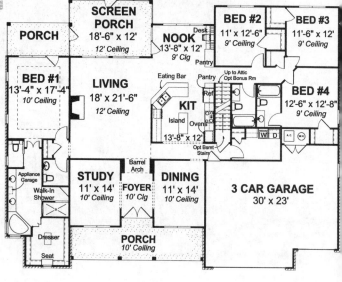

plan # HPK0100165

STYLE: COUNTRY COTTAGE
SQUARE FOOTAGE: 1,768
BEDROOMS: 3
BATHROOMS: 2
WIDTH: 49' - 0"
DEPTH: 66' - 0"

SEARCH ONLINE @ EPLANS.COM

ORDER BLUEPRINTS 24 HOURS, 7 DAYS A WEEK, AT 1-800-521-6797

plan# HPK0100166

STYLE: TRADITIONAL
SQUARE FOOTAGE: 3,175
BEDROOMS: 4
BATHROOMS: 2½
WIDTH: 79' - 0"
DEPTH: 65' - 4"
FOUNDATION: BASEMENT,
CRAWLSPACE, SLAB

SEARCH ONLINE @ EPLANS.COM

This European design features an arched entryway and matching windows with keystone moldings. Once inside, the dining room and study enclose the foyer, which leads to the living room and porch. To the left, an island kitchen is accompanied by a very large family room, also functioning as a breakfast nook. The master suite resides at the left of the plan, with views to the rear of the home. The master bath features dual vanities and two spacious walk-in closets.

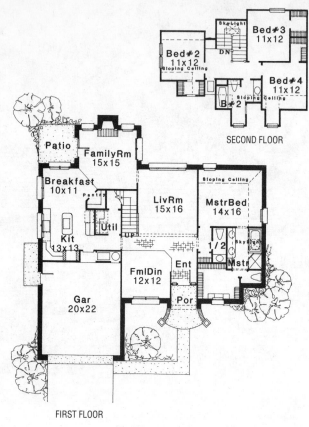

SECOND FLOOR

Bed#2 11x12 Sloping Ceiling

Bed#3 11x12

Bed#4 11x12 Sloping Ceiling

B#2 Sloping Ceiling

Patio

FamilyRm 15x15

Breakfast 10x11

Pantry

Kit 13x13

Util

LivRm 15x16

MstrBed 14x16

1/2

Mstr

FmlDin 12x12

Ent

Por

Gar 20x22

FIRST FLOOR

plan# HPK0100167

STYLE: TRADITIONAL
FIRST FLOOR: 1,649 SQ. FT.
SECOND FLOOR: 660 SQ. FT.
TOTAL: 2,309 SQ. FT.
BEDROOMS: 4
BATHROOMS: 2½
WIDTH: 55' - 0"
DEPTH: 54' - 4"
FOUNDATION: BASEMENT,
CRAWLSPACE, SLAB

SEARCH ONLINE @ EPLANS.COM

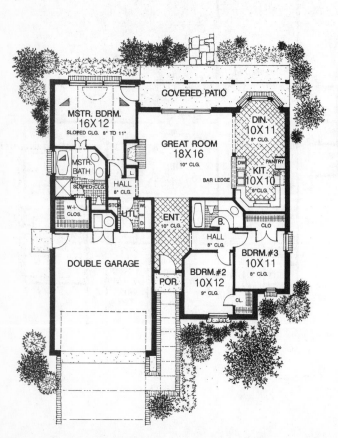

COVERED PATIO

MSTR. BDRM. 16X12 SLOPED CLG. 8" TO 11"

GREAT ROOM 18X16 10" CLG.

DIN. 10X11 8" CLG.

MSTR. BATH SLOPED CLG.

HALL 8" CLG.

DW

PANTRY

KIT. 10X10 8" CLG.

BAR LEDGE

W·I· CLOS.

UTL

ENT 10" CLG.

B.

HALL 8" CLG.

CLO

DOUBLE GARAGE

POR.

BDRM.#2 10X12 9" CLG.

BDRM.#3 10X11 8" CLG.

CL.

plan# HPK0100168

STYLE: FRENCH
SQUARE FOOTAGE: 1,416
BEDROOMS: 3
BATHROOMS: 2
WIDTH: 45' - 0"
DEPTH: 49' - 10"
FOUNDATION: SLAB

SEARCH ONLINE @ EPLANS.COM

plan # HPK0100169

STYLE: FRENCH
SQUARE FOOTAGE: 4,095
BONUS SPACE: 599 SQ. FT.
BEDROOMS: 4
BATHROOMS: 3½
WIDTH: 98' - 0"
DEPTH: 77' - 6"

SEARCH ONLINE @ EPLANS.COM

Step up to elegance in this gorgeous brick home. Varying rooflines and copper bays attract the eye on the exterior, and it gets even better inside. Formal areas set the tone at the front of the plan, with a dining room and study flanking the foyer, which opens to a gallery hall. The living room at the center of the plan, enjoys a dramatic 14-foot ceiling, a fireplace, and access to the rear porch. To the left, the island kitchen opens to a dining nook and is loaded with a pantry and abundant counter space. Three bedrooms share two baths on the far left of the plan, behind the three-car garage. The right wing is taken up completely by the master suite, which is expanded by a bayed sitting area that opens to the rear porch. Two walk-in closets provide plenty of wardrobe space, and the spacious bath pampers with its circular tub, glass-walled shower, and compartmented toilet. Upstairs, an optional game room awaits your expansion.

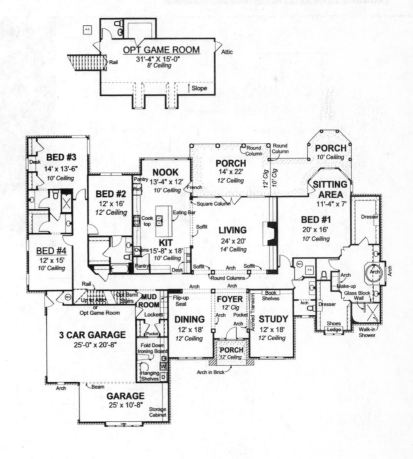

SECOND FLOOR

SUITE 4 12'-6" X 14'-0"

UNFINISHED STORAGE 16'-0" X 14'-4"

SUITE 3 12'-4" X 16'-8"

BATH

BATH

ACCESS

STUDY LOFT 7'-8" X 6'-8"

SUITE 2 13'-2" X 13'-8"

TERRACE

MASTER SUITE 12'-6" X 14'-0"

GATHERING ROOM 16'-0" X 14'-4"

BREAKFAST 12'-2" X 9'-4"

W.I.C.

KITCHEN 12'-4" X 14'-6"

MASTER BATH

PDR.

FOYER

P.

PORTICO

DINING ROOM 11'-6" X 8'-4"

LAUN

FIRST FLOOR

2 CAR GARAGE 21'-2" X 25'-10"

plan # HPK0100170

STYLE: TRADITIONAL
FIRST FLOOR: 1,723 SQ. FT.
SECOND FLOOR: 1,081 SQ. FT.
TOTAL: 2,804 SQ. FT.
BEDROOMS: 4
BATHROOMS: 3½
WIDTH: 56' - 4"
DEPTH: 72' - 0"
FOUNDATION: CRAWLSPACE

SEARCH ONLINE @ EPLANS.COM

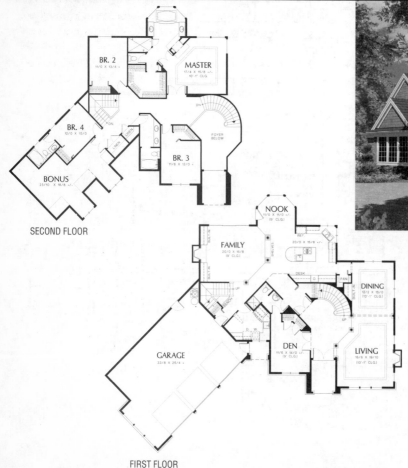

BR. 2 11/0 X 13/4

MASTER 17/4 X 15/8 +/- 10'-1" CLG.

BR. 4 12/0 X 10/0

DN

FOYER BELOW

BR. 3 11/8 X 12/0

BONUS 23/10 X 18/8 +/-

SECOND FLOOR

NOOK 11/0 X 11/0 (9' CLG.)

FAMILY 20/0 X 15/8 (9' CLG.)

REF.

DINING 13/2 X 15/0 (19'-1" CLG.)

DESK

GARAGE 33/8 X 25/4 +/-

DEN 11/8 X 14/0 (9' CLG.)

LIVING 16/8 X 18/0 (13'-1" CLG.)

D W

FIRST FLOOR

plan # HPK0100171

STYLE: NW CONTEMPORARY
FIRST FLOOR: 2,148 SQ. FT.
SECOND FLOOR: 1,541 SQ. FT.
TOTAL: 3,689 SQ. FT.
BONUS SPACE: 383 SQ. FT.
BEDROOMS: 4
BATHROOMS: 4
WIDTH: 85' - 5"
DEPTH: 50' - 0"
FOUNDATION: CRAWLSPACE

SEARCH ONLINE @ EPLANS.COM

ORDER BLUEPRINTS 24 HOURS, 7 DAYS A WEEK, AT 1-800-521-6797

plan# HPK0100172

STYLE: TRADITIONAL
FIRST FLOOR: 2,304 SQ. FT.
SECOND FLOOR: 1,147 SQ. FT.
TOTAL: 3,451 SQ. FT.
BEDROOMS: 4
BATHROOMS: 3½
WIDTH: 64' - 0"
DEPTH: 55' - 0"

SEARCH ONLINE @ EPLANS.COM

Live large in this four-bedroom beauty. Entertain in the formal dining room and elegant study that greet you at the front of the plan, accented by columns. The hearth-warmed living room features a specialty ceiling and a triple window that looks out to the porch. The kitchen is at the heart of the plan, and enjoys conveniences such as an island counter, pantry, desk, and snack bar. To the left lie a handy utility room and the master bedroom with a private bath and a huge walk-in closet with a built-in dresser! Upstairs, three bedrooms all enjoy walk-in closets and share two baths.

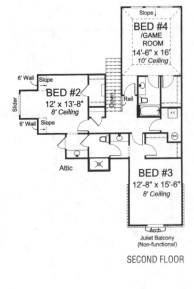

SECOND FLOOR

FIRST FLOOR

From the brick-and-siding exterior to the country-size kitchen, this two-story home will easily win your family's accolades. The kitchen readily serves the informal family snack counter and the formal dining room. The spacious living room welcomes friends as they step through the foyer. Off the kitchen is a laundry area and a bath with a shower. Upstairs, the sheer size of the walk-in closet in the master bedroom will sweep you off your feet. A lavish bath with an oversize tub, a shower, and a double-sink vanity serves all three second-floor bedrooms. Adjoining space is available for a fourth bedroom or playroom over the garage.

plan# HPK0100173

STYLE: EUROPEAN COTTAGE
FIRST FLOOR: 816 SQ. FT.
SECOND FLOOR: 812 SQ. FT.
TOTAL: 1,628 SQ. FT.
BEDROOMS: 3
BATHROOMS: 2
WIDTH: 32' - 0"
DEPTH: 38' - 0"
FOUNDATION: BASEMENT

SEARCH ONLINE @ EPLANS.COM

FIRST FLOOR

SECOND FLOOR

ORDER BLUEPRINTS 24 HOURS, 7 DAYS A WEEK, AT 1-800-521-6797

plan# HPK0100174

STYLE: CONTEMPORARY
SQUARE FOOTAGE: 1,129
BEDROOMS: 2
BATHROOMS: 1
WIDTH: 49' - 0"
DEPTH: 37' - 4"
FOUNDATION: BASEMENT

SEARCH ONLINE @ EPLANS.COM

Refreshing style and thoughtful planning make this two-bedroom home a great choice. A glass front door lit by an overhead arched window opens to a foyer that either leads up to the main level or downstairs to an unfinished basement. The living room is enchanting with a bay window, perfect for a window seat. A central freestanding fireplace defines this area and separates it from the kitchen and dining room, each with ample space for family and guests. Two good-size bedrooms share a luxurious bath on the left.

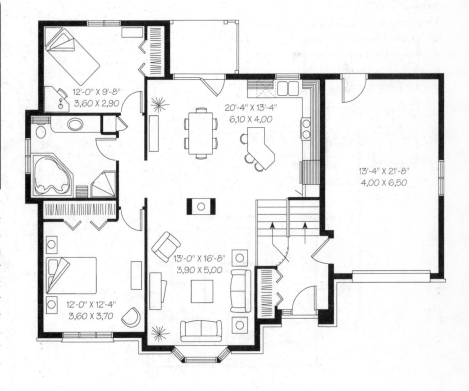

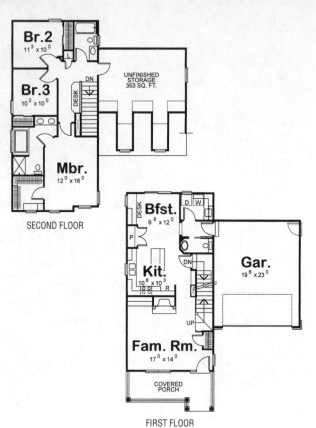

SECOND FLOOR

Br.2
11³ x 10⁰

Br.3
10⁰ x 10⁰

UNFINISHED STORAGE
353 SQ. FT.

Mbr.
12⁰ x 16⁰

Bfst.
9⁸ x 12⁰

Kit.
10⁸ x 10³

Gar.
19⁸ x 23⁰

Fam. Rm.
17⁰ x 14⁰

COVERED PORCH

FIRST FLOOR

plan # HPK0100175

STYLE: TRADITIONAL
FIRST FLOOR: 787 SQ. FT.
SECOND FLOOR: 788 SQ. FT.
TOTAL: 1,575 SQ. FT.
BONUS SPACE: 353 SQ. FT.
BEDROOMS: 3
BATHROOMS: 2½
WIDTH: 40' - 0"
DEPTH: 48' - 0"

SEARCH ONLINE @ EPLANS.COM

COMPUTER LOFT

TWO STORY FOYER

BEDROOM 2
10'-4" x 11'-4"

BEDROOM 3
13'-0" x 16'-0"

W.I.C.

SECOND FLOOR

BREAKFAST

KITCHEN

GRAND ROOM
15'-4" x 18'-4"

MASTER BEDROOM
13'-1" x 14'-1"

TWO STORY FOYER

DINING ROOM
10'-1" x 12'-3"

M. BATH

P.R.

LNDRY.

W.I.C.

FIRST FLOOR

TWO CAR GARAGE

©2001, 02, 03, 04 By Designer

plan # HPK0100004

STYLE: TRADITIONAL
FIRST FLOOR: 1,314 SQ. FT.
SECOND FLOOR: 616 SQ. FT.
TOTAL: 1,930 SQ. FT.
BEDROOMS: 3
BATHROOMS: 2½
WIDTH: 40' - 0"
DEPTH: 54' - 6"
FOUNDATION: BASEMENT

SEARCH ONLINE @ EPLANS.COM

ORDER BLUEPRINTS 24 HOURS, 7 DAYS A WEEK, AT 1-800-521-6797

plan# HPK0100176

STYLE: TRADITIONAL
FIRST FLOOR: 2,188 SQ. FT.
SECOND FLOOR: 922 SQ. FT.
TOTAL: 3,110 SQ. FT.
BEDROOMS: 4
BATHROOMS: 3½
WIDTH: 69' - 0"
DEPTH: 53' - 10"
FOUNDATION: SLAB

SEARCH ONLINE @ EPLANS.COM

A rustic appeal radiates from the stone exterior of this two-story beauty, yet, the interior is astounding for its modernity. Those just-right social affairs can extend beyond the front dining and living rooms to the hearth-warmed great room with a soaring cathedral ceiling. From here visitors can easily enter the rear patio. For relaxed family dining and hanging out, the kitchen and adjoining dining area, which accesses a second patio are perfect. A main-floor master suite enjoys His and Hers walk-in closets and a lavish bath. Up a spiral stairway, three more bedrooms and two baths can be found. Ample linen closets and a plant ledge are also on this floor.

SECOND FLOOR

FIRST FLOOR

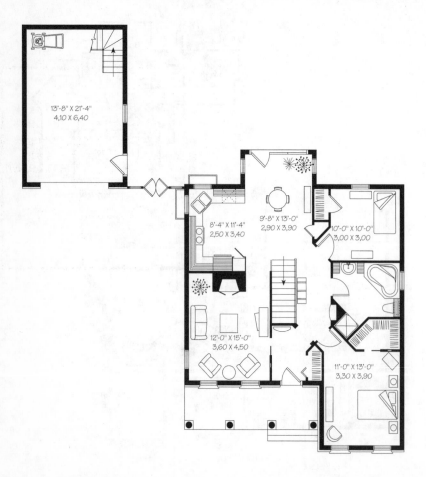

13'-8" X 21'-4"
4,10 X 6,40

8'-4" X 11'-4"
2,50 X 3,40

9'-8" X 13'-0"
2,90 X 3,90

10'-0" X 10'-0"
3,00 X 3,00

12'-0" X 15'-0"
3,60 X 4,50

11'-0" X 13'-0"
3,30 X 3,90

plan# HPK0100177

STYLE: COUNTRY COTTAGE
SQUARE FOOTAGE: 1,072
BEDROOMS: 2
BATHROOMS: 1
WIDTH: 32' - 0"
DEPTH: 42' - 0"
FOUNDATION: BASEMENT

SEARCH ONLINE @ EPLANS.COM

Gentle arches separating front-porch columns and
hipped rooflines distinguish this handsome one-story
home, perfect for a new family. From the warming
fireplace in the front living room to the open space of
the combined kitchen and dining area, this plan
promises both comfort and convenience. The master
bedroom, which enjoys a walk-in wardrobe, shares a
splendid bath with a second bedroom. It includes a
walk-in shower, but winning marks go to the magnificent corner garden tub. A rear deck and unat-
tached garage complete this plan.

plan# HPK0100178

STYLE: CRAFTSMAN
FIRST FLOOR: 1,283 SQ. FT.
SECOND FLOOR: 1,010 SQ. FT.
TOTAL: 2,293 SQ. FT.
BEDROOMS: 4
BATHROOMS: 3½
WIDTH: 38' - 0"
DEPTH: 59' - 0"
FOUNDATION: BASEMENT

SEARCH ONLINE @ EPLANS.COM

This four-bedroom home has everything a family needs. Enter through the front porch or the garage and walk right in to the living room, which enjoys a fireplace and a two-story ceiling. This space flows right in to the spacious kitchen and dining room, complete with an island counter, pantry closet, and bayed window. A powder room and laundry closet flank the hallway to the master suite, which features a walk-in closet and twin-sink vanity. Upstairs, three bedrooms surround a study loft and share two bathrooms. Each bedroom has a large walk-in closet.

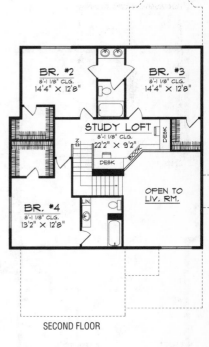

SECOND FLOOR

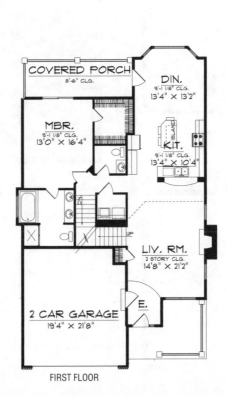

FIRST FLOOR

plan# HPK0100179

STYLE: BUNGALOW
SQUARE FOOTAGE: 1,019
BEDROOMS: 2
BATHROOMS: 1
WIDTH: 46' - 0"
DEPTH: 37' - 0"
FOUNDATION: BASEMENT

SEARCH ONLINE @ EPLANS.COM

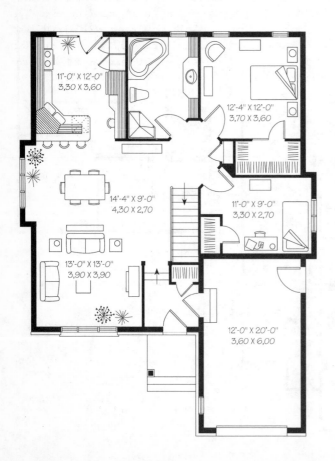

plan# HPK0100180

STYLE: CONTEMPORARY
SQUARE FOOTAGE: 1,138
BEDROOMS: 2
BATHROOMS: 1
WIDTH: 34' - 0"
DEPTH: 48' - 0"
FOUNDATION: BASEMENT

SEARCH ONLINE @ EPLANS.COM

plan # HPK0100181

STYLE: COUNTRY COTTAGE
FIRST FLOOR: 1,192 SQ. FT.
SECOND FLOOR: 1,152 SQ. FT.
TOTAL: 2,344 SQ. FT.
BEDROOMS: 4
BATHROOMS: 2½
WIDTH: 47' - 4"
DEPTH: 40' - 8"
FOUNDATION: BASEMENT, CRAWLSPACE

SEARCH ONLINE @ EPLANS.COM

Columns, inside and out, give this charming country cottage a distinguished look that complements its homey coziness. Designed to impress, the spacious two-story foyer has entries to a convenient coat room and half-bath and leads into the splendid dining and living rooms. The hearth-warmed family room, together with the kitchen and breakfast area, stretches across the back of the house. Upstairs four bedrooms, including a posh master suite, afford comfortable sleeping space. A huge corner tub, shower with a seat, and plant shelves make the master bath a very special retreat. A laundry and pantry behind the kitchen and a two-car garage round out this plan.

FIRST FLOOR

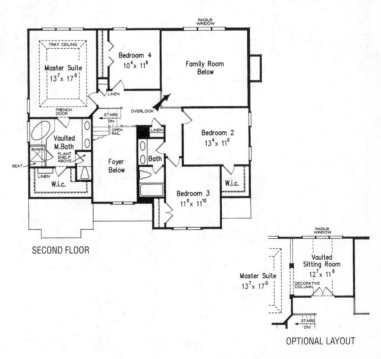

SECOND FLOOR

OPTIONAL LAYOUT

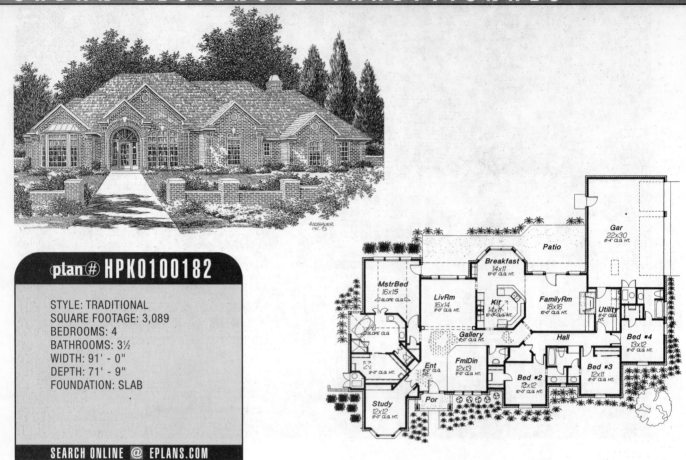

plan# HPK0100182

STYLE: TRADITIONAL
SQUARE FOOTAGE: 3,089
BEDROOMS: 4
BATHROOMS: 3½
WIDTH: 91' - 0"
DEPTH: 71' - 9"
FOUNDATION: SLAB

SEARCH ONLINE @ EPLANS.COM

SECOND FLOOR

FIRST FLOOR

plan# HPK0100183

STYLE: COUNTRY COTTAGE
FIRST FLOOR: 1,790 SQ. FT.
SECOND FLOOR: 797 SQ. FT.
TOTAL: 2,587 SQ. FT.
BEDROOMS: 4
BATHROOMS: 3½
WIDTH: 64' - 4"
DEPTH: 50' - 0"
FOUNDATION: BASEMENT

SEARCH ONLINE @ EPLANS.COM

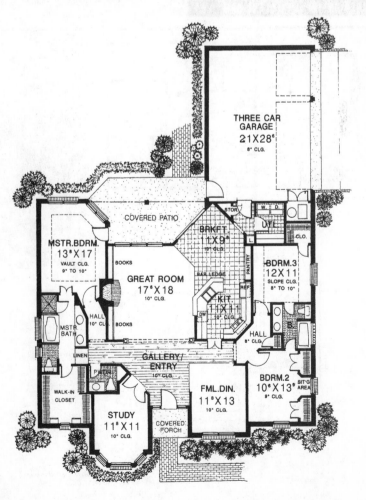

plan # HPK0100184

STYLE: TRADITIONAL
SQUARE FOOTAGE: 2,214
BEDROOMS: 3
BATHROOMS: 2½
WIDTH: 55' - 0"
DEPTH: 77' - 11"
FOUNDATION: SLAB

SEARCH ONLINE @ EPLANS.COM

Hipped and gabled rooflines, combined with an arch-topped window and an elegant window bay with a flared top, herald a charming interior to this European-style beauty. A spacious gallery entry opens to the formal dining room to the right and the cozy great room straight ahead. Through French doors to the left enter the study set into the window bay. The great room boasts a fireplace flanked by rows of built-in bookshelves. Sliding doors lead to the rear covered patio. An angled counter ties the great room together with the kitchen and breakfast nook in a smoothly working unit. A master suite on the left side of the plan is thoughtfully separated from the other two bedrooms located on the other side of the plan.

FREILING

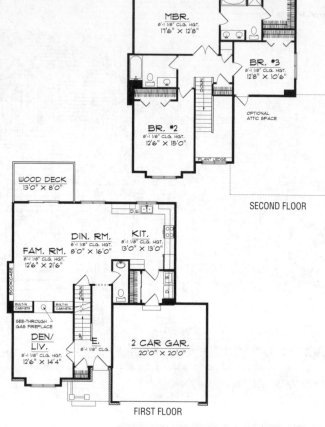

SECOND FLOOR

plan# HPK0100185

STYLE: TRADITIONAL
FIRST FLOOR: 1,016 SQ. FT.
SECOND FLOOR: 926 SQ. FT.
TOTAL: 1,942 SQ. FT.
BEDROOMS: 3
BATHROOMS: 2½
WIDTH: 40' - 8"
DEPTH: 40' - 0"
FOUNDATION: BASEMENT

SEARCH ONLINE @ EPLANS.COM

FIRST FLOOR

MAIN LEVEL

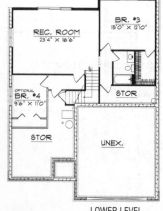

LOWER LEVEL

plan# HPK0100186

STYLE: TRADITIONAL
MAIN LEVEL: 1,382 SQ. FT.
LOWER LEVEL: 766 SQ. FT.
TOTAL: 2,148 SQ. FT.
BEDROOMS: 3
BATHROOMS: 3
WIDTH: 40' - 4"
DEPTH: 52' - 0"
FOUNDATION: BASEMENT

SEARCH ONLINE @ EPLANS.COM

ORDER BLUEPRINTS 24 HOURS, 7 DAYS A WEEK, AT 1-800-521-6797

plan# HPK0100187

STYLE: TRADITIONAL
FIRST FLOOR: 935 SQ. FT.
SECOND FLOOR: 1,150 SQ. FT.
TOTAL: 2,085 SQ. FT.
BEDROOMS: 4
BATHROOMS: 2½
WIDTH: 50' - 0"
DEPTH: 36' - 8"
FOUNDATION: BASEMENT

SEARCH ONLINE @ EPLANS.COM

This wonderful floor plan offers convenience and style to provide many years of enjoyment and comfort for the growing family. The foyer introduces a turned staircase with wood trim and a large great room with a corner fireplace and windows to the rear yard. The grand opening to the dining area and snack bar expands the gathering space for a roomy look and feel. The kitchen offers an abundance of counter space, cabinets, and a pantry for added storage. Entry from the garage through a hall creates an orderly and accessible traffic flow. The second-floor master suite showcases a raised ceiling and dressing area with whirlpool tub, double-bowl vanity, shower enclosure, and two walk-in closets. Three additional bedrooms complete this wonderfully designed home.

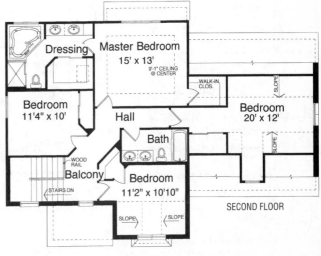

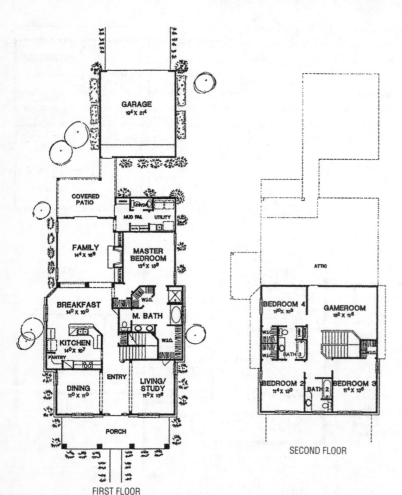

FIRST FLOOR

SECOND FLOOR

plan# HPK0100188

STYLE: COUNTRY COTTAGE
FIRST FLOOR: 1,742 SQ. FT.
SECOND FLOOR: 958 SQ. FT.
TOTAL: 2,700 SQ. FT.
BEDROOMS: 4
BATHROOMS: 3½
WIDTH: 38' - 7"
DEPTH: 96' - 3"
FOUNDATION: BASEMENT, CRAWLSPACE, SLAB

SEARCH ONLINE @ EPLANS.COM

With a low-pitched hipped roof and symmetrical facade, this design serves as a fine example of an American Foursquare home, one of the earliest Prairie-style designs. Its simple floor plan begins with formal rooms—the dining room and living room/study—to either side of the foyer. Next, the kitchen/breakfast area flows gracefully into the family room, which includes a fireplace and built-in shelves and opens to a covered patio. The master suite boasts two walk-in closets and a private bath; upstairs, three bedrooms—all with walk-in closets—join a game room.

plan# HPK0100189

STYLE: PRAIRIE
FIRST FLOOR: 1,217 SQ. FT.
SECOND FLOOR: 1,057 SQ. FT.
TOTAL: 2,274 SQ. FT.
BEDROOMS: 3
BATHROOMS: 2½
WIDTH: 38' - 0"
DEPTH: 40' - 5"
FOUNDATION: BASEMENT,
CRAWLSPACE, SLAB

SEARCH ONLINE @ EPLANS.COM

Tall windows in every room bring plenty of natural light into this Prairie design, and a wide, covered front porch provides a place to enjoy the outdoors. The dining room, to the right of the entry, is convenient to the kitchen, which includes a pantry and a niche. Nearby, the breakfast area opens to the rear patio, and the spacious family room is a comfortable gathering spot. Upstairs, the elegant master suite features a private bath and a walk-in closet with built-in shelves; two additional bedrooms share a full bath.

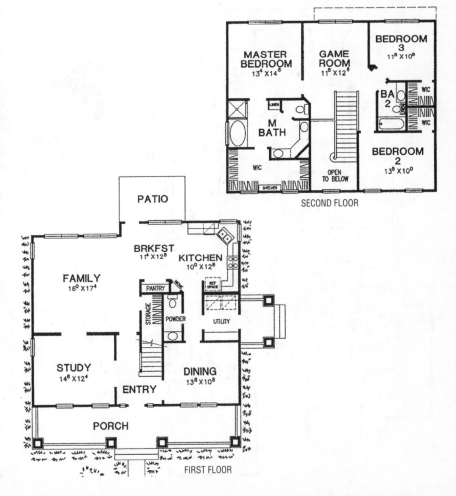

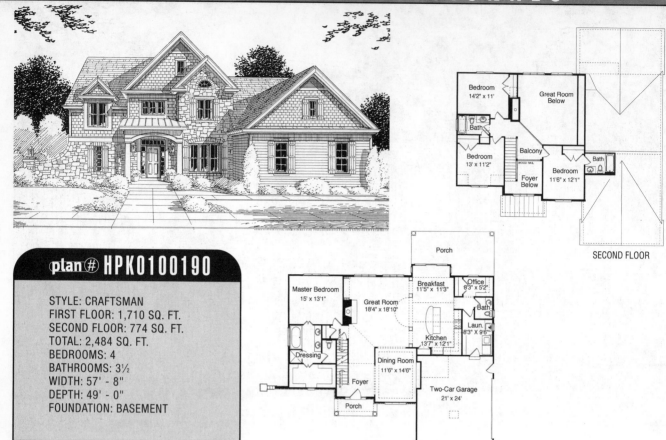

SECOND FLOOR

FIRST FLOOR

plan # HPK0100190

STYLE: CRAFTSMAN
FIRST FLOOR: 1,710 SQ. FT.
SECOND FLOOR: 774 SQ. FT.
TOTAL: 2,484 SQ. FT.
BEDROOMS: 4
BATHROOMS: 3½
WIDTH: 57' - 8"
DEPTH: 49' - 0"
FOUNDATION: BASEMENT

SEARCH ONLINE @ EPLANS.COM

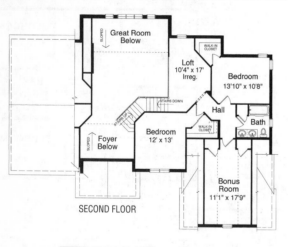

SECOND FLOOR

FIRST FLOOR

plan # HPK0100191

STYLE: TRADITIONAL
FIRST FLOOR: 1,808 SQ. FT.
SECOND FLOOR: 698 SQ. FT.
TOTAL: 2,506 SQ. FT.
BONUS SPACE: 217 SQ. FT.
BEDROOMS: 3
BATHROOMS: 2½
WIDTH: 62' - 8"
DEPTH: 49' - 0"
FOUNDATION: BASEMENT

SEARCH ONLINE @ EPLANS.COM

ORDER BLUEPRINTS 24 HOURS, 7 DAYS A WEEK, AT 1-800-521-6797

plan# HPK0100192

STYLE: FRENCH
FIRST FLOOR: 2,019 SQ. FT.
SECOND FLOOR: 468 SQ. FT.
TOTAL: 2,487 SQ. FT.
BONUS SPACE: 286 SQ. FT.
BEDROOMS: 5
BATHROOMS: 3
WIDTH: 59' - 0"
DEPTH: 58' - 0"

SEARCH ONLINE @ EPLANS.COM

Brick, varying rooflines, and stunning window details make the most of this traditional facade. Enter the foyer and find a formal dining room with a window seat on the left, and a study/optional bedroom on the right. The living room enjoys a 12-foot ceiling and a fireplace, as well as a view of the screen porch, which is accessed from the dining nook. The kitchen features a handy snack bar and spacious pantry. The master suite takes up the rest of the left wing, with its elegant bath and large walk-in closet. Another bedroom is found on the right of the first floor. The second floor is home to two bedrooms that share a bath, as well as optional game room space.

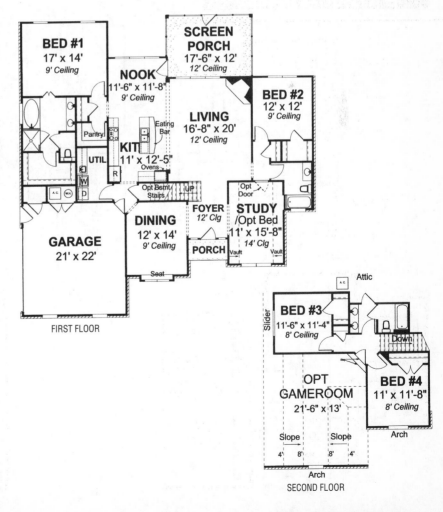

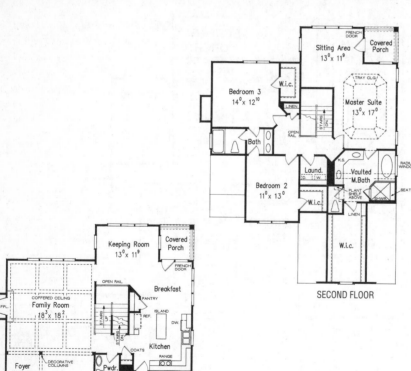

SECOND FLOOR

FIRST FLOOR

plan # HPK0100193

STYLE: COUNTRY COTTAGE
FIRST FLOOR: 1,120 SQ. FT.
SECOND FLOOR: 1,250 SQ. FT.
TOTAL: 2,370 SQ. FT.
BEDROOMS: 3
BATHROOMS: 2½
WIDTH: 41' - 4"
DEPTH: 51' - 0"
FOUNDATION: BASEMENT, CRAWLSPACE

SEARCH ONLINE @ EPLANS.COM

The stone-and-siding facade give this country home a rustic feel; the arched entry promises a grand interior. Decorative columns define the formal dining area from the main living room, which sits under an impressive coffered ceiling. The kitchen, keeping room, and breakfast area form a big open space that offers great flexibility in furniture arrangement and usage. This living area extends outside to the covered porch through a French door. Upstairs, the master suite accesses a second-level covered porch. An oversize walk-in closet with ample space for seasonal storage is one of the many amenities of this suite. Two more bedrooms, each with walk-in closets, share a bath.

plan# HPK0100194

STYLE: COUNTRY COTTAGE
FIRST FLOOR: 50 SQ. FT.
SECOND FLOOR: 1,714 SQ. FT.
TOTAL: 1,764 SQ. FT.
BEDROOMS: 3
BATHROOMS: 2
WIDTH: 51' - 0"
DEPTH: 40' - 4"
FOUNDATION: BASEMENT

SEARCH ONLINE @ EPLANS.COM

Gabled rooflines and a brick-and-siding facade give class to this country cottage, which is matched by the intriguing ceilings and columns inside. An open layout draws the vaulted family room together with both the casual breakfast area and formal dining room, as well as the expansive foyer. The kitchen's convenient serving bar meets the family room and breakfast area where they intersect. A tray ceiling in the bedchamber, a cozy sitting corner, and a lavish private bath underline the master suite's elegance and comfort. Two front-facing bedrooms share a linen closet and bath.

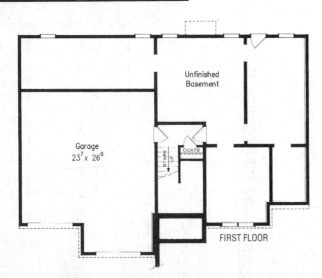

An ornately railed wraparound porch with graceful columns, a charming bay window with a flared metal hood, and a dignified brick-and-siding facade suggest that the interior of this home is extraordinary...and that is right! An impressive foyer leads you into elegant dining and living rooms, with tastefully placed columns. The delightful kitchen, which enjoys a walk-in pantry, easily serves the cheery breakfast area and the two-story family room warmed by a fireplace. A bedroom—or make it a study—is tucked into the rear left corner. The magnificent master suite on the second floor pampers with His and Hers vanities and walk-in closets and a separate tub and shower. Hanging plants on a built-in shelf will make you think you're in paradise. Two more bedrooms share a bath.

plan# HPK0100195

STYLE: COUNTRY COTTAGE
FIRST FLOOR: 1,555 SQ. FT.
SECOND FLOOR: 1,269 SQ. FT.
TOTAL: 2,824 SQ. FT.
BEDROOMS: 4
BATHROOMS: 3½
WIDTH: 62' - 3"
DEPTH: 46' - 6"
FOUNDATION: BASEMENT, CRAWLSPACE

SEARCH ONLINE @ EPLANS.COM

FIRST FLOOR

SECOND FLOOR

plan# HPK0100196

STYLE: SOUTHERN COLONIAL
FIRST FLOOR: 1,364 SQ. FT.
SECOND FLOOR: 1,398 SQ. FT.
TOTAL: 2,762 SQ. FT.
BEDROOMS: 5
BATHROOMS: 4
WIDTH: 51' - 0"
DEPTH: 45' - 4"
FOUNDATION: BASEMENT,
CRAWLSPACE

SEARCH ONLINE @ EPLANS.COM

This sturdy Southern Colonial home is perfect for a large family that likes to stretch out—and it's great for entertaining too. Upstairs, four bedrooms, including a ravishing master suite, provide ample sleeping quarters. A laundry is conveniently located on this level. Downstairs a den that could serve as a guest bedroom enjoys hall access to a full bath. Nearby is a study. The two-story family room opens one way to the formal dining area, and the other way to the casual eating area and kitchen, outfitted with a time-saving island counter.

FIRST FLOOR

SECOND FLOOR

SECOND FLOOR

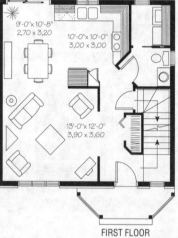

FIRST FLOOR

plan# HPK0100197

STYLE: FRENCH
FIRST FLOOR: 585 SQ. FT.
SECOND FLOOR: 585 SQ. FT.
TOTAL: 1,170 SQ. FT.
BEDROOMS: 3
BATHROOMS: 1½
WIDTH: 24' - 0"
DEPTH: 24' - 0"
FOUNDATION: BASEMENT

SEARCH ONLINE @ EPLANS.COM

SECOND FLOOR

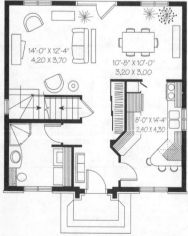

FIRST FLOOR

plan# HPK0100198

STYLE: CONTEMPORARY
FIRST FLOOR: 689 SQ. FT.
SECOND FLOOR: 676 SQ. FT.
TOTAL: 1,365 SQ. FT.
BEDROOMS: 3
BATHROOMS: 2
WIDTH: 26' - 0"
DEPTH: 26' - 4"
FOUNDATION: BASEMENT

SEARCH ONLINE @ EPLANS.COM

plan# HPK0100199

STYLE: CONTEMPORARY
SQUARE FOOTAGE: 1,433
BEDROOMS: 4
BATHROOMS: 1
WIDTH: 30' - 0"
DEPTH: 50' - 0"
FOUNDATION: BASEMENT

SEARCH ONLINE @ EPLANS.COM

Looking for the perfect starter home? How about a great retreat? For anyone who wants a budget-friendly plan, this brick-and-siding design is a dream come true. The foyer is adorned by columns and a half-wall that gracefully separate it from the living room. The kitchen flows easily from here, with a step-saving layout and sliding glass doors that let the light in. Four bedrooms line the left side of the house and share a marvelous spa bath.

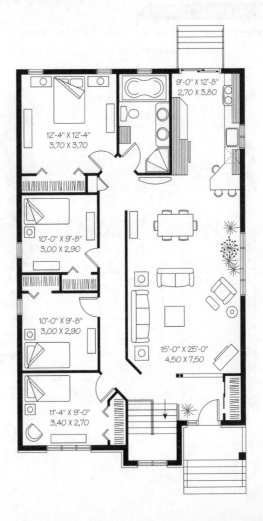

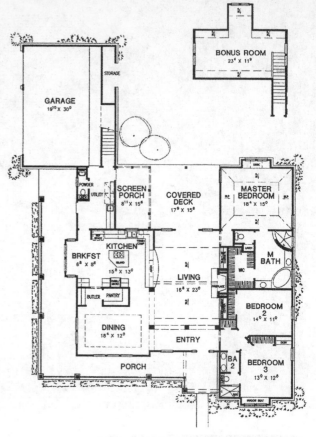

plan # HPK0100200

STYLE: FARMHOUSE
SQUARE FOOTAGE: 2,405 SQ. FT.
BONUS SPACE: 375 SQ. FT.
BEDROOMS: 3
BATHROOMS: 2½
WIDTH: 70' - 7"
DEPTH: 89' - 5"
FOUNDATION: CRAWLSPACE, SLAB

SEARCH ONLINE @ EPLANS.COM

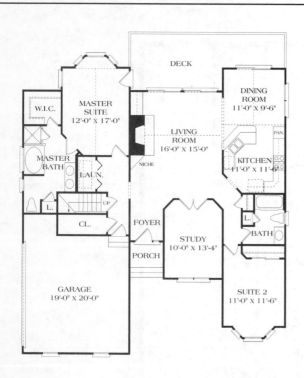

plan # HPK0100201

STYLE: CRAFTSMAN
SQUARE FOOTAGE: 1,570
BONUS SPACE: 326 SQ. FT.
BEDROOMS: 2
BATHROOMS: 2
WIDTH: 47' - 6"
DEPTH: 52' - 0"
FOUNDATION: CRAWLSPACE

SEARCH ONLINE @ EPLANS.COM

plan # HPK0100202

STYLE: TRADITIONAL
FIRST FLOOR: 1,583 SQ. FT.
SECOND FLOOR: 1,431 SQ. FT.
TOTAL: 3,014 SQ. FT.
BEDROOMS: 4
BATHROOMS: 3½
WIDTH: 63' - 8"
DEPTH: 59' - 4"
FOUNDATION: CRAWLSPACE

SEARCH ONLINE @ EPLANS.COM

A wraparound porch offers additional outside living and gives this design, oriented for front and side views, a great informal feel. Inside is an economical layout featuring a spacious gathering room and open living and dining rooms. The full kitchen is easily accessible from both the dining room and breakfast room. A vaulted ceiling gives added dimension to the large sunroom. The upstairs master suite offers a spacious bedroom with a tray ceiling and His and Hers walk-in closets. Outside the master suite are a seating area and balcony. There are three additional suites upstairs, including one with a private bath.

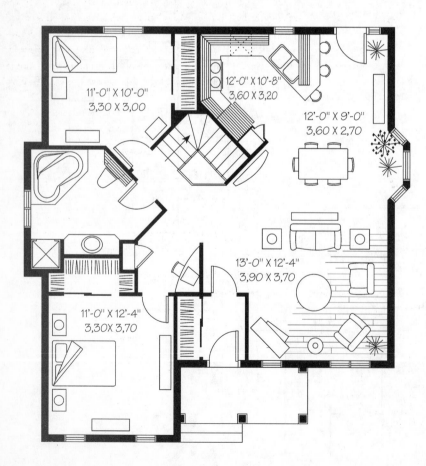

plan # HPK0100203

STYLE: BUNGALOW
SQUARE FOOTAGE: 1,102
BEDROOMS: 2
BATHROOMS: 1
WIDTH: 32' - 8"
DEPTH: 37' - 0"
FOUNDATION: BASEMENT

SEARCH ONLINE @ EPLANS.COM

With hipped rooflines and stylish windows— including an octagonal one on the front porch—this one-story home makes for an elegant family vacation retreat. The living room, dining area, and kitchen flow smoothly together, creating a relaxed atmosphere. A bow-bay window opens the dining area to a cascade of natural light. The kitchen enjoys a snack bar, perfect for casual breakfasts and late-evening conversation. A magnificent oversize tub is nestled in the corner of the luxurious bath that serves both bedrooms. The bath also includes a walk-in shower. The bedrooms have ample closets with sliding doors.

plan# HPK0100204

STYLE: FRENCH
FIRST FLOOR: 1,558 SQ. FT.
SECOND FLOOR: 546 SQ. FT.
TOTAL: 2,104 SQ. FT.
BONUS SPACE: 233 SQ. FT.
BEDROOMS: 3
BATHROOMS: 2½
WIDTH: 48' - 0"
DEPTH: 52' - 0"
FOUNDATION: BASEMENT

SEARCH ONLINE @ EPLANS.COM

This sturdy home with a brick exterior and intriguing gable lines is well suited to make life comfortable and enjoyable for most any family. The huge island kitchen, with French-door access to the backyard, opens to a cozy dining area that will surely be a center for family socializing. A fireplace joins the dining area with the living room. A front study or home office is an especially attractive feature. The master suite with a lavish bath and a walk-in closet is also located on the first level. Above, on the second floor, two more bedrooms share a bath. Off the kitchen, a laundry and a half-bath are near the entry to the garage.

SECOND FLOOR

FIRST FLOOR

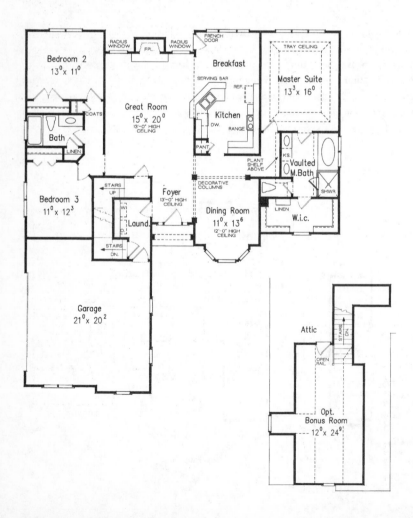

ptan# HPK0100205

STYLE: TRADITIONAL
SQUARE FOOTAGE: 1,725
BONUS SPACE: 377 SQ. FT.
BEDROOMS: 3
BATHROOMS: 2
WIDTH: 53' - 6"
DEPTH: 59' - 0"
FOUNDATION: BASEMENT,
CRAWLSPACE

SEARCH ONLINE @ EPLANS.COM

The handsome brick facade, stylish multipane bay window, and arched entry say that this is no ordinary design...and the wonderful interior layout fully confirms this expectation. Decorative columns invite guests into the elegant formal dining room just to the right of the foyer. Plants will hang from shelves in the hallway leading to the master suite. A walk-in closet with room for linen, twin vanities, a huge tub, and a separate shower are some of the amenities found here. With lots of space and a warming fireplace flanked by radius windows, the great room will host many memorable social activities, as well as family gatherings. The casual eating area flows into the kitchen and enjoys French-door access to the backyard. Two family bedrooms share a bath, which includes an ample linen closet, and a hallway coatroom.

plan# HPK0100206

STYLE: FRENCH
FIRST FLOOR: 1,807 SQ. FT.
SECOND FLOOR: 1,970 SQ. FT.
TOTAL: 3,777 SQ. FT.
BEDROOMS: 4
BATHROOMS: 3½
WIDTH: 57' - 4"
DEPTH: 53' - 6"
FOUNDATION: BASEMENT

SEARCH ONLINE @ EPLANS.COM

For sheer magnificence, this chateau-style mansion is unbeatable. Guests will be enchanted, both by the pillared entry and the inside splendor. The two-story grand room, with an extended-hearth fireplace, is well designed for unforgettable soiree's. A front dining room and living room (or make it a library) radiate a gracious welcome. The kitchen can easily serve gourmet dinners and informal family meals. It opens to an exquisite breakfast bay with five windows and to a keeping room with a fireplace. All four bedrooms are situated upstairs, and the posh master suite enjoys His and Hers walk-in closets and vanities. The laundry is conveniently located on this floor.

SECOND FLOOR

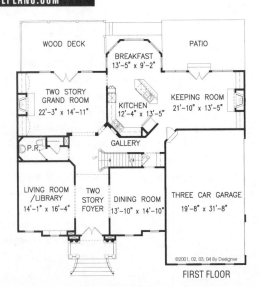

FIRST FLOOR

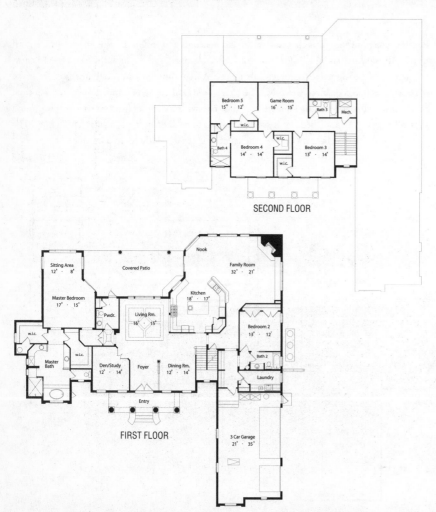

SECOND FLOOR

FIRST FLOOR

plan# HPK0100207

STYLE: FEDERAL
FIRST FLOOR: 3,505 SQ. FT.
SECOND FLOOR: 1,302 SQ. FT.
TOTAL: 4,807 SQ. FT.
BEDROOMS: 5
BATHROOMS: 4½
WIDTH: 89' - 4"
DEPTH: 87' - 0"
FOUNDATION: SLAB

SEARCH ONLINE @ EPLANS.COM

This majestic Early American mansion presents a sturdy, formal outside appearance; inside, it is especially well suited for a large family that likes big informal get-togethers. The huge family room, with a corner fire-place that merges with a dining nook and adjoins the country-style kitchen, will surely be the center of activity. Five bedrooms are placed throughout the home's two levels, including a glorious master suite with all the comforts you've ever dreamed about. A game room joins three bedrooms upstairs. For formal socializing, the dining area and living room are easily entered from the foyer, which guests reach through the impressive pillars of the covered entry. A den, or make it a study, is also located near the front. To the rear is a covered patio, perfect for meals alfresco.

plan # HPK0100208

STYLE: PLANTATION
FIRST FLOOR: 1,773 SQ. FT.
SECOND FLOOR: 1,676 SQ. FT.
TOTAL: 3,449 SQ. FT.
BEDROOMS: 5
BATHROOMS: 4
WIDTH: 68' - 7"
DEPTH: 62' - 8"
FOUNDATION: BASEMENT,
CRAWLSPACE

SEARCH ONLINE @ EPLANS.COM

From a Colonial past to a contemporary future, this Southern-style home perfectly combines elements of history and modernity. Brick facing graces the entry, where a double-decker porch invites casual relaxation. A two-story foyer opens on the left to an elegant dining room; a butler's pantry makes entertaining simple. The kitchen is a dream come true for the chef who wants room to move and miles of counter space. Adjacent to the bayed breakfast nook, the vaulted keeping room warms with a cozy hearth. The family room completes the living areas with a fireplace and lots of natural light. Upstairs, the master suite is a romantic getaway with a fireplace, room-sized walk-in closet, and a luxuriant vaulted bath.

SECOND FLOOR

FIRST FLOOR

The grand facade of this Colonial wonder is only the beginning. A gracious formality reigns inside. Enjoy entertaining in the study or dining room, both of which flank the foyer. The huge living room is made cozy by a fireplace and access to the dining nook and kitchen. The master suite sits to the left with its deluxe private bath, enormous walk-in closet, and double shower. To the right of the plan lie the four-car garage and a convenient mudroom and utility area. Upstairs, three bedrooms with private baths reside, along with a game room and a Juliet balcony.

plan# HPK0100209

STYLE: COLONIAL
FIRST FLOOR: 2,706 SQ. FT.
SECOND FLOOR: 1,480 SQ. FT.
TOTAL: 4,186 SQ. FT.
BEDROOMS: 4
BATHROOMS: 4½
WIDTH: 102' - 0"
DEPTH: 63' - 0"

SEARCH ONLINE @ EPLANS.COM

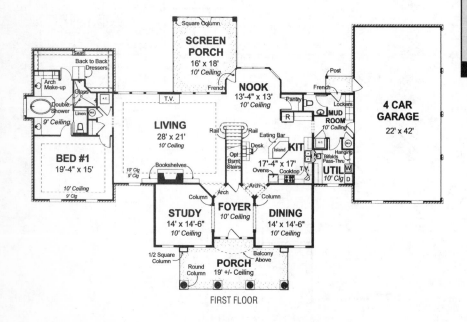

FIRST FLOOR

SECOND FLOOR

plan# HPK0100210

STYLE: TRADITIONAL
FIRST FLOOR: 1,639 SQ. FT.
SECOND FLOOR: 1,835 SQ. FT.
TOTAL: 3,474 SQ. FT.
BONUS SPACE: 628 SQ. FT.
BEDROOMS: 5
BATHROOMS: 4
WIDTH: 64' - 0"
DEPTH: 59' - 2"
FOUNDATION: CRAWLSPACE

SEARCH ONLINE @ EPLANS.COM

This stately brick exterior is softened by decorative touches on the windows and the balcony. Enter the foyer through the columned loggia and find a formal dining room to the left and a study to the right. A convenient bath sits behind the staircase. The rear of the plan is devoted to family living space. The hearth-warmed gathering room opens to the rear covered porch and flows right into the island kitchen and breakfast nook. The kitchen enjoys ample counter space and a pantry, as well as access to the laundry room and garage. The second floor is home to two suites that share a double-sink bath, a suite with its own bath, and a luxurious master suite. The master bath is a room unto itself, with double walk-in closets, a circular tub, and a compartmented toilet. The very top floor is bonus space that can easily be converted to guest quarters.

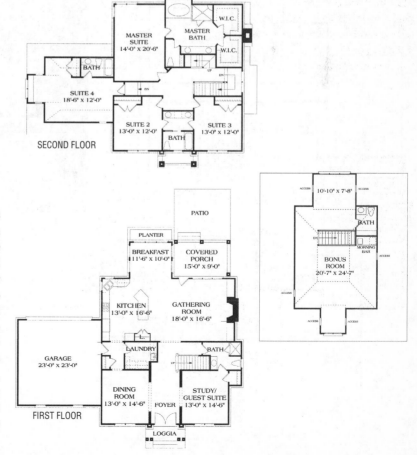

SECOND FLOOR

plan# HPK0100211

STYLE: COLONIAL
FIRST FLOOR: 1,393 SQ. FT.
SECOND FLOOR: 1,332 SQ. FT.
TOTAL: 2,725 SQ. FT.
BEDROOMS: 5
BATHROOMS: 4
WIDTH: 58' - 0"
DEPTH: 47' - 6"
FOUNDATION: BASEMENT,
CRAWLSPACE

SEARCH ONLINE @ EPLANS.COM

FIRST FLOOR

SECOND FLOOR

plan# HPK0100212

STYLE: COUNTRY COTTAGE
FIRST FLOOR: 1,063 SQ. FT.
SECOND FLOOR: 929 SQ. FT.
TOTAL: 1,992 SQ. FT.
BONUS SPACE: 246 SQ. FT.
BEDROOMS: 4
BATHROOMS: 3
WIDTH: 52' - 4"
DEPTH: 38' - 6"
FOUNDATION: BASEMENT,
CRAWLSPACE

SEARCH ONLINE @ EPLANS.COM

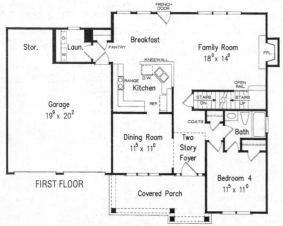

FIRST FLOOR

ORDER BLUEPRINTS 24 HOURS, 7 DAYS A WEEK, AT 1-800-521-6797

© William E. Poole Designs, Inc.

plan# HPK0100213

STYLE: FARMHOUSE
FIRST FLOOR: 1,978 SQ. FT.
SECOND FLOOR: 1,320 SQ. FT.
TOTAL: 3,298 SQ. FT.
BONUS SPACE: 352 SQ. FT.
BEDROOMS: 4
BATHROOMS: 3½
WIDTH: 66' - 8"
DEPTH: 62' - 0"
FOUNDATION: CRAWLSPACE

SEARCH ONLINE @ EPLANS.COM

High above the Suwannee River sits an old Southern Plantation home replete with Spanish moss swaying in the gentle breezes and bougainvillea vines exploding with color. I remembered similar warm evenings when my father would take us to get a block of ice so we could make cream. With fireflies dancing, stories entrancing, swinging soothing and ice cream cooling—what a blissful way to end a day both then and now, down home at River Road.

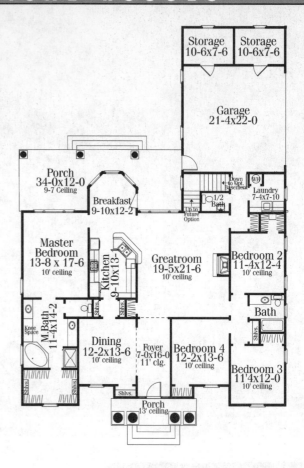

Storage 10-6x7-6 Storage 10-6x7-6

Garage 21-4x22-0

Porch 34-0x12-0 9-7 Ceiling

Breakfast 9-10x12-2

1/2 Bath

Down to Opt Basement

Up to Future Option

WH

Laundry 7-4x7-10

Master Bedroom 13-8 x 17-6 10' ceiling

Kitchen 9-10x13-

Greatroom 19-5x21-6 10' ceiling

Bedroom 2 11-4x12-4 10' ceiling

M.Bath 11-4x14-2

Knee Space

Shlvs.

Shlvs.

Bath

Dining 12-2x13-6 10' ceiling

Foyer 7-0x16-0 11' clg.

Bedroom 4 12-2x13-6 10' ceiling

Shlvs.

Bedroom 3 11'4x12-0 10' ceiling

Shlvs.

Porch 13' ceiling

plan# HPK0100214

STYLE: GOTHIC REVIVAL
SQUARE FOOTAGE: 2,402
BONUS SPACE: 294 SQ. FT.
BEDROOMS: 4
BATHROOMS: 2½
WIDTH: 56' - 6"
DEPTH: 82' - 0"
FOUNDATION: BASEMENT, CRAWLSPACE, SLAB

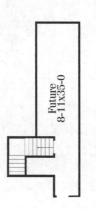

Future 8-11x35-0

SEARCH ONLINE @ EPLANS.COM

Attic 39-0x20-0

Raised floor to accomodate higher ceiling in foyer.

Optional Gameroom 11-8x33-4

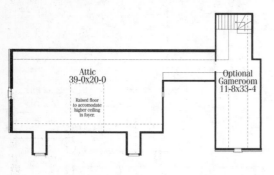

Bedroom 11-6x13-0 9' ceiling

Bedroom 11-6x13-0 9' ceiling

Porch 22-6x12-8 9' ceiling

Breakfast 11-6x10-6 9' ceiling

Shlvs

Master Bedroom 15-2x18-0 9' ceiling

Family Room 21-8x16-9 9' ceiling

Kitchen 11-6x14-6 9' ceiling

See Stair Opt. for Future and/or Basement Stair

Bath

Laundry 5-8x11-1 8' ceiling

Storage 7-8x4-10 8' ceiling

M.Bath 9-3x10-6

DW

Ref.

Broom Closet

Closet 15-2x7-10

Foyer 7-10x11-8 11' clg.

Dining 15-4x11-8 9' ceiling

Pantry

1/2 Bath

Garage 23-5x23-6

Porch 41-7x8-0 10' ceiling with Arched Center

plan# HPK0100215

STYLE: TRADITIONAL
SQUARE FOOTAGE: 2,373
BONUS SPACE: 1,178 SQ. FT.
BEDROOMS: 3
BATHROOMS: 2½
WIDTH: 73' - 1"
DEPTH: 58' - 6"
FOUNDATION: BASEMENT, CRAWLSPACE, SLAB

SEARCH ONLINE @ EPLANS.COM

© William E. Poole Designs, Inc.

plan# HPK0100216

STYLE: GREEK REVIVAL
FIRST FLOOR: 2,337 SQ. FT.
SECOND FLOOR: 1,016 SQ. FT.
TOTAL: 3,353 SQ. FT.
BONUS SPACE: 394 SQ. FT.
BEDROOMS: 4
BATHROOMS: 3½
WIDTH: 66' - 2"
DEPTH: 71' - 2"
FOUNDATION: CRAWLSPACE

SEARCH ONLINE @ EPLANS.COM

We were looking for the perfect home. It had to be both charming and cozy, classical in proportion and timeless in design—not too big and not too little. It had to be just right and, above all, it had to be built of brick. One house rambled. One was too formal and all were wrong for us in one way or another until suddenly we saw it—the Shields Town House in Natchez, Mississippi— the home of our dreams.

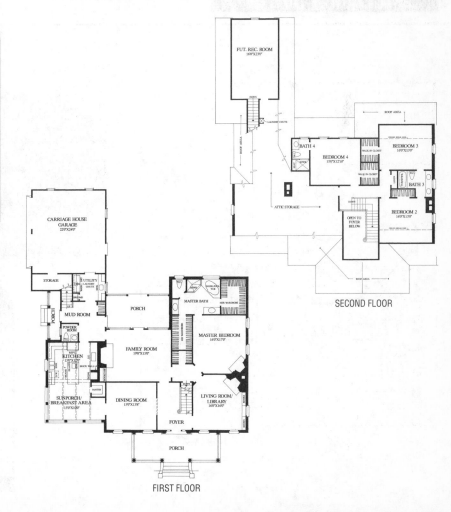

SECOND FLOOR

FIRST FLOOR

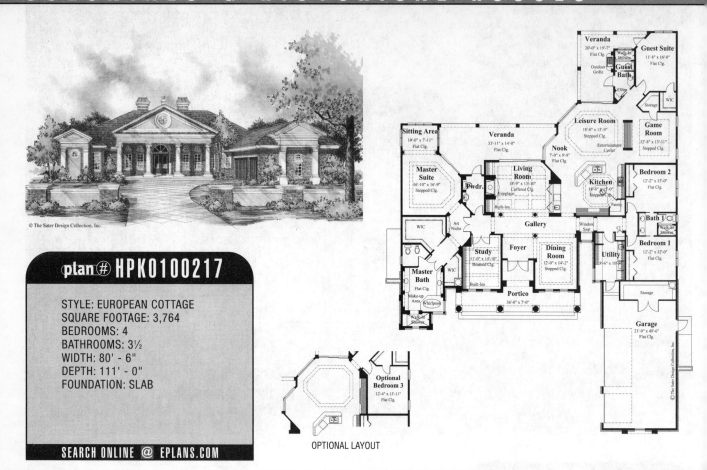

© The Sater Design Collection, Inc.

plan# HPK0100217

STYLE: EUROPEAN COTTAGE
SQUARE FOOTAGE: 3,764
BEDROOMS: 4
BATHROOMS: 3½
WIDTH: 80' - 6"
DEPTH: 111' - 0"
FOUNDATION: SLAB

SEARCH ONLINE @ EPLANS.COM

Optional Bedroom 3
12'-4" x 13'-11"
Flat Clg.

OPTIONAL LAYOUT

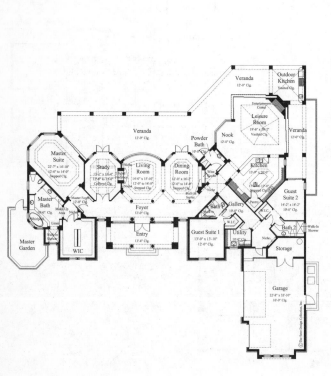

© The Sater Design Collection, Inc.

plan# HPK0100218

STYLE: EUROPEAN COTTAGE
SQUARE FOOTAGE: 3,640
BEDROOMS: 3
BATHROOMS: 3½
WIDTH: 106' - 4"
DEPTH: 102' - 4"
FOUNDATION: SLAB

SEARCH ONLINE @ EPLANS.COM

ORDER BLUEPRINTS 24 HOURS, 7 DAYS A WEEK, AT 1-800-521-6797

© William E. Poole Designs, Inc.

plan# HPK0100219

STYLE: COLONIAL
FIRST FLOOR: 1,816 SQ. FT.
SECOND FLOOR: 968 SQ. FT.
TOTAL: 2,784 SQ. FT.
BONUS SPACE: 402 SQ. FT.
BEDROOMS: 4
BATHROOMS: 3½
WIDTH: 54' - 6"
DEPTH: 52' - 8"
FOUNDATION: CRAWLSPACE

SEARCH ONLINE @ EPLANS.COM

Picnics. Parades. Fireworks. Flags. Fourth of July celebrations. Nowhere are patriotic commemorations more evident than in the areas surrounding our nation's capital. The patina of old brick, the diversity of classical design and the lushness of mature plantings provide the serenity requisite to these older homes that whisper a fond farewell in the morning and a warm welcome every evening—as the family gathers at home in the Arlington once again.

SECOND FLOOR

FIRST FLOOR

plan# HPK0100220

STYLE: COUNTRY COTTAGE
FIRST FLOOR: 2,600 SQ. FT.
SECOND FLOOR: 1,174 SQ. FT.
TOTAL: 3,774 SQ. FT.
BONUS SPACE: 340 SQ. FT.
BEDROOMS: 4
BATHROOMS: 4
WIDTH: 58' - 1"
DEPTH: 125' - 4"
FOUNDATION: CRAWLSPACE

SEARCH ONLINE @ EPLANS.COM

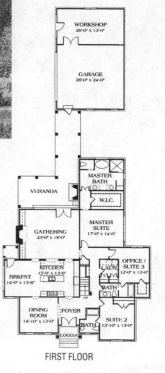

FIRST FLOOR

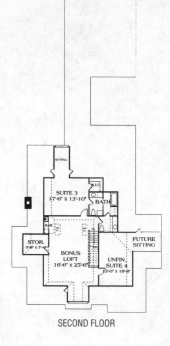

SECOND FLOOR

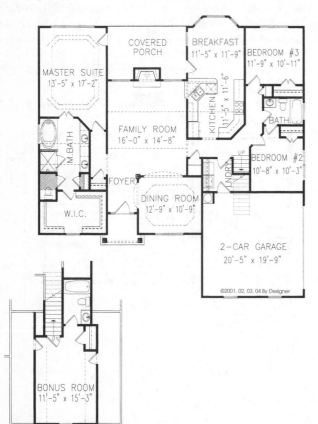

plan# HPK0100221

STYLE: COUNTRY COTTAGE
SQUARE FOOTAGE: 1,821
BONUS SPACE: 191 SQ. FT.
BEDROOMS: 3
BATHROOMS: 2
WIDTH: 54' - 0"
DEPTH: 54' - 0"
FOUNDATION: SLAB

SEARCH ONLINE @ EPLANS.COM

ORDER BLUEPRINTS 24 HOURS, 7 DAYS A WEEK, AT 1-800-521-6797

plan# HPK0100222

STYLE: GEORGIAN
FIRST FLOOR: 1,327 SQ. FT.
SECOND FLOOR: 1,099 SQ. FT.
TOTAL: 2,426 SQ. FT.
BONUS SPACE: 290 SQ. FT.
BEDROOMS: 4
BATHROOMS: 3
WIDTH: 54' - 4"
DEPTH: 42' - 10"
FOUNDATION: BASEMENT,
CRAWLSPACE

SEARCH ONLINE @ EPLANS.COM

A Southern classic, this lovely home will become a treasured place to call your own. The entry makes a grand impression; double doors open to the foyer where French doors reveal a study. To the right, the dining room is designed for entertaining with easy access to the angled serving-bar kitchen. A bayed breakfast nook leads into the hearth-warmed family room. Tucked to the rear, a bedroom with a full bath makes an ideal guest room. The master suite is upstairs and enjoys a private vaulted spa bath. Two additional bedrooms reside on this level and join a full bath and an optional bonus room, perfect as a kid's retreat, home gym, or crafts room.

SECOND FLOOR

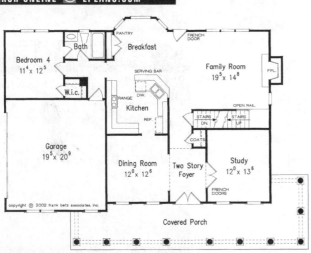

FIRST FLOOR

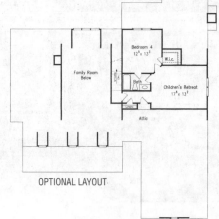

plan# HPK0100223

STYLE: COLONIAL
SQUARE FOOTAGE: 2,477
BEDROOMS: 3
BATHROOMS: 2½
WIDTH: 65' - 4"
DEPTH: 68' - 0"
FOUNDATION: BASEMENT,
CRAWLSPACE

SEARCH ONLINE @ EPLANS.COM

OPTIONAL LAYOUT

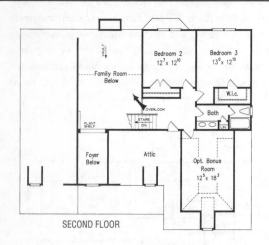

SECOND FLOOR

FIRST FLOOR

plan# HPK0100224

STYLE: COUNTRY COTTAGE
FIRST FLOOR: 1,805 SQ. FT.
SECOND FLOOR: 593 SQ. FT.
TOTAL: 2,398 SQ. FT.
BONUS SPACE: 255 SQ. FT.
BEDROOMS: 4
BATHROOMS: 3
WIDTH: 55' - 0"
DEPTH: 48' - 0"
FOUNDATION: BASEMENT,
CRAWLSPACE

SEARCH ONLINE @ EPLANS.COM

© William E. Poole Designs, Inc.

plan# HPK0100225

STYLE: COUNTRY COTTAGE
FIRST FLOOR: 2,357 SQ. FT.
SECOND FLOOR: 772 SQ. FT.
TOTAL: 3,129 SQ. FT.
BONUS SPACE: 450 SQ. FT.
BEDROOMS: 4
BATHROOMS: 3
WIDTH: 69' - 4"
DEPTH: 67' - 4"
FOUNDATION: CRAWLSPACE

SEARCH ONLINE @ EPLANS.COM

Miss Helen taught my mother in second grade, taught me in second grade (as well as Sunday School) and was our friend and neighbor. She lived in her old homeplace and we were always welcomed with a cookie when we dropped in for a visit. Once I came with my first-born and Miss Helen pulled out some old primers that had my name written on the inside cover. She gave them to my child and he has them to this day. Many stories abound about Miss Helen (all with wit and charm) and fond memories of her and her homeplace, Mulberry Farm.

SECOND FLOOR

FIRST FLOOR

© William E. Poole Designs, Inc.

SECOND FLOOR

FIRST FLOOR

plan# HPK0100226

STYLE: GREEK REVIVAL
FIRST FLOOR: 2,473 SQ. FT.
SECOND FLOOR: 1,447 SQ. FT.
TOTAL: 3,920 SQ. FT.
BONUS SPACE: 428 SQ. FT.
BEDROOMS: 4
BATHROOMS: 3½
WIDTH: 68' - 8"
DEPTH: 80' - 0"
FOUNDATION: BASEMENT,
CRAWLSPACE

SEARCH ONLINE @ EPLANS.COM

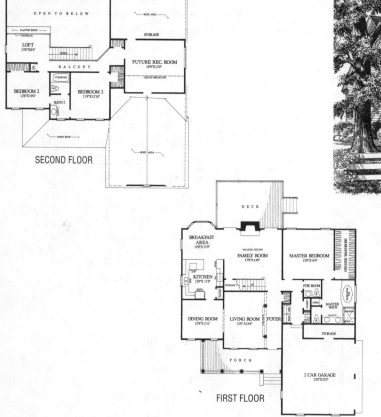

SECOND FLOOR

FIRST FLOOR

© William E. Poole Designs, Inc.

plan# HPK0100002

STYLE: COUNTRY COTTAGE
FIRST FLOOR: 1,714 SQ. FT.
SECOND FLOOR: 683 SQ. FT.
TOTAL: 2,397 SQ. FT.
BONUS SPACE: 287 SQ. FT.
BEDROOMS: 3
BATHROOMS: 2½
WIDTH: 53' - 8"
DEPTH: 56' - 8"
FOUNDATION: CRAWLSPACE

SEARCH ONLINE @ EPLANS.COM

ORDER BLUEPRINTS 24 HOURS, 7 DAYS A WEEK, AT 1-800-521-6797

© William E. Poole Designs, Inc.

plan # HPK0100227

STYLE: COLONIAL
FIRST FLOOR: 1,122 SQ. FT.
SECOND FLOOR: 1,068 SQ. FT.
TOTAL: 2,190 SQ. FT.
BONUS SPACE: 360 SQ. FT.
BEDROOMS: 3
BATHROOMS: 2½
WIDTH: 54' - 8"
DEPTH: 38' - 4"
FOUNDATION: CRAWLSPACE

SEARCH ONLINE @ EPLANS.COM

A single, gabled dormer tops the facade of this colonial home. The Georgian sense of understatement is evident inside as well, with a sinsible living room and famil room separated by French doors. Upstairs, the master suite enjoys views of the rear of the house and is attended by a whirlpool bath and dual vanities. Two other bedrooms share a full bath. A future rec room, with access via a rear stairway, awaits above the two-car garage.

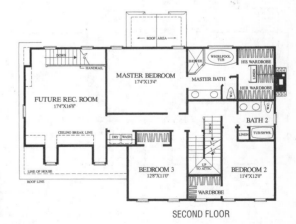

SECOND FLOOR

FIRST FLOOR

© William E. Poole Designs, Inc.

Cutting blooms from her flowerbed, the lady in a straw hat paused and looked out at the New England Sea with such serenity and pleasure that we were momentarily transfixed. Flags were snapping in the brisk breeze and the sky was so blue that darkness seemed improbable. Her home, overlooking the sea and facing the town square, was picture perfect. With this memory firmly etched in my mind, the Stonington was created for you to enjoy for your own special homeplace.

plan# HPK0100228

STYLE: GEORGIAN
FIRST FLOOR: 1,209 SQ. FT.
SECOND FLOOR: 1,005 SQ. FT.
TOTAL: 2,214 SQ. FT.
BONUS SPACE: 366 SQ. FT.
BEDROOMS: 3
BATHROOMS: 2½
WIDTH: 65' - 4"
DEPTH: 40' - 4"
FOUNDATION: CRAWLSPACE

SEARCH ONLINE @ EPLANS.COM

FIRST FLOOR

SECOND FLOOR

ORDER BLUEPRINTS 24 HOURS, 7 DAYS A WEEK, AT 1-800-521-6797

ptan# HPK0100229

STYLE: GEORGIAN
SQUARE FOOTAGE: 2,869
BONUS SPACE: 541 SQ. FT.
BEDROOMS: 3
BATHROOMS: 2½
WIDTH: 68' - 6"
DEPTH: 79' - 8"
FOUNDATION: CRAWLSPACE

SEARCH ONLINE @ EPLANS.COM

Here is a beautiful example of Classical Revival architecture complete with shuttered, jack-arch windows and a column-supported pediment over the entry. Inside, the foyer opens to the living room and leads to the family room at the rear. Here a panoramic view is complemented by an impressive fireplace framed by built-ins. To the left, the efficient island kitchen is situated between the sunny breakfast nook and the formal dining room. The right side of the plan holds two bedrooms and the lavish master suite.

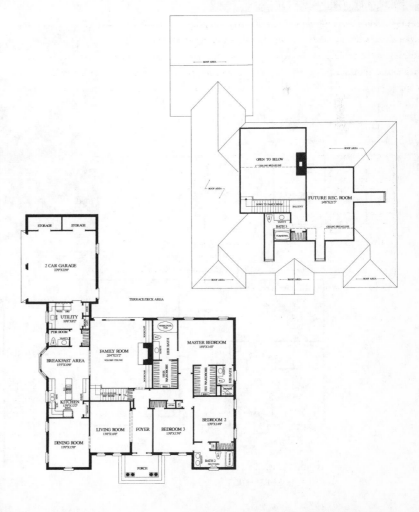

SECOND FLOOR

BED #2
14'-6" x 19'-6"
9' Ceiling

BED #3
17'-4" x 14'-6"
9' Ceiling

GAME ROOM
29'-8" x 14'-6"
9' Ceiling

BED #4
17'-4" x 14'-6"
9' Ceiling

DECK
32' x 12'

Square Pediment
Centered Over
1st Floor Columns

plan# HPK0100230

STYLE: COLONIAL
FIRST FLOOR: 3,725 SQ. FT.
SECOND FLOOR: 2,208 SQ. FT.
TOTAL: 5,933 SQ. FT.
BEDROOMS: 4
BATHROOMS: 5½ + ½
WIDTH: 132' - 0"
DEPTH: 78' - 0"

SEARCH ONLINE @ EPLANS.COM

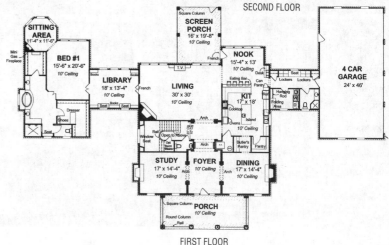

SITTING AREA
11'-4" x 11'-6"

SCREEN PORCH
16' x 19'-8"
10' Ceiling

NOOK
15'-4" x 13'
10' Ceiling

4 CAR GARAGE
24' x 46'

BED #1
15'-6" x 20'-6"
10' Ceiling

LIBRARY
18' x 13'-4"
10' Ceiling

LIVING
30' x 30'
10' Ceiling

KIT
17' x 18'
10' Ceiling

STUDY
17' x 14'-4"
10' Ceiling

FOYER
10' Ceiling

DINING
17' x 14'-4"
10' Ceiling

PORCH
10' Ceiling

FIRST FLOOR

SECOND FLOOR

CLOSET
9'-0" x 7'-0"
9' CH

BEDROOM 4
11'-0" x 11'-0"
9' CH

BEDROOM 3
11'-8" x 12'-1"
9' CH

MASTER BATH
9' CH

BATH 1
9' CH

UNFINISHED STORAGE
5'-9" CH

MASTER BEDROOM
12'-0" x 15'-8"
9'-11" CH

BEDROOM 2
12'-2" x 11'-4"
9' CH

COMPUTER ALCOVE
10'-6" CH

plan# HPK0100231

STYLE: FEDERAL
FIRST FLOOR: 1,285 SQ. FT.
SECOND FLOOR: 1,345 SQ. FT.
TOTAL: 2,630 SQ. FT.
BONUS SPACE: 352 SQ. FT.
BEDROOMS: 4
BATHROOMS: 2½
WIDTH: 59' - 2"
DEPTH: 51' - 9"

SEARCH ONLINE @ EPLANS.COM

BREAKFAST
9' CH
11'-8" x 9'-2"

FAMILY ROOM
18'-2" x 14'-1"
9' CH

KITCHEN
14'-6" x 14'-0"
9' CH

3-CAR GARAGE
21'-4" x 31'-4"
9' CH

PWD
9' CH

UTIL
9' CH

STUDY
12'-0" x 12'-8"
9' CH

DINING ROOM
12'-0" x 12'-8"
9' CH

ENTRY

PORCH
9' CH

FIRST FLOOR

© William E. Poole Designs, Inc.

MILES

plan# HPK0100232

STYLE: COLONIAL
FIRST FLOOR: 2,273 SQ. FT.
SECOND FLOOR: 1,391 SQ. FT.
TOTAL: 3,664 SQ. FT.
BONUS SPACE: 547 SQ. FT.
BEDROOMS: 4
BATHROOMS: 4½
WIDTH: 77' - 2"
DEPTH: 48' - 0"
FOUNDATION: CRAWLSPACE

SEARCH ONLINE @ EPLANS.COM

An easy and charming interpretation of the Late Georgian style, this plan is carefully adapted to meet the practical requirements of a modern lifestyle. Cased openings, high ceilings, and well-placed windows keep the expansive, comfortable interiors well-lighted and open. The spacious family room, which enjoys a fireplace flanked by built-in shelves, opens to the rear terrace. The lavish master suite enjoys privacy on the first level; the other three bedrooms—each with private baths—are comfortably situated on the second floor. Additional space is available upstairs to develop a recreation room.

SECOND FLOOR

FIRST FLOOR

SECOND FLOOR

FIRST FLOOR

plan# HPK0100233

STYLE: COUNTRY COTTAGE
FIRST FLOOR: 1,252 SQ. FT.
SECOND FLOOR: 1,125 SQ. FT.
TOTAL: 2,377 SQ. FT.
BONUS SPACE: 328 SQ. FT.
BEDROOMS: 3
BATHROOMS: 3½
WIDTH: 42' - 4"
DEPTH: 53' - 0"
FOUNDATION: BASEMENT,
CRAWLSPACE

SEARCH ONLINE @ EPLANS.COM

SECOND FLOOR

FIRST FLOOR

plan# HPK0100234

STYLE: CAPE COD
FIRST FLOOR: 1,461 SQ. FT.
SECOND FLOOR: 1,132 SQ. FT.
TOTAL: 2,593 SQ. FT.
BONUS SPACE: 365 SQ. FT.
BEDROOMS: 4
BATHROOMS: 4
WIDTH: 44' - 0"
DEPTH: 62' - 4"
FOUNDATION: BASEMENT,
CRAWLSPACE

SEARCH ONLINE @ EPLANS.COM

plan# HPK0100235

STYLE: SOUTHERN COLONIAL
FIRST FLOOR: 1,645 SQ. FT.
SECOND FLOOR: 563 SQ. FT.
TOTAL: 2,208 SQ. FT.
BONUS SPACE: 255 SQ. FT.
BEDROOMS: 3
BATHROOMS: 2½
WIDTH: 50' - 0"
DEPTH: 54' - 0"
FOUNDATION: BASEMENT,
CRAWLSPACE, SLAB

SEARCH ONLINE @ EPLANS.COM

This Southern country home will charm you from the curb, but don't stop there! Inside, a wonderful floor plan offers natural light, spacious rooms, and options to expand. The two-story foyer opens on the right to an elegant dining room. Continue past an art niche to the vaulted family room, lit by radius windows that frame a fireplace. The island kitchen is conveniently located near the breakfast nook and large laundry room. A keeping room offers a cozy place to relax. The master suite claims the entire left side of the home, with a lavish spa bath and abundant closet space. Two bedrooms on the second floor share a full bath and access optional bonus space.

SECOND FLOOR

FIRST FLOOR

This colonial home gets a Victorian treatment with an expansive covered porch complete with a gazebo-like terminus. Inside, the impressive foyer is flanked by the living room and the formal dining room. The spacious island kitchen is ideally situated between the dining room and the sunny breakfast area. Completing the living area, the family room enjoys a fireplace, built ins, and a generous view. The lavish master suite resides on the far right with a private bath and a huge walk-in closet.

plan# HPK0100236

STYLE: VICTORIAN
FIRST FLOOR: 2,099 SQ. FT.
SECOND FLOOR: 1,260 SQ. FT.
TOTAL: 3,359 SQ. FT.
BONUS SPACE: 494 SQ. FT.
BEDROOMS: 4
BATHROOMS: 3½
WIDTH: 68' - 4"
DEPTH: 54' - 0"
FOUNDATION: CRAWLSPACE

SEARCH ONLINE @ EPLANS.COM

FIRST FLOOR

SECOND FLOOR

ORDER BLUEPRINTS 24 HOURS, 7 DAYS A WEEK, AT 1-800-521-6797

© William E. Poole Designs, Inc.

plan# HPK0100237

STYLE: PLANTATION
FIRST FLOOR: 2,359 SQ. FT.
SECOND FLOOR: 1,112 SQ. FT.
TOTAL: 3,471 SQ. FT.
BONUS SPACE: 559 SQ. FT.
BEDROOMS: 4
BATHROOMS: 3½
WIDTH: 81' - 8"
DEPTH: 77' - 8"
FOUNDATION: CRAWLSPACE

SEARCH ONLINE @ EPLANS.COM

Collaboration with the developer of Kilgore Plantation in Greenville, South Carolina resulted in the design of this modern iteration of Southern charm. The Georgian facade has been dressed with a columned porch and balcony, and augmented with wings to house the master bath and kitchen areas. A mudroom and utility areas lead to the two-car garage, with room upstairs for a rec room.

SECOND FLOOR

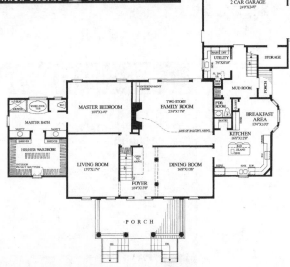

FIRST FLOOR

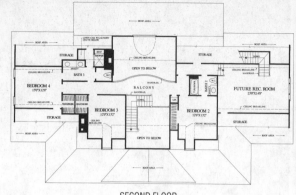

SECOND FLOOR

FIRST FLOOR

plan# HPK0100238

STYLE: GREEK REVIVAL
FIRST FLOOR: 2,449 SQ. FT.
SECOND FLOOR: 1,094 SQ. FT.
TOTAL: 3,543 SQ. FT.
BONUS SPACE: 409 SQ. FT.
BEDROOMS: 4
BATHROOMS: 3½
WIDTH: 89' - 0"
DEPTH: 53' - 10"
FOUNDATION: CRAWLSPACE

SEARCH ONLINE @ EPLANS.COM

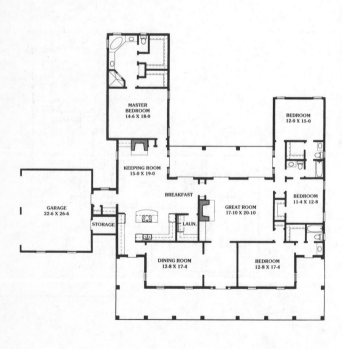

plan# HPK0100239

STYLE: PLANTATION
SQUARE FOOTAGE: 3,064
BEDROOMS: 4
BATHROOMS: 3
WIDTH: 94' - 0"
DEPTH: 83' - 0"
FOUNDATION: CRAWLSPACE

SEARCH ONLINE @ EPLANS.COM

ORDER BLUEPRINTS 24 HOURS, 7 DAYS A WEEK, AT 1-800-521-6797

plan# HPK0100240

STYLE: COUNTRY COTTAGE
FIRST FLOOR: 1,773 SQ. FT.
SECOND FLOOR: 2,293 SQ. FT.
TOTAL: 4,066 SQ. FT.
BEDROOMS: 5
BATHROOMS: 4½
WIDTH: 69' - 0"
DEPTH: 54' - 4"
FOUNDATION: BASEMENT,
CRAWLSPACE

SEARCH ONLINE @ EPLANS.COM

This a great home for a large, active family that is continually inviting friends over. Five bedrooms, four of them upstairs, offer lots of sleeping space. A large entertainment room is designed for games, music, and movies. On the main floor, a spacious family room with a fireplace and coffered ceiling, and a formal dining room will provide many memorable get-togethers. The study offers a quiet retreat, and the nearby bedroom, which adjoins a full bath, works well as a guest room. The casual eating area flows into the kitchen, which is well designed for effortless food preparation.

plan# HPK0100241

STYLE: TRANSITIONAL
FIRST FLOOR: 1,066 SQ. FT.
SECOND FLOOR: 1,070 SQ. FT.
TOTAL: 2,136 SQ. FT.
BEDROOMS: 3
BATHROOMS: 2½
WIDTH: 56' - 0"
DEPTH: 42' - 0"
FOUNDATION: CRAWLSPACE

SEARCH ONLINE @ EPLANS.COM

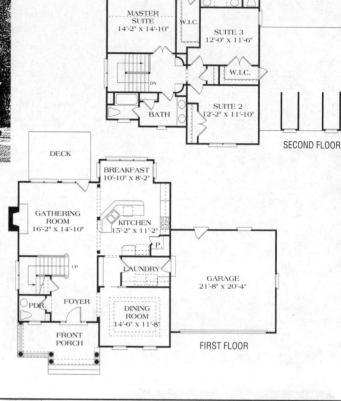

SECOND FLOOR

FIRST FLOOR

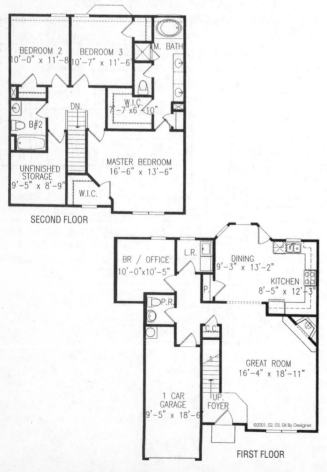

SECOND FLOOR

FIRST FLOOR

plan# HPK0100242

STYLE: TRADITIONAL
FIRST FLOOR: 876 SQ. FT.
SECOND FLOOR: 834 SQ. FT.
TOTAL: 1,710 SQ. FT.
BEDROOMS: 3
BATHROOMS: 2½
WIDTH: 35' - 0"
DEPTH: 39' - 8"
FOUNDATION: SLAB

SEARCH ONLINE @ EPLANS.COM

ORDER BLUEPRINTS 24 HOURS, 7 DAYS A WEEK, AT 1-800-521-6797

© William E. Poole Designs, Inc.

plan # HPK0100243

STYLE: COLONIAL
FIRST FLOOR: 1,625 SQ. FT.
SECOND FLOOR: 849 SQ. FT.
TOTAL: 2,474 SQ. FT.
BONUS SPACE: 283 SQ. FT.
BEDROOMS: 4
BATHROOMS: 3½
WIDTH: 50' - 2"
DEPTH: 71' - 1"
FOUNDATION: CRAWLSPACE

SEARCH ONLINE @ EPLANS.COM

This picturesque colonial offers a pleasing blend of historic charm and contemporary enjoyments. The large wood-burning fireplace in the great room is functional and quaint, and the adjoining porch allows for larger gatherings. The master suite enjoys a bath with dual vanities and a spacious walk-in closet. Three more bedrooms upstairs share two baths. The second floor is completed by a large rec room to the left of the plan.

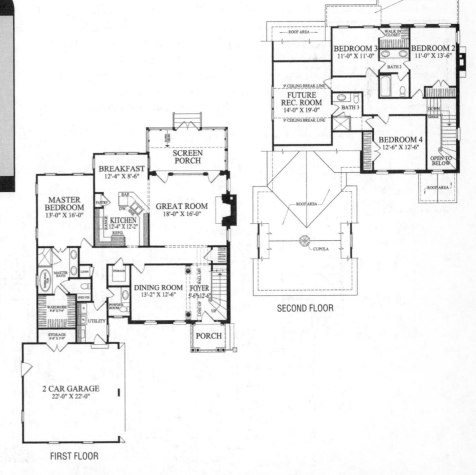

Stately and sophisticated, this home showcases drama in the entryway with bold columns and a barrel-vault arch that leads to the double front door. Elliptical transoms and a bonneted roof over the upper foyer soften the facade, contrasting with the hipped roof and gables. Upon entrance, the study and dining room flank a grand staircase. A see-through fireplace, bay window, and walk-in pantry add elegance and convenience. With the kitchen as the heart of the home, a center island allows room for two cooks. All bedrooms feature cathedral ceilings and Palladian windows. The master suite includes twin walk-in closets and a spacious master bath with lush amenities. Note the additional bonus room and garage storage.

plan# HPK0100244

STYLE: TRADITIONAL
FIRST FLOOR: 2,160 SQ. FT.
SECOND FLOOR: 951 SQ. FT.
TOTAL: 3,111 SQ. FT.
BONUS SPACE: 491 SQ. FT.
BEDROOMS: 4
BATHROOMS: 3½
WIDTH: 61' - 11"
DEPTH: 63' - 11"

SEARCH ONLINE @ EPLANS.COM

FIRST FLOOR

SECOND FLOOR

ORDER BLUEPRINTS 24 HOURS, 7 DAYS A WEEK, AT 1-800-521-6797

plan# HPK0100245

STYLE: COUNTRY COTTAGE
FIRST FLOOR: 1,894 SQ. FT.
SECOND FLOOR: 683 SQ. FT.
TOTAL: 2,577 SQ. FT.
BONUS SPACE: 210 SQ. FT.
BEDROOMS: 4
BATHROOMS: 3
WIDTH: 57' - 0"
DEPTH: 53' - 6"
FOUNDATION: BASEMENT,
CRAWLSPACE

SEARCH ONLINE @ EPLANS.COM

Perfectly proportionate and definitely distinctive, this country home offers an open floor plan, abundant natural light, and plenty of space to kick back and relax. The plan begins with a two-story foyer that leads ahead to a family room lit by second-floor radius windows. Decorative columns define the nearby dining room, and a freestanding pantry is all that separates the welcoming island kitchen. The breakfast nook flows easily into the vaulted keeping room, surrounded by sparkling windows. Two bedrooms reside on this level, including a secondary bedroom with a box-bay window and a master suite with a sitting bay and a vaulted bath. Upstairs, two bedrooms enjoy privacy and share a full bath and a loft. Optional bonus space is available to expand as your family's needs change.

SECOND FLOOR

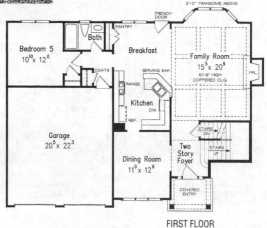

FIRST FLOOR

plan# HPK0100246

STYLE: COUNTRY COTTAGE
FIRST FLOOR: 1,108 SQ. FT.
SECOND FLOOR: 1,253 SQ. FT.
TOTAL: 2,361 SQ. FT.
BEDROOMS: 5
BATHROOMS: 3
WIDTH: 50' - 4"
DEPTH: 37' - 9"
FOUNDATION: BASEMENT,
CRAWLSPACE

SEARCH ONLINE @ EPLANS.COM

SECOND FLOOR

FIRST FLOOR

plan# HPK0100247

STYLE: SOUTHERN COLONIAL
FIRST FLOOR: 2,113 SQ. FT.
SECOND FLOOR: 583 SQ. FT.
TOTAL: 2,696 SQ. FT.
BONUS SPACE: 341 SQ. FT.
BEDROOMS: 4
BATHROOMS: 3
WIDTH: 58' - 4"
DEPTH: 61' - 0"
FOUNDATION: BASEMENT,
CRAWLSPACE

SEARCH ONLINE @ EPLANS.COM

ORDER BLUEPRINTS 24 HOURS, 7 DAYS A WEEK, AT 1-800-521-6797

© William E. Poole Designs, Inc.

plan# HPK0100248

STYLE: COUNTRY COTTAGE
FIRST FLOOR: 1,291 SQ. FT.
SECOND FLOOR: 1,006 SQ. FT.
TOTAL: 2,297 SQ. FT.
BONUS SPACE: 351 SQ. FT.
BEDROOMS: 3
BATHROOMS: 2½
WIDTH: 45' - 0"
DEPTH: 64' - 3"
FOUNDATION: CRAWLSPACE

SEARCH ONLINE @ EPLANS.COM

Gabled dormers and a pedimented entryway give this home undeniable colonial character. Once past the dining room, the kitchen, breakfast area, and great room form an uninterrupted space in the heart of this home. The porch at the rear of the plan provides even more room for large gatherings. The home's three bedrooms are on the second floor, attended by two full baths. A future rec room awaits above the garage.

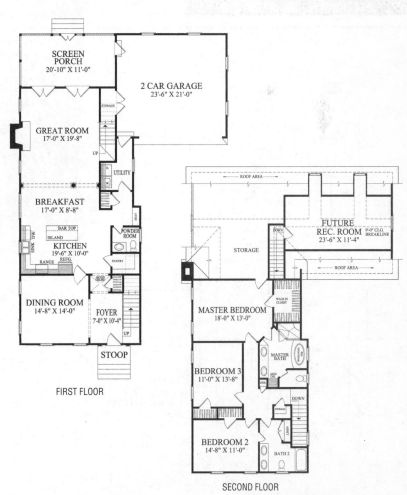

FIRST FLOOR

SECOND FLOOR

SECOND FLOOR

FIRST FLOOR

plan# HPK0100249

STYLE: CAPE COD
FIRST FLOOR: 1,672 SQ. FT.
SECOND FLOOR: 788 SQ. FT.
TOTAL: 2,460 SQ. FT.
BEDROOMS: 4
BATHROOMS: 2½
WIDTH: 56' - 10"
DEPTH: 46' - 6"
FOUNDATION: BASEMENT,
CRAWLSPACE

SEARCH ONLINE @ EPLANS.COM

plan# HPK0100250

STYLE: EUROPEAN COTTAGE
SQUARE FOOTAGE: 2,684
BEDROOMS: 3
BATHROOMS: 2
WIDTH: 71' - 10"
DEPTH: 69' - 7"
FOUNDATION: BASEMENT,
CRAWLSPACE, SLAB

SEARCH ONLINE @ EPLANS.COM

ORDER BLUEPRINTS 24 HOURS, 7 DAYS A WEEK, AT 1-800-521-6797

plan# HPK0100251

STYLE: COLONIAL
FIRST FLOOR: 889 SQ. FT.
SECOND FLOOR: 896 SQ. FT.
TOTAL: 1,785 SQ. FT.
BEDROOMS: 4
BATHROOMS: 2
WIDTH: 32' - 0"
DEPTH: 28' - 0"
FOUNDATION: BASEMENT

SEARCH ONLINE @ EPLANS.COM

A brick facade with corner quoins and shuttered front windows give this respectable two-story home an aura of permanence. The sleeping quarters are located on the second level—three family bedrooms and a master bedroom share hallway access to a full bath with a separate shower and tub. Downstairs, the living room enjoys a corner fireplace and flows through an open doorway to the dining area. Counters and cabinets wrap almost entirely around the kitchen, very handy for the family cooks; a snack bar opens onto the dining room. A downstairs bath with a shower is also home to the washer and dryer.

SECOND FLOOR

FIRST FLOOR

© William E. Poole Designs, Inc.

SECOND FLOOR

FIRST FLOOR

plan# HPK0100252

STYLE: GEORGIAN
FIRST FLOOR: 2,767 SQ. FT.
SECOND FLOOR: 1,179 SQ. FT.
TOTAL: 3,946 SQ. FT.
BONUS SPACE: 591 SQ. FT.
BEDROOMS: 4
BATHROOMS: 3½ + ½
WIDTH: 79' - 11"
DEPTH: 80' - 6"
FOUNDATION: CRAWLSPACE

SEARCH ONLINE @ EPLANS.COM

SECOND FLOOR

FIRST FLOOR

plan# HPK0100253

STYLE: PLANTATION
FIRST FLOOR: 1,510 SQ. FT.
SECOND FLOOR: 1,486 SQ. FT.
TOTAL: 2,996 SQ. FT.
BEDROOMS: 5
BATHROOMS: 4
WIDTH: 53' - 0"
DEPTH: 53' - 4"
FOUNDATION: BASEMENT, CRAWLSPACE

SEARCH ONLINE @ EPLANS.COM

ORDER BLUEPRINTS 24 HOURS, 7 DAYS A WEEK, AT 1-800-521-6797

plan# HPK0100254

STYLE: COUNTRY COTTAGE
FIRST FLOOR: 1,480 SQ. FT.
SECOND FLOOR: 1,651 SQ. FT.
TOTAL: 3,131 SQ. FT.
BEDROOMS: 4
BATHROOMS: 3½
WIDTH: 67' - 5"
DEPTH: 61' - 5"
FOUNDATION: CRAWLSPACE

SEARCH ONLINE @ EPLANS.COM

The designer of this colonial-style home found inspiration from a Victorian manor in Southport, North Carolina. The cupola, turret, gazebo, balustrades, porches, delicate details accurately portray the Victorian period in a home plan of today. Inside, living and family area are spacious and sunny. Upstairs, four bedrooms share three bathrooms and access to the porch.

SECOND FLOOR

FIRST FLOOR

SECOND FLOOR

plan# HPK0100255

STYLE: FARMHOUSE
FIRST FLOOR: 1,176 SQ. FT.
SECOND FLOOR: 1,278 SQ. FT.
TOTAL: 2,454 SQ. FT.
BEDROOMS: 4
BATHROOMS: 3½
WIDTH: 42' - 0"
DEPTH: 42' - 0"
FOUNDATION: CRAWLSPACE

SEARCH ONLINE @ EPLANS.COM

FIRST FLOOR

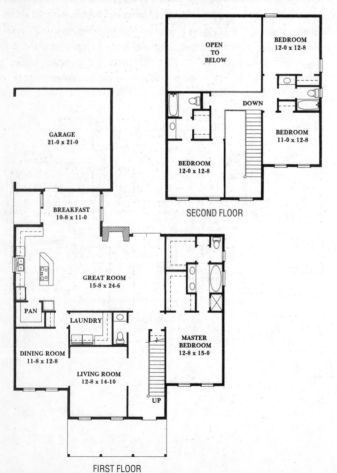

SECOND FLOOR

FIRST FLOOR

plan# HPK0100256

STYLE: FARMHOUSE
FIRST FLOOR: 1,812 SQ. FT.
SECOND FLOOR: 779 SQ. FT.
TOTAL: 2,591 SQ. FT.
BEDROOMS: 4
BATHROOMS: 3½
WIDTH: 47' - 0"
DEPTH: 78' - 0"
FOUNDATION: CRAWLSPACE

SEARCH ONLINE @ EPLANS.COM

ORDER BLUEPRINTS 24 HOURS, 7 DAYS A WEEK, AT 1-800-521-6797

plan# HPK0100257

STYLE: FARMHOUSE
FIRST FLOOR: 1,352 SQ. FT.
SECOND FLOOR: 1,238 SQ. FT.
TOTAL: 2,590 SQ. FT.
BONUS SPACE: 459 SQ. FT.
BEDROOMS: 3
BATHROOMS: 2½
WIDTH: 62' - 0"
DEPTH: 44' - 0"
FOUNDATION: BASEMENT

SEARCH ONLINE @ EPLANS.COM

A Victorian porch and turret embellish this otherwise modern country home with the style and charm of yesterday. A beautiful foyer with porch views greets family and friends, offering access to the living and dining rooms. Continue past a central powder room to the hearth-warmed family room. A well-equipped kitchen with a walk-in pantry is situated nearby and leads out to the rear porch. Upstairs, bedrooms are arranged with privacy in mind. The master suite revels in a resplendent bath and enormous walk-in closet. A two-car garage completes this special plan.

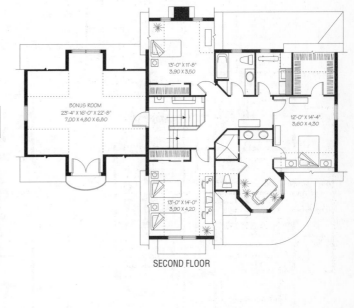

SECOND FLOOR

FIRST FLOOR

A Victorian beauty! With an impressive front-corner tower, bay windows, and a circular chimney with a decorative top, the exterior radiates grandeur. Formal entertaining will be done in the front dining and great rooms. Nearby is a guest bedroom with a bath for overnight guests. To the rear is the family area: a large keeping room, bayed breakfast alcove, and a kitchen surrounded by counter space. Upstairs, the deluxe master suite is what you've always dreamed about. The sleeping area is set in a huge bay with four windows; the oversize garden tub is also set in a bay lighted by three windows. There is also a shower, dual sinks, and a closeted toilet. Three other bedrooms are located on this level; one has a private bath, the other two share a bath. They all have walk-in closets.

ptan# HPK0100258

STYLE: VICTORIAN
FIRST FLOOR: 1,578 SQ. FT.
SECOND FLOOR: 1,418 SQ. FT.
TOTAL: 2,996 SQ. FT.
BEDROOMS: 5
BATHROOMS: 4
WIDTH: 42' - 0"
DEPTH: 56' - 0"
FOUNDATION: CRAWLSPACE

SEARCH ONLINE @ EPLANS.COM

LAUN

BREAKFAST

KITCHEN

KEEPING ROOM
15-6 x 15-6

DINING ROOM
12-0 X 13-6

UP

GUEST ROOM
11-0 X12-6

GREAT ROOM
15-0 X 19-0

FIRST FLOOR

BEDROOM
11-0 X 13-6

BEDROOM
12-6 X 13-6

BEDROOM
12-0 X 13-6

DOWN

UP

MASTER
BEDROOM
15-0 x 15-0

SECOND FLOOR

plan# HPK0100259

STYLE: EUROPEAN COTTAGE
FIRST FLOOR: 2,788 SQ. FT.
SECOND FLOOR: 1,116 SQ. FT.
TOTAL: 3,904 SQ. FT.
BEDROOMS: 4
BATHROOMS: 3½
WIDTH: 68' - 10"
DEPTH: 76' - 4"
FOUNDATION: BASEMENT,
CRAWLSPACE, SLAB

SEARCH ONLINE @ EPLANS.COM

Straight from the hills of the French countryside, this whimsical estate features every amenity on your wish list with the style and grace you've been searching for. Enter through French doors to a two-story foyer; on the left, a dining room is defined by columns. The living room is ahead, adorned with columns and leading into a gallery with rear-property access. The master suite is entered via the gallery and delights in a bayed sitting area, lavish whirlpool bath, and two generous walk-in closets. Living areas on the opposite side of the home include a kitchen with a unique serving island and a sunlit family room with a fireplace. The upper level hosts two bedrooms, a game room, and a full bath. A balcony overlook to the living room is an elegant touch.

FIRST FLOOR

SECOND FLOOR

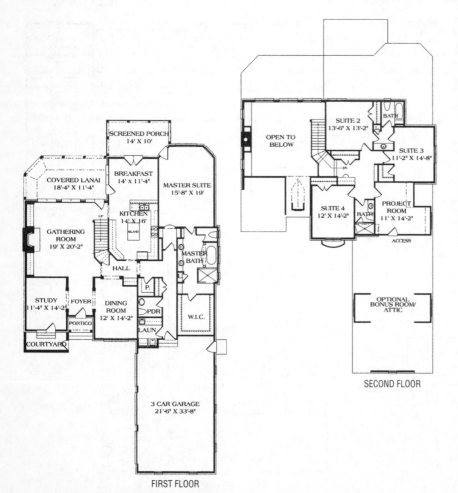

FIRST FLOOR

SECOND FLOOR

plan# HPK0100260

STYLE: FRENCH COUNTRY
FIRST FLOOR: 2,423 SQ. FT.
SECOND FLOOR: 1,197 SQ. FT.
TOTAL: 3,620 SQ. FT.
BONUS SPACE: 551 SQ. FT.
BEDROOMS: 4
BATHROOMS: 3½
WIDTH: 56' - 6"
DEPTH: 97' - 3"
FOUNDATION: CRAWLSPACE

SEARCH ONLINE @ EPLANS.COM

This home was transplanted right from the French countryside! Stone, sloping rooflines, and window detail give the facade great curb appeal. Enter the foyer through the delightful portico and find a study with its own courtyard to the left, and a formal dining room to the right. Ahead is a large gathering room, with a fireplace and access to the rear covered lanai. To the right of the staircase lies the kitchen and breakfast room, which opens to the screened porch. The island kitchen enjoys a pantry and ample counter space. The master suite rounds out the first floor and is nicely accommodated with a deluxe bath and large walk-in closet. Upstairs, three bedrooms and two baths share space with a convenient project room, as well as optional attic space.

© 2002 Donald A. Gardner, Inc.

plan# HPK0100261

STYLE: CHATEAU STYLE
FIRST FLOOR: 2,062 SQ. FT.
SECOND FLOOR: 1,279 SQ. FT.
TOTAL: 3,341 SQ. FT.
BONUS SPACE: 386 SQ. FT.
BEDROOMS: 5
BATHROOMS: 4½
WIDTH: 73' - 8"
DEPTH: 50' - 0"

SEARCH ONLINE @ EPLANS.COM

A five-story chateau-style home may be exactly what you are looking for to entertain guests in grand style and accommodate a growing family. When visitors pass through the elegant columns on the front porch into the foyer with its spiral staircase and art niche, they know this is a special place. To the left is the formal dining room, and straight ahead is the spacious, two-story-high great room with a centered fireplace flanked by built-in shelves. The huge kitchen with an island counter and handy pantry easily serves the dining room and the sunlit breakfast nook. The absolutely magnificent master suite assumes the entire right wing of the plan. Upstairs, four bedrooms (make one a study) and three baths offer plenty of comfort. A balcony overlooks the great room.

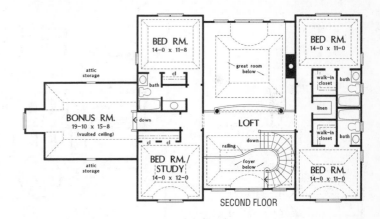

SECOND FLOOR

FIRST FLOOR

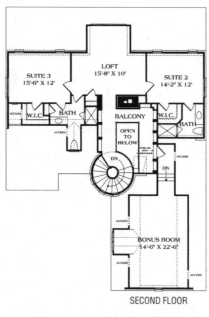

SECOND FLOOR

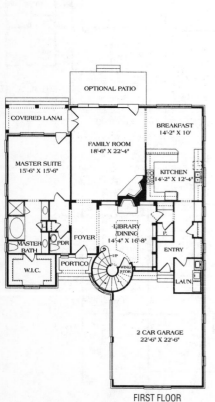

FIRST FLOOR

plan # HPK0100262

STYLE: FRENCH
FIRST FLOOR: 1,980 SQ. FT.
SECOND FLOOR: 1,186 SQ. FT.
TOTAL: 3,166 SQ. FT.
BONUS SPACE: 433 SQ. FT.
BEDROOMS: 3
BATHROOMS: 3½
WIDTH: 50' - 8"
DEPTH: 69' - 0"
FOUNDATION: CRAWLSPACE

SEARCH ONLINE @ EPLANS.COM

The stone turret is the gorgeous centerpiece of this home's facade. It houses a dazzling spiral staircase that is accessed from the elegant library/dining room to the right of the foyer. In the center of the plan lies the hearth-warmed family room, which leads to the breakfast room and kitchen to right. A spacious mudroom/utility area lies conveniently between the kitchen and two-car garage. A deluxe master suite takes up the left wing of the plan, boasting its own covered lanai and pampering bath. On the second floor, two suites with private baths share a loft and convertible bonus space.

© 2003 Donald A. Gardner, Inc.

plan# HPK0100263

STYLE: CHATEAU STYLE
SQUARE FOOTAGE: 2,330
BEDROOMS: 3
BATHROOMS: 3
WIDTH: 55' - 0"
DEPTH: 72' - 4"

SEARCH ONLINE @ EPLANS.COM

Capturing a bit of the French countryside, this design beautifully combines stone and stucco for a striking facade. An impressive court with a fountain leads to a grand entryway with double doors and a large transom. The family-efficient floor plan divides the sleeping and living quarters. Tray ceilings and columns throughout the home add elegance. Views of the warming fireplace can be enjoyed from the kitchen and breakfast nook. A dramatic barrel-vault crowns a Palladian window in the master suite, and dual walk-ins and twin vanities ease morning routines in the master bath.

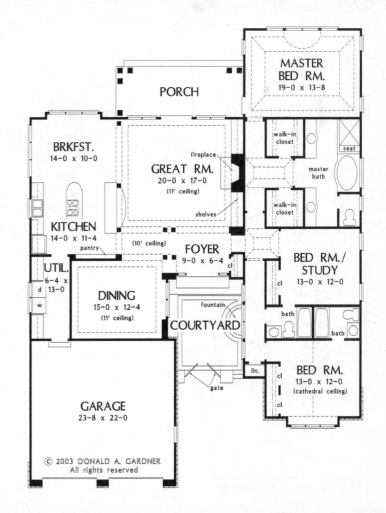

SECOND FLOOR

plan# HPK0100264

STYLE: EUROPEAN COTTAGE
FIRST FLOOR: 2,950 SQ. FT.
SECOND FLOOR: 1,278 SQ. FT.
TOTAL: 4,228 SQ. FT.
BEDROOMS: 4
BATHROOMS: 4½
WIDTH: 91' - 8"
DEPTH: 71' - 10"
FOUNDATION: BASEMENT,
CRAWLSPACE, SLAB

SEARCH ONLINE @ EPLANS.COM

FIRST FLOOR

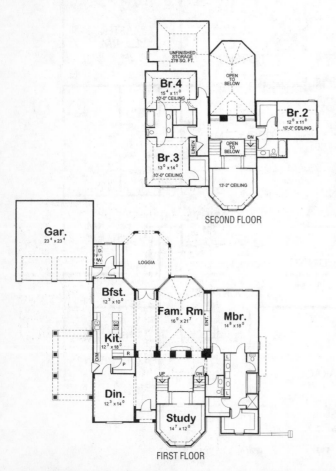

SECOND FLOOR

FIRST FLOOR

plan# HPK0100265

STYLE: FRENCH
FIRST FLOOR: 2,292 SQ. FT.
SECOND FLOOR: 1,010 SQ. FT.
TOTAL: 3,302 SQ. FT.
BONUS SPACE: 278 SQ. FT.
BEDROOMS: 4
BATHROOMS: 3½
WIDTH: 75' - 0"
DEPTH: 72' - 8"

SEARCH ONLINE @ EPLANS.COM

plan # HPK0100266

STYLE: EUROPEAN COTTAGE
FIRST FLOOR: 2,025 SQ. FT.
SECOND FLOOR: 1,310 SQ. FT.
TOTAL: 3,335 SQ. FT.
BEDROOMS: 3
BATHROOMS: 3½
WIDTH: 59' - 8"
DEPTH: 78' - 8"
FOUNDATION: CRAWLSPACE

SEARCH ONLINE @ EPLANS.COM

European flair lights up this stately manor. Shutters, stone, and charming details enliven the facade. Inside, find a unique arrangement of space. The kitchen and gathering room flow together on the right, enjoying a fireplace and access to the rear covered veranda, where a second fireplace awaits. The elegant dining room is at the center of the plan, and leads out to the terrace. The master suite stretches the entire length of the plan on the right, with a huge walk-in closet, deluxe bath, and private pergola, as well as terrace access. The large second floor is home to two bedrooms with private baths and a study/recreation room. Plenty of storage space surrounds these rooms, and a balcony overlook adds drama.

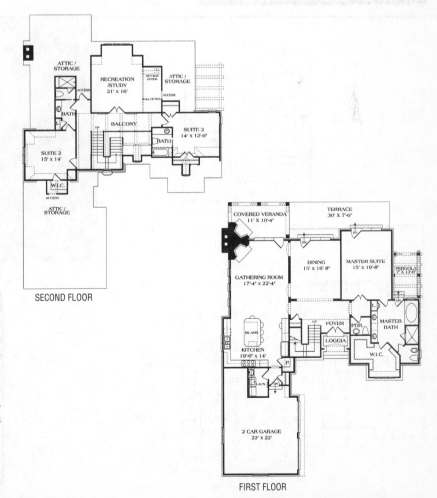

SECOND FLOOR

FIRST FLOOR

plan# HPK0100267

STYLE: TRADITIONAL
SQUARE FOOTAGE: 2,331
BEDROOMS: 3
BATHROOMS: 2½
WIDTH: 74' - 11"
DEPTH: 68' - 9"

SEARCH ONLINE @ EPLANS.COM

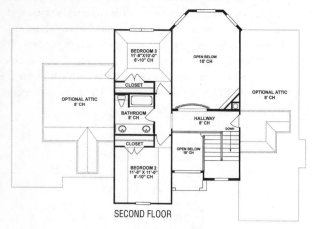

SECOND FLOOR

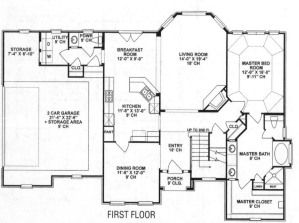

FIRST FLOOR

plan# HPK0100268

STYLE: FRENCH
FIRST FLOOR: 1,487 SQ. FT.
SECOND FLOOR: 497 SQ. FT.
TOTAL: 1,984 SQ. FT.
BEDROOMS: 3
BATHROOMS: 2½
WIDTH: 62' - 0"
DEPTH: 42' - 6"

SEARCH ONLINE @ EPLANS.COM

plan# HPK0100269

STYLE: TRADITIONAL
FIRST FLOOR: 1,373 SQ. FT.
SECOND FLOOR: 1,150 SQ. FT.
TOTAL: 2,523 SQ. FT.
BEDROOMS: 4
BATHROOMS: 2½
WIDTH: 64' - 1"
DEPTH: 39' - 9"

SEARCH ONLINE @ EPLANS.COM

Imaginative, ambitious, and definitely unique, this four-bedroom design was created for families that don't want just another cookie-cutter home. An entry tower makes a grand impression and opens to the family room, with a cathedral ceiling and warming fireplace. A library alcove is the perfect place to settle down with a good book or simply gaze out the full-length windows. The kitchen is a chef's dream come true, with a cooktop island and oversized pantry. Direct access to the bayed breakfast nook and elegant dining room make it simple to cater to any occasion. Up the dramatic T-shaped stair, three bedrooms line the front of the home. The master suite is situated at the rear and indulges in a spa bath and massive walk-in closet.

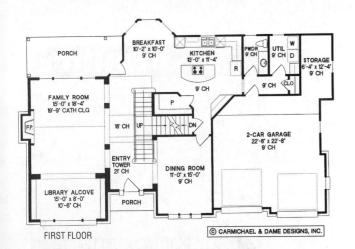

FIRST FLOOR

© CARMICHAEL & DAME DESIGNS, INC.

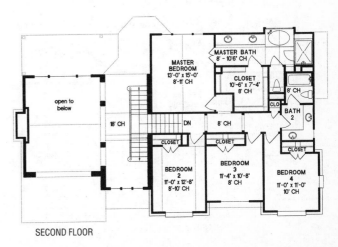

SECOND FLOOR

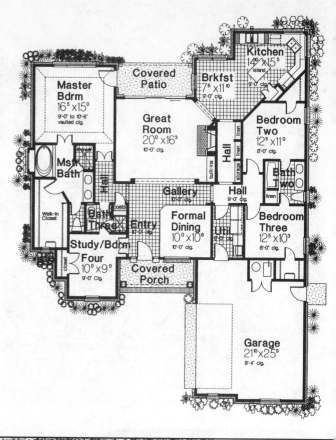

plan # HPK0100270

STYLE: TRADITIONAL
SQUARE FOOTAGE: 2,193
BEDROOMS: 4
BATHROOMS: 3
WIDTH: 55' - 0"
DEPTH: 71' - 0"
FOUNDATION: SLAB

SEARCH ONLINE @ EPLANS.COM

plan # HPK0100271

STYLE: FRENCH COUNTRY
SQUARE FOOTAGE: 2,526
BEDROOMS: 4
BATHROOMS: 3
WIDTH: 64' - 0"
DEPTH: 65' - 1"
FOUNDATION: SLAB

SEARCH ONLINE @ EPLANS.COM

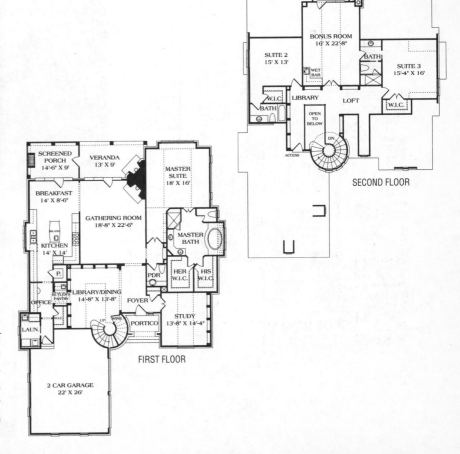

plan# HPK0100272

STYLE: FRENCH COUNTRY
FIRST FLOOR: 2,507 SQ. FT.
SECOND FLOOR: 1,472 SQ. FT.
TOTAL: 3,979 SQ. FT.
BEDROOMS: 3
BATHROOMS: 3½
WIDTH: 59' - 6"
DEPTH: 82' - 8"
FOUNDATION: CRAWLSPACE

SEARCH ONLINE @ EPLANS.COM

With the looks of a charming rural inn on the outside, this plan delights on the inside with a cozy yet elegant floor plan. The foyer graciously accesses both the formal study on the right and the library/dining room on the left, and looks ahead to the hearth-warmed gathering room. This room opens to the rear veranda with its own fireplace, and flows into the breakfast room and kitchen. The spacious island kitchen leads into an office area and the laundry room, both of which are surrounded by plenty of storage space. The master suite dazzles on the right of the plan with its enormous bath and double walk-in closets. The second floor is home to two suites with walk-in closets and private baths, as well as library and loft space. A bonus room awaits expansion with its own balcony.

SECOND FLOOR

FIRST FLOOR

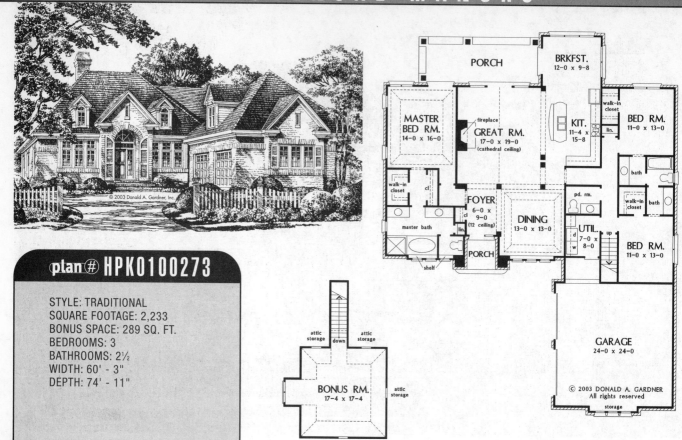

plan# HPK0100273

STYLE: TRADITIONAL
SQUARE FOOTAGE: 2,233
BONUS SPACE: 289 SQ. FT.
BEDROOMS: 3
BATHROOMS: 2½
WIDTH: 60' - 3"
DEPTH: 74' - 11"

SEARCH ONLINE @ EPLANS.COM

plan# HPK0100274

STYLE: FRENCH COUNTRY
MAIN LEVEL: 2,563 SQ. FT.
UPPER LEVEL: 298 SQ. FT.
LOWER LEVEL: 1,870 SQ. FT.
TOTAL: 4,731 SQ. FT.
BONUS SPACE: 532 SQ. FT.
BEDROOMS: 3
BATHROOMS: 3½
WIDTH: 84' - 2"
DEPTH: 89' - 3"
FOUNDATION: BASEMENT

SEARCH ONLINE @ EPLANS.COM

ORDER BLUEPRINTS 24 HOURS, 7 DAYS A WEEK, AT 1-800-521-6797

© 2003 Donald A. Gardner, Inc.

plan# HPK0100275

STYLE: TRADITIONAL
FIRST FLOOR: 2,194 SQ. FT.
SECOND FLOOR: 971 SQ. FT.
TOTAL: 3,165 SQ. FT.
BONUS SPACE: 462 SQ. FT.
BEDROOMS: 5
BATHROOMS: 3½
WIDTH: 82' - 7"
DEPTH: 51' - 1"

SEARCH ONLINE @ EPLANS.COM

Sophisticated and stately, this traditional home has an abundance of architectural interest and an open, family-efficient floor plan. Columns and an elegant balustrade create a regal entryway, joined by a box-bay window crowned with a metal roof and accentuated by a Palladian window. The foyer features a two-story cathedral ceiling and grand staircase. Interior columns and a balcony separate the great room with its fireplace, French doors, and built-in cabinetry. The kitchen is complete with a convenient central island and is open to the breakfast bay. The master bedroom includes a tray ceiling; two secondary bedrooms showcase vaulted ceilings.

SECOND FLOOR

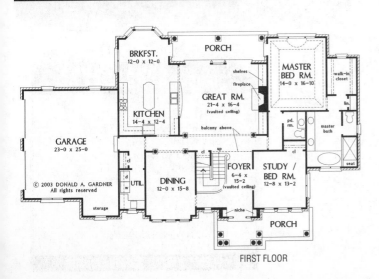

FIRST FLOOR

© The Sater Design Collection, Inc.

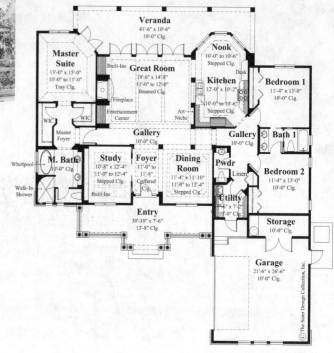

© The Sater Design Collection, Inc.

plan# HPK0100276

STYLE: EUROPEAN COTTAGE
SQUARE FOOTAGE: 2,194
BEDROOMS: 3
BATHROOMS: 2½
WIDTH: 62' - 10"
DEPTH: 73' - 6"
FOUNDATION: SLAB

SEARCH ONLINE @ EPLANS.COM

OPTIONAL LAYOUT

© The Sater Design Collection, Inc.

© The Sater Design Collection, Inc.

plan# HPK0100277

STYLE: ITALIANATE
SQUARE FOOTAGE: 3,790
BEDROOMS: 4
BATHROOMS: 3½
WIDTH: 80' - 8"
DEPTH: 107' - 8"
FOUNDATION: SLAB

SEARCH ONLINE @ EPLANS.COM

ORDER BLUEPRINTS 24 HOURS, 7 DAYS A WEEK, AT 1-800-521-6797

© The Sater Design Collection, Inc.

plan # HPK0100013

STYLE: ITALIANATE
SQUARE FOOTAGE: 3,942
BEDROOMS: 3
BATHROOMS: 4
WIDTH: 83' - 10"
DEPTH: 106' - 0"
FOUNDATION: SLAB

SEARCH ONLINE @ EPLANS.COM

Welcome home to a country manor with Renaissance flair. Full-length, squint-style windows and brick accents bring Old World charm to a modern plan. Designed for flexibility, the open foyer, living room, and dining room have infinite decor options. Down a gallery (with art niches) two bedroom suites enjoy private baths. The bon-vivant island kitchen is introduced with a wet bar and pool bath. In the leisure room, family and friends will revel in expansive views of the rear property. An outdoor kitchen on the lanai invites alfresco dining. Separated for ultimate privacy, the master suite is an exercise in luxurious living. Past the morning kitchen and into the grand bedroom, an octagonal sitting area is bathed in light. The bath is gracefully set in the turret, with a whirlpool tub and views of the master garden.

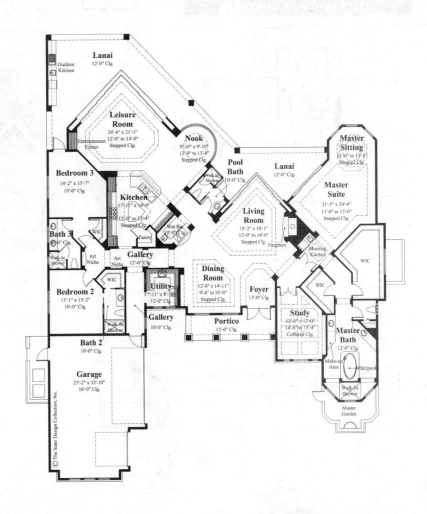

plan# HPK0100278

STYLE: FRENCH
SQUARE FOOTAGE: 2,908
BONUS SPACE: 430 SQ. FT.
BEDROOMS: 4
BATHROOMS: 3½
WIDTH: 73' - 0"
DEPTH: 73' - 7"
FOUNDATION: SLAB

SEARCH ONLINE @ EPLANS.COM

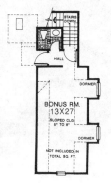

SECOND FLOOR

FIRST FLOOR

plan# HPK0100279

STYLE: TRADITIONAL
FIRST FLOOR: 2,293 SQ. FT.
SECOND FLOOR: 907 SQ. FT.
TOTAL: 3,200 SQ. FT.
BEDROOMS: 4
BATHROOMS: 3½
WIDTH: 76' - 0"
DEPTH: 56' - 0"
FOUNDATION: BASEMENT

SEARCH ONLINE @ EPLANS.COM

ORDER BLUEPRINTS 24 HOURS, 7 DAYS A WEEK, AT 1-800-521-6797

plan# HPK0100280

STYLE: TRADITIONAL
SQUARE FOOTAGE: 2,435
BEDROOMS: 4
BATHROOMS: 3
WIDTH: 76' - 0"
DEPTH: 66' - 5"
FOUNDATION: SLAB

SEARCH ONLINE @ EPLANS.COM

Antique French Country meets comfortable family design in this distinctive home. A gorgeous exterior opens to an entry accented by brick paver flooring. The great room is just ahead, warmed by a fireplace and bathed in natural light. The kitchen and breakfast nook are both complemented by brick pavers for a low-maintenance workspace. Two nearby bedrooms share a full bath between them, thoughtfully separated from the decadent master suite on the right. Here, a vaulted ceiling, patio access, and a lavish bath create a soothing escape. The study is also convenient as a nursery, due to its proximity to the master suite.

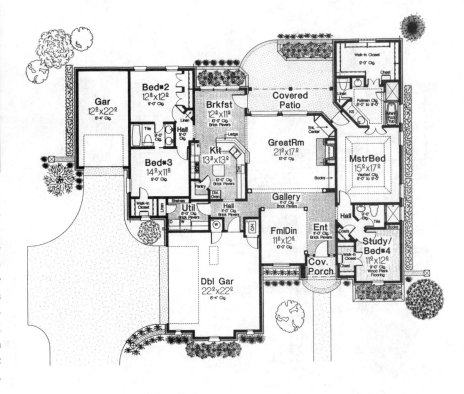

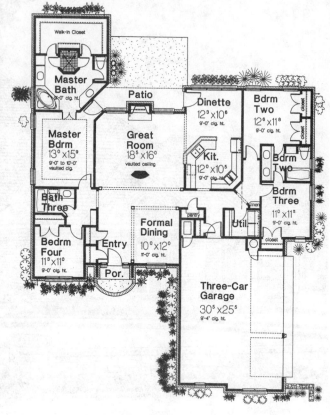

plan# HPK0100281

STYLE: FRENCH
SQUARE FOOTAGE: 2,279
BEDROOMS: 4
BATHROOMS: 3
WIDTH: 60' - 0"
DEPTH: 78' - 0"
FOUNDATION: SLAB

SEARCH ONLINE @ EPLANS.COM

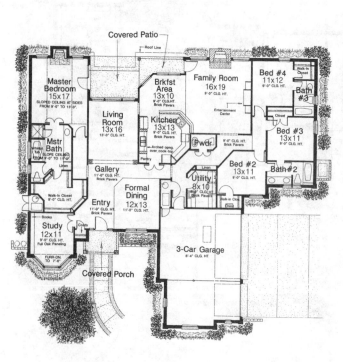

plan# HPK0100282

STYLE: TRADITIONAL
SQUARE FOOTAGE: 2,885
BEDROOMS: 4
BATHROOMS: 3½
WIDTH: 75' - 0"
DEPTH: 68' - 4"
FOUNDATION: SLAB

SEARCH ONLINE @ EPLANS.COM

plan # HPK0100283

STYLE: EUROPEAN COTTAGE
SQUARE FOOTAGE: 2,553
BEDROOMS: 3
BATHROOMS: 2½
WIDTH: 80' - 0"
DEPTH: 56' - 10"
FOUNDATION: SLAB

SEARCH ONLINE @ EPLANS.COM

Contrasting brick lends itself to the ornate shapes of Old World arches and angles, creating a compelling example of European architecture, right in your own neighborhood. An arched window and sidelights brighten the entry, which opens on either side to the dining room and study. The great room emphasizes a grand stone hearth and clear views of the rear property. The island-cooktop kitchen is truly a chef's delight, opening to the uniquely angled breakfast nook. Bedrooms are designed to value peace and quiet; the master suite—remarkable with patio access and a magnificent bath—resides to the right, as two additional bedrooms occupy the left wing. The three-car garage is large enough to hold cars, garden equipment... even a small boat!

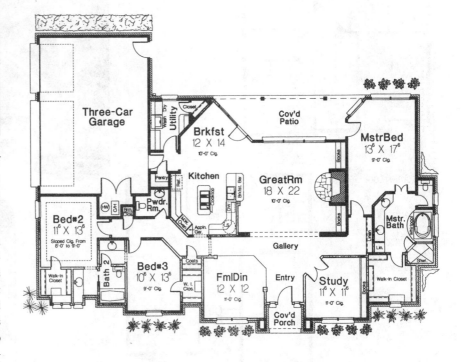

SECOND FLOOR

FIRST FLOOR

plan# HPK0100284

STYLE: FRENCH
FIRST FLOOR: 845 SQ. FT.
SECOND FLOOR: 768 SQ. FT.
TOTAL: 1,613 SQ. FT.
BONUS SPACE: 288 SQ. FT.
BEDROOMS: 3
BATHROOMS: 1½
WIDTH: 36' - 0"
DEPTH: 40' - 0"
FOUNDATION: BASEMENT

SEARCH ONLINE @ EPLANS.COM

SECOND FLOOR

FIRST FLOOR

plan# HPK0100285

STYLE: EUROPEAN COTTAGE
FIRST FLOOR: 805 SQ. FT.
SECOND FLOOR: 937 SQ. FT.
TOTAL: 1,742 SQ. FT.
BEDROOMS: 3
BATHROOMS: 2½
WIDTH: 33' - 0"
DEPTH: 35' - 0"
FOUNDATION: BASEMENT

SEARCH ONLINE @ EPLANS.COM

ORDER BLUEPRINTS 24 HOURS, 7 DAYS A WEEK, AT 1-800-521-6797

plan# HPK0100286

STYLE: EUROPEAN COTTAGE
FIRST FLOOR: 1,010 SQ. FT.
SECOND FLOOR: 898 SQ. FT.
TOTAL: 1,908 SQ. FT.
BEDROOMS: 3
BATHROOMS: 2
WIDTH: 40' - 8"
DEPTH: 34' - 0"
FOUNDATION: BASEMENT

SEARCH ONLINE @ EPLANS.COM

This handsome two-story home with a brick exterior offers special amenities and uniquely shaped rooms to provide a warm and relaxed ambiance. A freestanding, see-through fireplace serves as a divider between the living room and formal dining area. An angled island counter with a rounded snack bar at one end not only dresses up the kitchen but is readily accessible to the food-preparation areas. A laundry and half-bath are conveniently set off the kitchen. Toward the front, a home office or study highlight this plan's versatility. The master bedroom on the second floor enjoys an ample walk-in closet and shares a comfort-filled bath with two other bedrooms. One of these rooms also has a walk-in closet, as well as a cozy nook in the front dormer and a triangular-shaped space for a desk.

FIRST FLOOR

SECOND FLOOR

SECOND FLOOR

plan # HPK0100287

STYLE: CONTEMPORARY
FIRST FLOOR: 997 SQ. FT.
SECOND FLOOR: 1,124 SQ. FT.
TOTAL: 2,121 SQ. FT.
BEDROOMS: 3
BATHROOMS: 2
WIDTH: 40' - 0"
DEPTH: 48' - 0"
FOUNDATION: BASEMENT

SEARCH ONLINE @ EPLANS.COM

FIRST FLOOR

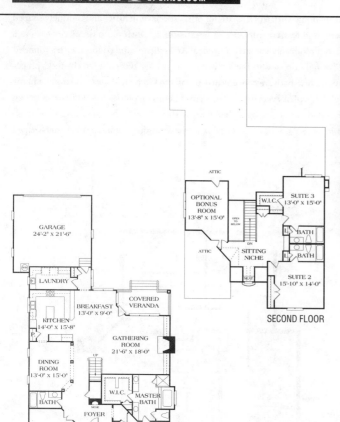

FIRST FLOOR

SECOND FLOOR

plan # HPK0100288

STYLE: EUROPEAN COTTAGE
FIRST FLOOR: 2,326 SQ. FT.
SECOND FLOOR: 955 SQ. FT.
TOTAL: 3,281 SQ. FT.
BONUS SPACE: 253 SQ. FT.
BEDROOMS: 4
BATHROOMS: 4
WIDTH: 84' - 2"
DEPTH: 51' - 4"
FOUNDATION: CRAWLSPACE

SEARCH ONLINE @ EPLANS.COM

plan # HPK0100289

STYLE: FRENCH
FIRST FLOOR: 917 SQ. FT.
SECOND FLOOR: 889 SQ. FT.
TOTAL: 1,806 SQ. FT.
BEDROOMS: 3
BATHROOMS: 2½
WIDTH: 40' - 0"
DEPTH: 40' - 0"
FOUNDATION: BASEMENT

SEARCH ONLINE @ EPLANS.COM

A sturdy French Country home with an internal design that's perfect for relaxed entertaining and active family life. That's what you get with this plan. An angled planter with a built-in art niche partially defines the formal dining and living rooms. The country-size kitchen enjoys a built-in eating counter, which marks off a sunlit breakfast nook with French-door access to the rear yard. A second-level master suite includes a reading corner, walk-in closet, and bath fit for royalty. Two other bedrooms are served by a bath with a large shower. The plan comes with a one-car garage.

SECOND FLOOR

FIRST FLOOR

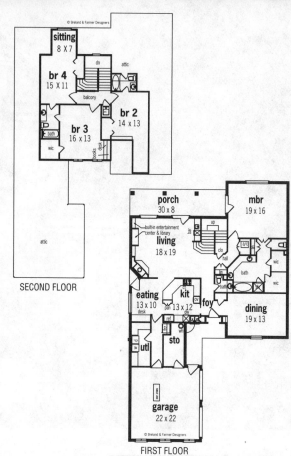

SECOND FLOOR

FIRST FLOOR

plan # HPK0100290

STYLE: EUROPEAN COTTAGE
FIRST FLOOR: 1,884 SQ. FT.
SECOND FLOOR: 1,034 SQ. FT.
TOTAL: 2,918 SQ. FT.
BEDROOMS: 4
BATHROOMS: 3½
WIDTH: 49' - 0"
DEPTH: 79' - 0"
FOUNDATION: SLAB

SEARCH ONLINE @ EPLANS.COM

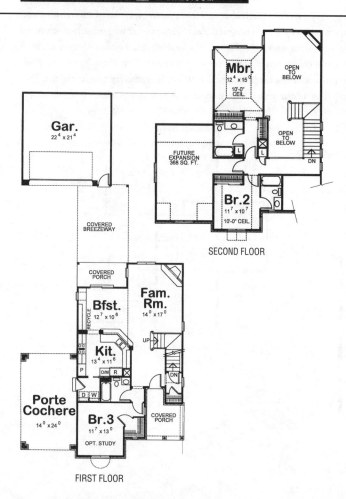

SECOND FLOOR

FIRST FLOOR

plan # HPK0100291

STYLE: EUROPEAN COTTAGE
FIRST FLOOR: 1,071 SQ. FT.
SECOND FLOOR: 657 SQ. FT.
TOTAL: 1,728 SQ. FT.
BONUS SPACE: 368 SQ. FT.
BEDROOMS: 3
BATHROOMS: 3
WIDTH: 41' - 8"
DEPTH: 48' - 4"

SEARCH ONLINE @ EPLANS.COM

© The Sater Design Collection, Inc.

plan# HPK0100292

STYLE: EUROPEAN COTTAGE
FIRST FLOOR: 2,219 SQ. FT.
SECOND FLOOR: 1,085 SQ. FT.
TOTAL: 3,304 SQ. FT.
BONUS SPACE: 404 SQ. FT.
BEDROOMS: 4
BATHROOMS: 3½
WIDTH: 91' - 0"
DEPTH: 52' - 8"
FOUNDATION: SLAB

SEARCH ONLINE @ EPLANS.COM

Stucco and stone combine with graceful details on this four-bedroom home. A covered front porch welcomes friends and family alike, and ushers you into the elegant foyer. A formal dining room is to your right, defined by columns and a grand ceiling treatment. Convenient to the front door, as well as to the lavish master suite, a study/office provides a bay window and lots of privacy. The spacious great room offers a warming fireplace, built-ins, and a pass-through to the efficient kitchen. Here, the gourmet of the family will be well pleased with a worktop island, plenty of wrapping counters, and a huge pantry nearby. A sunny bayed breakfast area will be perfect for early morning coffee. Separated on the first floor for privacy, the master suite is full of tempting amenities. Upstairs, two family bedrooms share a bath, and a guest suite revels in privacy.

SECOND FLOOR

FIRST FLOOR

© The Sater Design Collection, Inc.

plan# HPK0100293

STYLE: EUROPEAN COTTAGE
FIRST FLOOR: 2,250 SQ. FT.
SECOND FLOOR: 663 SQ. FT.
TOTAL: 2,913 SQ. FT.
BONUS SPACE: 351 SQ. FT.
BEDROOMS: 3
BATHROOMS: 3½
WIDTH: 72' - 0"
DEPTH: 68' - 3"
FOUNDATION: SLAB

SEARCH ONLINE @ EPLANS.COM

SECOND FLOOR

FIRST FLOOR

FIRST FLOOR

SECOND FLOOR

© The Sater Design Collection, Inc.

plan# HPK0100294

STYLE: EUROPEAN COTTAGE
FIRST FLOOR: 2,084 SQ. FT.
SECOND FLOOR: 652 SQ. FT.
TOTAL: 2,736 SQ. FT.
BONUS SPACE: 365 SQ. FT.
BEDROOMS: 3
BATHROOMS: 2½
WIDTH: 60' - 6"
DEPTH: 94' - 0"
FOUNDATION: SLAB

SEARCH ONLINE @ EPLANS.COM

ORDER BLUEPRINTS 24 HOURS, 7 DAYS A WEEK, AT 1-800-521-6797

plan # HPK0100295

STYLE: CONTEMPORARY
FIRST FLOOR: 825 SQ. FT.
SECOND FLOOR: 825 SQ. FT.
TOTAL: 1,650 SQ. FT.
BEDROOMS: 3
BATHROOMS: 2
WIDTH: 30' - 0"
DEPTH: 28' - 0"
FOUNDATION: BASEMENT

SEARCH ONLINE @ EPLANS.COM

The stately aura of this rustic European-style home, enhanced by the stone exterior, introduces an interior that is both comfortable and convenient. The family cooks will appreciate the thought that has gone into designing a kitchen that has more than adequate counter and cabinet space and easy access to the living room via the snack bar. A gas fireplace warms the living room. A downstairs bathroom with a shower has enough room for the washer and dryer. Three second-floor bedrooms share a deluxe bath with a corner garden tub, shower, and double-sink vanity. An alcove at the end of the hall is lighted by a circular window and can serve as a modest sitting area.

SECOND FLOOR

FIRST FLOOR

© 2002 Donald A. Gardner, Inc.

This rustic French Country exterior opens up to a plan full of modern amenities. The foyer, preceded by a petite porch, leads into a gallery hall that opens to a sunny, vaulted great room. With its fireplace and porch access, this will be the most popular room in the house. As an added convenience, the great room flows into the breakfast room, with its box-bay window and built-ins. The island kitchen features a pantry and plenty of counter space. A formal dining room is adjacent. The deluxe master suite awaits on the left of the plan, enjoying a pampering bath and double walk-in closets. Upstairs, two bedrooms boast ample closet space and a private bath. Bonus space awaits expansion over the garage.

plan# HPK0100296

STYLE: FRENCH COUNTRY
FIRST FLOOR: 1,834 SQ. FT.
SECOND FLOOR: 681 SQ. FT.
TOTAL: 2,515 SQ. FT.
BONUS SPACE: 365 SQ. FT.
BEDROOMS: 3
BATHROOMS: 3½
WIDTH: 50' - 8"
DEPTH: 66' - 8"

SEARCH ONLINE @ EPLANS.COM

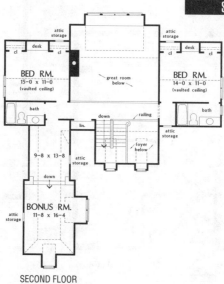

PORCH

MASTER BED RM.
15-0 x 15-0

fireplace

GREAT RM.
20-0 x 17-0
(vaulted ceiling)

BRKFST.
12-0 x 11-0

cl

cl

walk-in closet

walk-in closet

KITCHEN
14-0 x 13-8

cl

master bath

pd. rm.

sto.

up

FOYER
6-8 x 9-6

DINING
14-0 x 13-4

storage

UTILITY
9-0 x 8-0

d   w

GARAGE
21-0 x 21-0

© 2002 DONALD A. GARDNER
All rights reserved

FIRST FLOOR

attic storage

desk   cl

cl   cl

desk

attic storage

BED RM.
15-0 x 11-0
(vaulted ceiling)

great room below

BED RM.
14-0 x 11-0
(vaulted ceiling)

bath

down

railing

bath

lin.

attic storage

foyer below

9-8 x 13-8

attic storage

down

BONUS RM.
11-8 x 16-4

attic storage

SECOND FLOOR

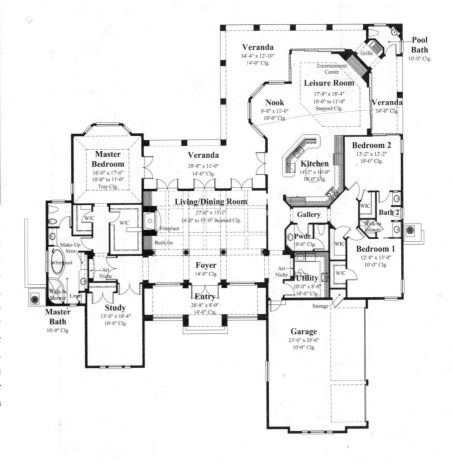

plan# HPK0100297

STYLE: MISSION
SQUARE FOOTAGE: 3,343
BEDROOMS: 3
BATHROOMS: 2½ + ½
WIDTH: 84' - 0"
DEPTH: 92' - 0"
FOUNDATION: SLAB

SEARCH ONLINE @ EPLANS.COM

This distinctive stucco home is reminiscent of early Mission-style architecture. Decorative vigas line the entry as double doors lead into an elongated columned foyer. A living/dining room combination ahead enjoys abundant light from three French doors, and the warmth of a Southwestern fireplace. An abbreviated hall leads either to the bedroom gallery or to the gourmet kitchen. A sunny nook and leisure room just beyond are bathed in natural light. A veranda grill is perfect in any season. Separated from the rest of the home for complete privacy, the master suite relishes a bay window, veranda access, and a lavish bath.

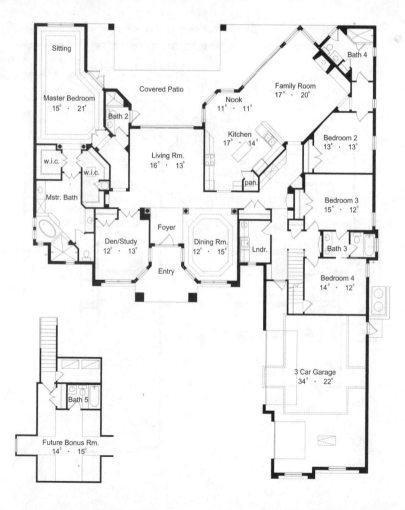

plan # HPK0100298

STYLE: ITALIANATE
SQUARE FOOTAGE: 3,589
BONUS SPACE: 430 SQ. FT.
BEDROOMS: 4
BATHROOMS: 4
WIDTH: 76' - 0"
DEPTH: 98' - 0"
FOUNDATION: SLAB

SEARCH ONLINE @ EPLANS.COM

Exquisite rooflines and arched front windows offer a hint of the marvelous treasures to be found inside this European-style beauty. A highlight is the spacious country-style kitchen with lots and lots of counter space—including a handy island—a walk-in pantry, a sunlit breakfast bay, and a wide opening to the family room. The charming master suite encompasses the entire left side of the home. Off the bedchamber is a sitting room with access to a covered rear patio and two ample walk-in closets. The master bath pampers with a shower big enough for two, an oversize tub, two vanities, and a compartmented toilet. On the opposite side of the house, three bedrooms and two baths provide sleeping quarters for family or visitors. A window wall offers views from the living room to the rear patio and gardens.

plan# HPK0100299

STYLE: MEDITERRANEAN
FIRST FLOOR: 2,926 SQ. FT.
SECOND FLOOR: 1,268 SQ. FT.
TOTAL: 4,194 SQ. FT.
BONUS SPACE: 353 SQ. FT.
BEDROOMS: 4
BATHROOMS: 4½
WIDTH: 75' - 0"
DEPTH: 85' - 4"
FOUNDATION: SLAB

SEARCH ONLINE @ EPLANS.COM

This magnificent Mediterranean-style home is full of the charms that make entertaining gracious and family life comfortable. From the elegant covered entry, pass into the foyer or, through separate French doors, into the den on the right and the formal dining room on the left. A superb kitchen, sunlit breakfast nook, and family room flow together, creating a relaxed unit. Splendor awaits in the master suite with its gracefully curved bedchamber, huge walk-in wardrobes, and luxuriant bath. On the opposite side of the house, a guest bedroom enjoys a full bath. Two more bedrooms share a bath on the second level, and additional space is available for another bedroom and bath. The rear covered patio can be entered from the living room, the master suite, or the breakfast nook. Three vehicles will easily fit into the side-loading garage.

FIRST FLOOR

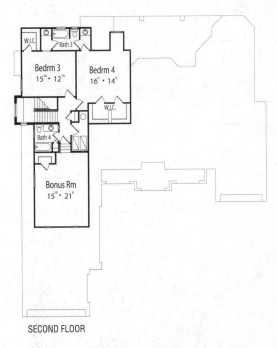

SECOND FLOOR

plan# HPK0100300

STYLE: CONTEMPORARY
SQUARE FOOTAGE: 3,220
BONUS SPACE: 522 SQ. FT.
BEDROOMS: 3
BATHROOMS: 3½
WIDTH: 81' - 4"
DEPTH: 102' - 6"
FOUNDATION: SLAB

SEARCH ONLINE @ EPLANS.COM

With an elegant Mediterranean flavor, this spacious home will be a joy to live in and a wonderful setting for gracious evenings of dining and talking with friends. Unusual-shaped rooms create interesting alcoves, nooks, and bays that can be used to dress up the interior with favorite pieces of furniture, handy cabinets, or plants. Built-in art niches, a built-in desk, and a built-in media/entertainment area are among the enhancements that make this home so special. A covered rear patio could be the site of a swimming pool; a bath with a shower opens to this area. The master suite also opens through French doors to the patio. It enjoys a regal bath with His and Hers walk-in closets and vanities, a shower, and a bumped-out garden tub. The huge kitchen, with a cooktop island and peninsular snack counter, will put a sparkle in the family chef's eye.

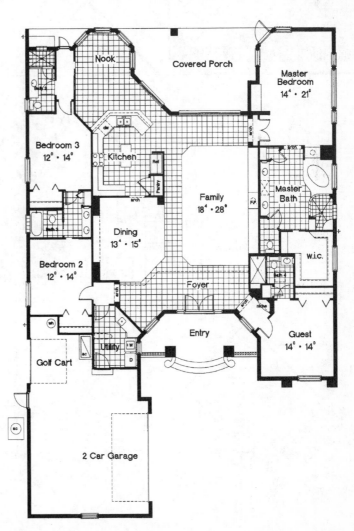

plan # HPK0100301

STYLE: CONTEMPORARY
SQUARE FOOTAGE: 3,119
BEDROOMS: 4
BATHROOMS: 4
WIDTH: 60' - 0"
DEPTH: 90' - 0"
FOUNDATION: SLAB

SEARCH ONLINE @ EPLANS.COM

Put a contemporary twist on Mediterranean style in this stylish luxury home. A grand sweeping entry ushers family and guests into the foyer; beautiful tile flooring stretches across the plan for low maintenance and high appeal. An open design places living areas in view of each other, from the island kitchen and bayed nook to the expansive family room and formal dining room. Bedrooms are arranged for full privacy; two family bedrooms share a bath to the left, and a guest room with a private bath resides toward the front of the home. Tucked to the rear, the master suite reigns with abundant natural light and an indulgent spa bath. Included in the plans is a two-car garage with space for a golf cart and extra storage.

© The Sater Design Collection, Inc.

plan# HPK0100302

STYLE: MEDITERRANEAN
FIRST FLOOR: 2,084 SQ. FT.
SECOND FLOOR: 652 SQ. FT.
TOTAL: 2,736 SQ. FT.
BONUS SPACE: 375 SQ. FT.
BEDROOMS: 3
BATHROOMS: 2½
WIDTH: 60' - 6"
DEPTH: 94' - 0"
FOUNDATION: SLAB

SEARCH ONLINE @ EPLANS.COM

FIRST FLOOR

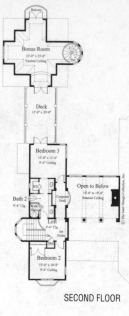

SECOND FLOOR

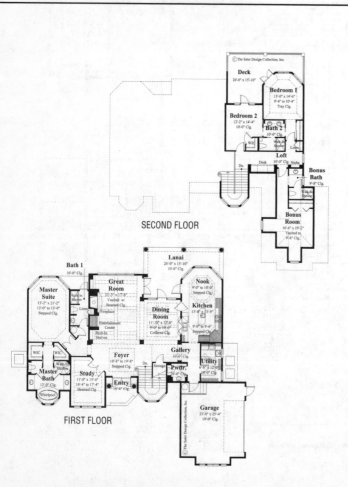

SECOND FLOOR

FIRST FLOOR

© The Sater Design Collection, Inc.

plan# HPK0100303

STYLE: ITALIANATE
FIRST FLOOR: 2,250 SQ. FT.
SECOND FLOOR: 663 SQ. FT.
TOTAL: 2,913 SQ. FT.
BONUS SPACE: 351 SQ. FT.
BEDROOMS: 3
BATHROOMS: 3½
WIDTH: 72' - 0"
DEPTH: 68' - 3"
FOUNDATION: SLAB

SEARCH ONLINE @ EPLANS.COM

plan# HPK0100304

STYLE: ITALIANATE
FIRST FLOOR: 2,567 SQ. FT.
SECOND FLOOR: 844 SQ. FT.
TOTAL: 3,411 SQ. FT.
BONUS SPACE: 297 SQ. FT.
BEDROOMS: 4
BATHROOMS: 3½ + ½
WIDTH: 56' - 8"
DEPTH: 85' - 4"
FOUNDATION: SLAB

SEARCH ONLINE @ EPLANS.COM

For serene beauty, both inside and out, this two-story European-style home can't be beat. The elegant front entry and the covered rear patio call out for the right combination of flowers and shrubs to enhance the home's graceful exterior features. Downstairs, the master suite gloriously offers twin walk-in closets and vanities, a gigantic tub, and a separate shower; upstairs, three bedrooms share two baths and a computer room. The living areas on the first level are designed for full comfort and ease for a busy family and for formal get-togethers. A good-sized laundry room and a two-car garage with the option of building a room above it complete this plan.

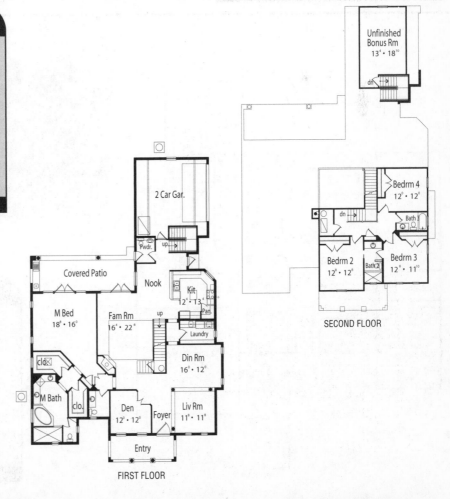

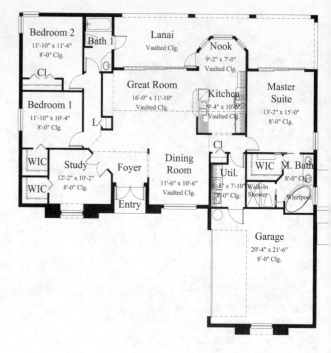

plan# HPK0100305

STYLE: TRADITIONAL
SQUARE FOOTAGE: 1,746
BEDROOMS: 3
BATHROOMS: 2
WIDTH: 58' - 0"
DEPTH: 59' - 4"
FOUNDATION: SLAB

SEARCH ONLINE @ EPLANS.COM

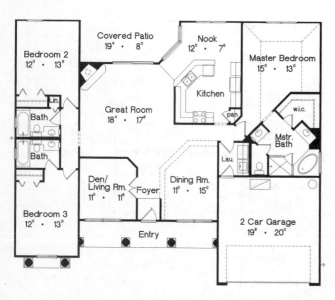

plan# HPK0100306

STYLE: CONTEMPORARY
SQUARE FOOTAGE: 2,052
BEDROOMS: 3
BATHROOMS: 3
WIDTH: 60' - 0"
DEPTH: 50' - 0"
FOUNDATION: SLAB

SEARCH ONLINE @ EPLANS.COM

plan# HPK0100307

STYLE: TRADITIONAL
FIRST FLOOR: 1,796 SQ. FT.
SECOND FLOOR: 771 SQ. FT.
TOTAL: 2,567 SQ. FT.
BONUS SPACE: 220 SQ. FT.
BEDROOMS: 4
BATHROOMS: 3½
WIDTH: 50' - 0"
DEPTH: 57' - 4"
FOUNDATION: SLAB

SEARCH ONLINE @ EPLANS.COM

Stucco, brick, and hipped rooflines give this home terrific curb appeal. Adding extra charm is the turreted entry, which leads into a uniquely angled foyer that opens directly into the dining room. To the right of the foyer is a cozy living room. Ahead, behind the staircase, awaits the spacious family room, boasting a corner hearth and a convenient snack-bar counter to the kitchen. A breakfast nook opens to the kitchen, with ample counter space and a handy pantry. A laundry room and powder room round out the left side of the plan. The right side is home to the deluxe master suite, complete with stunning private bath and two walk-in closets. Upstairs, three bedrooms share two baths, and an optional bonus room awaits expansion.

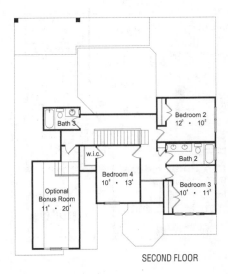

SECOND FLOOR

FIRST FLOOR

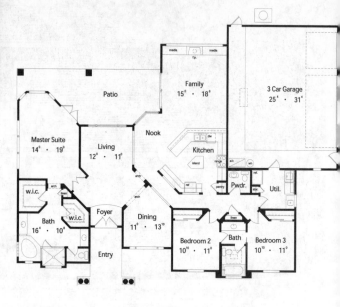

plan# HPK0100308

STYLE: FLORIDIAN
SQUARE FOOTAGE: 2,173
BEDROOMS: 3
BATHROOMS: 2½
WIDTH: 74' - 4"
DEPTH: 56' - 0"
FOUNDATION: SLAB

SEARCH ONLINE @ EPLANS.COM

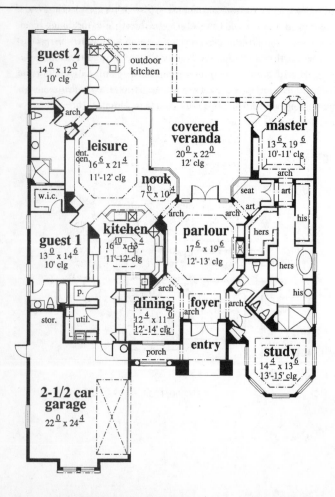

plan# HPK0100006

STYLE: ITALIANATE
SQUARE FOOTAGE: 3,230
BEDROOMS: 3
BATHROOMS: 3½
WIDTH: 65' - 0"
DEPTH: 94' - 10"
FOUNDATION: SLAB

SEARCH ONLINE @ EPLANS.COM

ORDER BLUEPRINTS 24 HOURS, 7 DAYS A WEEK, AT 1-800-521-6797

© The Sater Design Collection, Inc.

plan# HPK0100309

STYLE: EUROPEAN COTTAGE
FIRST FLOOR: 2,815 SQ. FT.
SECOND FLOOR: 1,130 SQ. FT.
TOTAL: 3,945 SQ. FT.
BEDROOMS: 4
BATHROOMS: 3½
WIDTH: 85' - 0"
DEPTH: 76' - 8"
FOUNDATION: SLAB

SEARCH ONLINE @ EPLANS.COM

Stone, stucco, beautiful windows, and a tile roof all combine to give this home plenty of classy curb appeal. An elegant entry leads to the grand foyer, which introduces the formal living room. Here, a bowed wall of windows shows off the rear veranda, and a two-sided fireplace warms cool evenings. A cozy study shares the fireplace and offers access to the rear veranda. Providing privacy as well as pampering, the first-floor master suite is complete with two walk-in closets, a deluxe bath, a stepped ceiling, and private access outdoors. For casual times, the leisure room features a fireplace, built-ins, a coffered ceiling, and outdoor access. Upstairs, Bedrooms 2 and 3 share a bath; the guest suite has a private bath.

SECOND FLOOR

FIRST FLOOR

© 2002 Donald A. Gardner, Inc.

LOGGIA

BED RM.
10-0 x 12-0

BRKFST.
8-10 x 13-1

MASTER
BED RM.
16-2 x 14-0
(10' ceiling)

master
bath

bath

fireplace

GREAT RM.
17-0 x 18-0
(13' ceiling)

KIT.
11-2 x
10-8

walk-in
closet

w d

UTIL.

BED RM./
STUDY
13-0 x 12-0

FOYER
6-8 x
10-4

DINING
13-0 x 12-0
(10' ceiling)

GARAGE
21-0 x 21-0

© 2002 DONALD A. GARDNER
All rights reserved

LOGGIA

COURTYARD

plan# HPK0100310

STYLE: SANTA FE
SQUARE FOOTAGE: 1,895
BEDROOMS: 3
BATHROOMS: 2
WIDTH: 65' - 10"
DEPTH: 59' - 9"

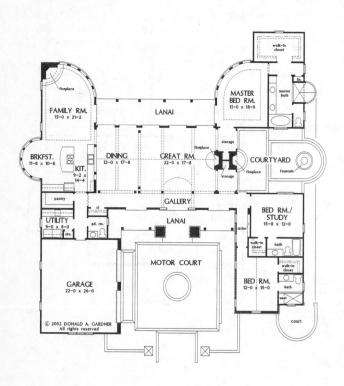

fireplace

FAMILY RM.
15-0 x 21-2

LANAI

MASTER
BED RM.
15-0 x 18-0

walk-in
closet

master
bath

BRKFST.
11-8 x 10-8

KIT.
9-2 x
14-4

DINING
12-0 x 17-8

GREAT RM.
22-0 x 17-8

storage

COURTYARD

fireplace

storage

fountain

pantry

GALLERY

BED RM./
STUDY
15-0 x 12-0

UTILITY
9-0 x 8-0

LANAI

niche

walk-in
closet

bath

GARAGE
22-0 x 26-0

MOTOR COURT

BED RM.
12-0 x 15-0

walk-in
closet

bath

seat

© 2002 Donald A. Gardner
All rights reserved

court

© 2002 Donald A. Gardner, Inc.

plan# HPK0100311

STYLE: RANCH
SQUARE FOOTAGE: 3,061
BEDROOMS: 3
BATHROOMS: 3½
WIDTH: 86' - 1"
DEPTH: 84' - 8"

© 2002 Donald A. Gardner, Inc.

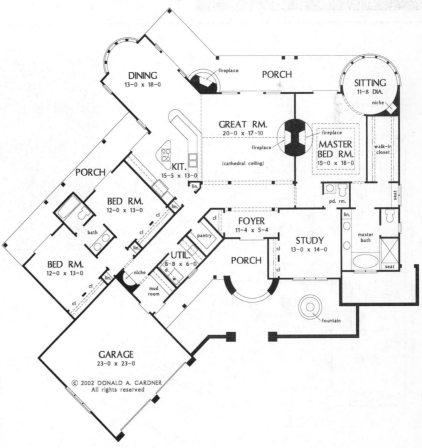

plan# HPK0100312

STYLE: SANTA FE
SQUARE FOOTAGE: 2,792
BEDROOMS: 3
BATHROOMS: 2½
WIDTH: 89' - 2"
DEPTH: 88' - 9"

SEARCH ONLINE @ EPLANS.COM

Angles and arcs are intriguingly juxtaposed in this innovative new Santa Fe design. A Spanish-turret entry presents the formal foyer and quiet study. In the great room, a cathedral ceiling soars. The half-moon fireplace completes its circle in the sumptuous master suite; the sitting room benefits from circumambient light. The left wing comprises a gourmet island kitchen, bayed dining room, and generous twin bedrooms. Not to be missed: a side-entry mudroom and a fireplace on the rear porch.

© 2002 DONALD A. GARDNER
All rights reserved

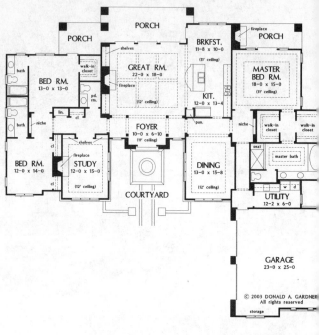

plan# HPK0100313

STYLE: SANTA FE
SQUARE FOOTAGE: 2,911
BEDROOMS: 3
BATHROOMS: 3½
WIDTH: 84' - 8"
DEPTH: 78' - 2"

SEARCH ONLINE @ EPLANS.COM

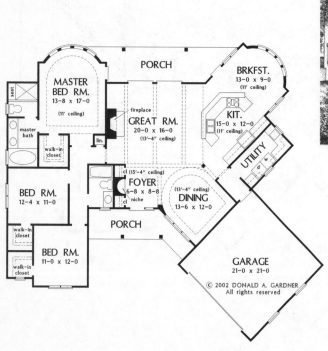

plan# HPK0100314

STYLE: SANTA FE
SQUARE FOOTAGE: 1,883
BEDROOMS: 3
BATHROOMS: 2
WIDTH: 66' - 2"
DEPTH: 59' - 8"

SEARCH ONLINE @ EPLANS.COM

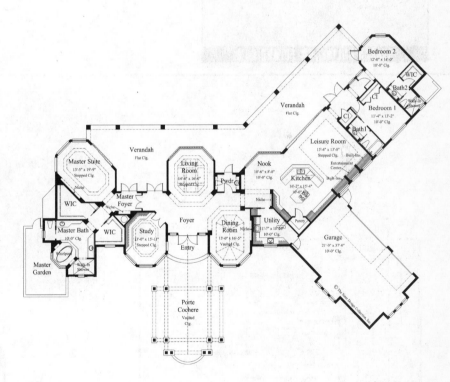

plan# HPK0100315

STYLE: SW CONTEMPORARY
SQUARE FOOTAGE: 3,368
BEDROOMS: 3
BATHROOMS: 3½
WIDTH: 121' - 5"
DEPTH: 99' - 6"
FOUNDATION: SLAB

SEARCH ONLINE @ EPLANS.COM

This magnificent Sun Country home is designed for families that want to break down the barriers between outdoor and indoor living. At the center, three octagonal rooms—the living room, formal dining area, and study/library—are linked by an expansive foyer. To the left, the master suite includes an octagonal master bedchamber, His and Hers walk-in closets, and a bath with a tub set in a bay overlooking the master garden. A wide veranda stretches across the entire back of the home, from the master suite to two family bedrooms with private baths on the far right. A family leisure room, an island kitchen, a breakfast nook, and a utility room also are found in the home's right wing. A classy porte cochere dresses up the front of the house.

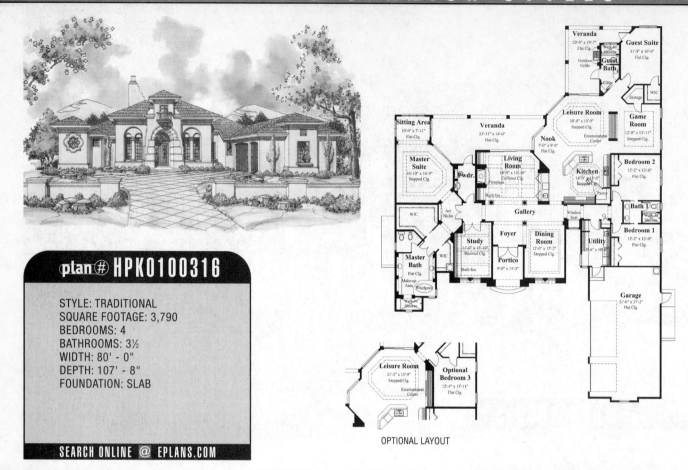

plan# HPK0100316

STYLE: TRADITIONAL
SQUARE FOOTAGE: 3,790
BEDROOMS: 4
BATHROOMS: 3½
WIDTH: 80' - 0"
DEPTH: 107' - 8"
FOUNDATION: SLAB

SEARCH ONLINE @ EPLANS.COM

OPTIONAL LAYOUT

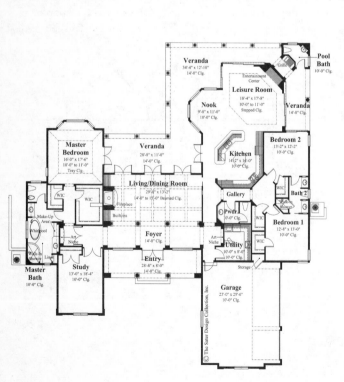

© The Sater Design Collection, Inc.

plan# HPK0100317

STYLE: ITALIANATE
SQUARE FOOTAGE: 3,351
BEDROOMS: 3
BATHROOMS: 2½ + ½
WIDTH: 84' - 0"
DEPTH: 92' - 2"
FOUNDATION: SLAB

SEARCH ONLINE @ EPLANS.COM

ORDER BLUEPRINTS 24 HOURS, 7 DAYS A WEEK, AT 1-800-521-6797

plan# HPK0100318

STYLE: EUROPEAN COTTAGE
FIRST FLOOR: 2,219 SQ. FT.
SECOND FLOOR: 1,085 SQ. FT.
TOTAL: 3,304 SQ. FT.
BONUS SPACE: 404 SQ. FT.
BEDROOMS: 4
BATHROOMS: 3½
WIDTH: 91' - 0"
DEPTH: 52' - 8"
FOUNDATION: SLAB

SEARCH ONLINE @ EPLANS.COM

This home features two levels of pampering luxury filled with the most up-to-date amenities. Touches of Mediterranean detail add to the striking facade. A wrapping front porch welcomes you inside to a formal dining room and two-story great room warmed by a fireplace. Double doors from the master suite, great room, and breakfast nook access the rear veranda. The first-floor master suite enjoys a luxury bath, roomy walk-in closet, and close access to the front-facing office/study. Three additional bedrooms reside upstairs. The bonus room above the garage is great for an apartment or storage space.

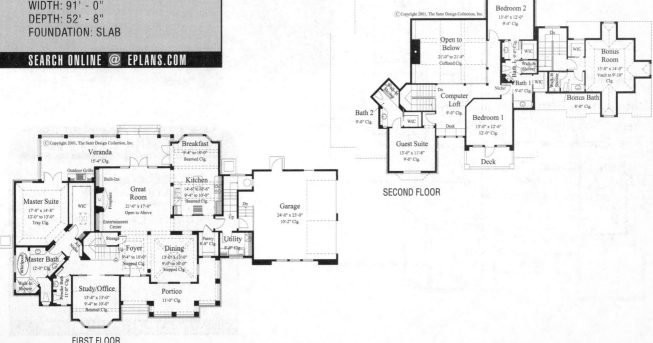

SECOND FLOOR

FIRST FLOOR

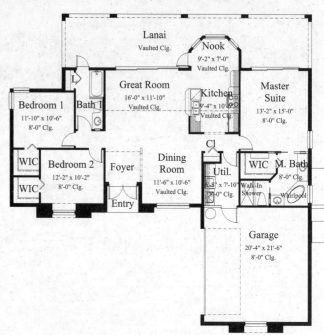

Lanai
Vaulted Clg.

Nook
9'-2" x 7'-0"
Vaulted Clg.

Great Room
16'-0" x 11'-10"
Vaulted Clg.

Kitchen
9'-4" x 10'-0"
Vaulted Clg.

Master Suite
13'-2" x 15'-0"
8'-0" Clg.

Bedroom 1
11'-10" x 10'-6"
8'-0" Clg.

Bath

Bedroom 2
12'-2" x 10'-2"
8'-0" Clg.

Foyer

Dining Room
11'-6" x 10'-6"
Vaulted Clg.

WIC

WIC

Cl

Util.

WIC

M. Bath
8'-0" Clg.

Walk-In Shower

Whirlpool

Entry

Garage
20'-4" x 21'-6"
8'-0" Clg.

plan# HPK0100319

STYLE: TRADITIONAL
SQUARE FOOTAGE: 1,515
BEDROOMS: 3
BATHROOMS: 2
WIDTH: 58' - 0"
DEPTH: 59' - 4"
FOUNDATION: SLAB

office/br
16 x 11

porch
38 x 14

eating
13 x 11

mbr
19 x 15
9' tray clg

util

storage

sto

br 3
12 x 11

built in entertainment center & library

living
23 x 20
12' clg

kit
18x12

3 car garage
32 x 22

br 2
16 x 12

grand foyer 19 x 6
12' clg

porch

dining
16 x 14
10' tray clg

bath

plan# HPK0100320

STYLE: TRADITIONAL
SQUARE FOOTAGE: 2,936
BEDROOMS: 4
BATHROOMS: 2½
WIDTH: 83' - 0"
DEPTH: 78' - 0"
FOUNDATION: SLAB

plan# HPK0100321

STYLE: SW CONTEMPORARY
SQUARE FOOTAGE: 3,105
BEDROOMS: 4
BATHROOMS: 3½
WIDTH: 66' - 0"
DEPTH: 91' - 8"
FOUNDATION: SLAB

SEARCH ONLINE @ EPLANS.COM

Spanish allure lends a magnificent quality to this Southwestern design. An inviting foyer leads to a formal dining room on the left and beamed-ceiling study on the right. Ahead, a unique ceiling treatment defines the living room. An oversized island and space for a six-burner range create divine haute cuisine in no time. An outdoor grill is great in any season. From the leisure room, enter the nearby guest suite or follow sliding glass doors to the veranda. The outstanding master suite opens through French doors; on the left, the bedroom includes outdoor access. To the right, walk-in closets and a whirlpool bath view the privacy garden.

plan# HPK0100322

STYLE: TRADITIONAL
SQUARE FOOTAGE: 2,394
BEDROOMS: 4
BATHROOMS: 2
WIDTH: 88' - 0"
DEPTH: 64' - 0"
FOUNDATION: CRAWLSPACE, SLAB

SEARCH ONLINE @ EPLANS.COM

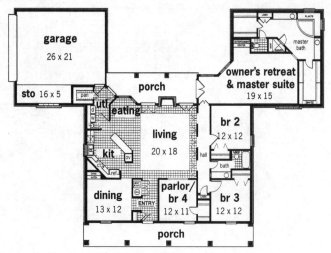

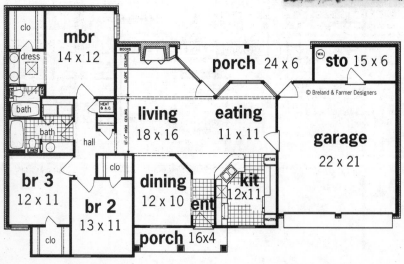

© Breland & Farmer Designers

plan# HPK0100323

STYLE: TRADITIONAL
SQUARE FOOTAGE: 1,507
BEDROOMS: 3
BATHROOMS: 2
WIDTH: 68' - 0"
DEPTH: 41' - 0"
FOUNDATION: CRAWLSPACE, SLAB

SEARCH ONLINE @ EPLANS.COM

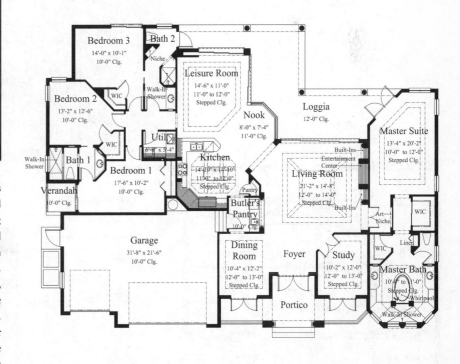

plan # HPK0100012

STYLE: SW CONTEMPORARY
SQUARE FOOTAGE: 2,908
BEDROOMS: 4
BATHROOMS: 3
WIDTH: 80' - 10"
DEPTH: 59' - 10"
FOUNDATION: SLAB

SEARCH ONLINE @ EPLANS.COM

Mediterranean influences grace the exterior of this contemporary Southwestern home. Enter past a grand portico to the sunburst-lit foyer; a study and dining room to either side both enjoy stepped ceilings and French doors. A convenient butler's pantry leads from the dining room to the exquisitely appointed kitchen. A sunny bayed nook lies between the living room, with a built-in entertainment center and leisure room. Three nearby bedrooms share two full baths. The right wing is entirely devoted to the master suite. Here, the comfortable bedroom accesses the rear lanai; for pure luxury, the private bath features an extravagant whirlpool tub and walk-in shower. A three-car garage completes the plan.

plan# HPK0100324

STYLE: TRADITIONAL
SQUARE FOOTAGE: 2,366
BEDROOMS: 4
BATHROOMS: 3
WIDTH: 50' - 0"
DEPTH: 86' - 0"
FOUNDATION: SLAB

SEARCH ONLINE @ EPLANS.COM

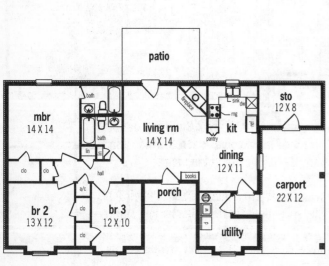

plan# HPK0100325

STYLE: TRADITIONAL
SQUARE FOOTAGE: 1,212
BEDROOMS: 3
BATHROOMS: 2
WIDTH: 60' - 0"
DEPTH: 31' - 0"
FOUNDATION: SLAB, CRAWLSPACE

SEARCH ONLINE @ EPLANS.COM

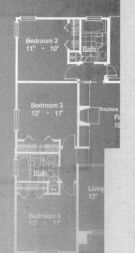

eplans.com

THE GATEWAY TO YOUR NEW HOME

Looking for more plans? Got questions? Try our one-stop home plans resource—eplans.com.

We'll help you streamline the plan selection process, so your dreams can become reality faster than you ever imagined. From choosing your home plan and ideal location to finding an experienced contractor, eplans.com will guide you every step of the way.

Mix and match! Explore! At eplans.com you can combine all your top criteria to find your perfect match. Search for your ideal home plan by any or all of the following:
> Number of bedrooms or baths,
> Total square feet,
> House style,
> Designer, and
> Cost.

With over 10,000 plans, the options are endless. Colonial, ranch, country, and Victorian are just a few of the house styles offered. Keep in mind your essential lifestyle features—whether to include a porch, fireplace, bonus room or main floor laundry room. And the garage—how many cars must it accommodate, if any? By filling out the preference page on eplans.com, we'll help you narrow your search. And, don't forget to enjoy a virtual home tour before any decisions are set in stone.

At eplans.com we'll make the building process a snap to understand. At the click of a button you'll find a complete building guide. And our eplan task planner will create a construction calendar just for you. Here you'll find links to tips and other valuable information to help you every step of the way—from choosing a site to moving day.

For your added convenience, our home plans experts are available for live, one-on-one chats at eplans.com. Building a home may seem like a complicated project, but it doesn't have to be—particularly if you'll let us help you from start to finish.

1 **BIGGEST & BEST**

1001 of our Best-Selling Plans in One Volume. 1,074 to 7,275 square feet. 704 pgs. $12.95 1K1

2 **ONE-STORY**

450 designs for all lifestyles. 810 to 5,400 square feet. 448 pgs. $9.95 OS2

3 **MORE ONE-STORY**

475 Superb One-Level Plans from 800 to 5,000 square feet. 448 pgs. $9.95 MO2

4 **TWO-STORY**

450 Best-Selling Designs for 1½ and 2-stories. 448 pgs. $9.95 TS2

5 **VACATION**

430 designs for Recreation, Retirement, and Leisure. 448 pgs. $9.95 VS3

6 **HILLSIDE**

208 designs for Split-Levels, Bi-Levels, Multi-Levels, and Walkouts. 224 pgs. $9.95 HH

7 **FARMHOUSE**

300 fresh designs from Classic to Modern. 320 pgs. $10.95 FCP

8 **COUNTRY HOUSES**

208 unique home plans that combine Traditional Style and Modern Livability. 224 pgs. $9.95 CN

9 **BUDGET-SMART**

200 Efficient Plans from 7 Top Designers, that you can really afford to build! 224 pgs. $8.95 BS

10 **BARRIER-FREE**

Over 1,700 products and 51 plans for Accessible Living. 128 pgs. $15.95 UH

11 **ENCYCLOPEDIA**

500 exceptional plans for all styles and budgets— The Best Book of its Kind! 528 pgs. $9.95 ENC3

12 **SUN COUNTRY**

175 Designs from Coastal Cottages to Stunning Southwesterns. 192 pgs. $9.95 SUN

13 **AFFORDABLE**

300 modest plans for savvy homebuyers. 256 pgs. $9.95 AH2

14 **VICTORIAN**

210 striking Victorian and Farmhouse designs from today's top designers. 224 pgs. $15.95 VDH2

15 **ESTATE**

Dream big! Eighteen designers showcase their biggest and best plans. 224 pgs. $16.95 EDH3

16 **LUXURY**

170 lavish designs, over 50% brand-new plans added to a most elegant collection. 192 pgs. $12.95 LD3

17 **WILLIAM E. POOLE**

100 classic house plans from William E. Poole. 224 pgs. $17.95 WP2

18 **HUGE SELECTION**

650 home plans— from Cottages to Mansions 464 pgs. $8.95 650

19 **SOUTHWEST**

120 designs in Santa Fe, Spanish, and Contemporary Styles. 192 pgs. $14.95 SI

20 **COUNTRY CLASSICS**

130 Best-Selling Home Plans from Donald A. Gardner. 192 pgs. $17.95 DAG2

21 **COTTAGES**

245 Delightful retreats from 825 to 3,500 square feet. 256 pgs. $10.95 COOL

22 **CONTEMPORARY**

The most complete and imaginative collection of contemporary designs available. 256 pgs. $10.95 CM2

23 **FRENCH COUNTRY**

Live every day in the French countryside using these plans, landscapes and interiors. 192 pgs. $14.95 PN

24 **SOUTHWESTERN**

138 designs that capture the spirit of the Southwest. 144 pgs. $10.95 SW

25 **SHINGLE-STYLE**

155 home plans from Classic Colonials to Breezy Bungalows. 192 pgs. $12.95 SNG

26 **NEIGHBORHOOD**

170 designs with the feel of main street America. 192 pgs. $12.95 TND

27 **CRAFTSMAN**

170 Home plans in the Craftsman and Bungalow style. 192 pgs. $12.95 CC

28 **GRAND VISTAS**

200 Homes with a View. 224 pgs. $10.95 GV

29 **MULTI-FAMILY**

115 Duplex, Multiplex & Townhome Designs. 128 pgs. $17.95 MFH

30 **WATERFRONT**

200 designs perfect for your Waterside Wonderland. 208 pgs. $10.95 WF

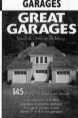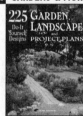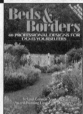

COPYRIGHT DOS & DON'TS

Blueprints for residential construction (or working drawings, as they are often called in the industry) are copyrighted intellectual property, protected under the terms of United States Copyright Law and, therefore, cannot be copied legally for use in building. However, we've made it easy for you to get what you need to build your home, without violating copyright law. Following are some guidelines to help you obtain the right number of copies for your chosen blueprint design.

COPYRIGHT DO

■ Do purchase enough copies of the blueprints to satisfy building requirements. As a rule for a home or project plan, you will need a set for yourself, two or three for your builder and sub-contractors, two for the local building department, and one to three for your mortgage lender. You may want to check with your local building department or your builder to see how many they need before you purchase. You may need to buy eight to 10 sets; note that some areas of the country require purchase of vellums (also called reproducibles) instead of blueprints. Vellums can be written on and changed more easily than blueprints. Also, remember, plans are only good for one-time construction.

■ Do consider reverse blueprints if you want to flop the plan. Lettering and numbering will appear backward, but the reversed sets will help you and your builder better visualize the design.

■ Do take advantage of multiple-set discounts at the time you place your order. Usually, purchasing additional sets after you receive your initial order is not as cost-effective.

■ Do take advantage of vellums. Though they are a little more expensive, they can be changed, copied, and used for one-time construction of a home. You will receive a copyright release letter with your vellums that will allow you to have them copied.

■ Do talk with one of our professional service representatives before placing your order. They can give you great advice about what packages are available for your chosen design and what will work best for your particular situation.

COPYRIGHT DON'T

■ Don't think you should purchase only one set of blueprints for a building project. One is fine if you want to study the plan closely, but will not be enough for actual building.

■ Don't expect your builder or a copy center to make copies of standard blueprints. They cannot legally—most copy centers are aware of this.

■ Don't purchase standard blueprints if you know you'll want to make changes to the plans; vellums are a better value.

■ Don't use blueprints or vellums more than one time. Additional fees apply if you want to build more than one time from a set of drawings. ■

hanley ▲ wood
HomePlanners

ORDERING IS EASY

HANLEY WOOD HOMEPLANNERS HAS EVERYTHING YOU NEED to build the home of your dreams, and with more than 50 years of experience in the industry, we make it as easy as possible for you to reach those goals. Just follow the steps on these pages and you'll receive a high-quality, ready-to-build set of home blueprints, plus everything else you need to make your home-building effort a success.

WHERE TO BEGIN?
1. CHOOSE YOUR PLAN

■ Browsing magazines, books, and eplans.com can be an exciting and rewarding part of the home-building process. As you search, make a list of the things you want in your dream home—everything from number of bedrooms and baths to details like fireplaces or a home office.

■ Take the time to consider your lot and your neighborhood, and how the home you choose will fit with both. And think about the future—how might your needs change if you plan to live in this house for five, 10, or 20 years?

■ With thousands of plans available, chances are that you'll have no trouble discovering your dream home. If you find something that's almost perfect, our Customization Program can help make it exactly what you want.

■ Most important, be sure to enjoy the process of picking out your new home!

WHAT YOU'LL GET WITH YOUR ORDER

Each designer's blueprint set is unique, but they all provide everything you'll need to build your home. Here are some standard elements you can expect to find in your plans:

1. FRONT PERSPECTIVE
This artist's sketch of the exterior of the house gives you an idea of how the house will look when built and landscaped.

2. FOUNDATION PLANS
This sheet shows the foundation layout including support walls, excavated and unexcavated areas, if any, and foundation notes. If your plan features slab construction rather than a basement, the plan shows footings and details for a monolithic slab. This page, or another in the set, may include a sample plot plan for locating your house on a building site.

3. DETAILED FLOOR PLANS
These plans show the layout of each floor of the house. Rooms and interior spaces are carefully dimensioned and keys are given for cross-section details provided later in the plans. The positions of electrical outlets and switches are shown.

4. HOUSE CROSS-SECTIONS
Large-scale views show sections or cutaways of the foundation, interior walls, exterior walls, floors, stairways, and roof details. Additional cross-sections may show important changes in floor, ceiling, or roof heights, or the relationship of one level to another. Extremely valuable during construction, these sections show exactly how the various parts of the house fit together.

5. INTERIOR ELEVATIONS
These elevations, or drawings, show the design and placement of kitchen and bathroom cabinets, laundry areas, fireplaces, bookcases, and other built-ins. Little extras, such as mantelpiece and wainscoting drawings, plus molding sections, provide details that give your home that custom touch.

6. EXTERIOR ELEVATIONS
Every blueprint set comes with drawings of the front exterior, and may include the rear and sides of your house as well. These drawings give necessary notes on exterior materials and finishes. Particular attention is given to cornice detail, brick, and stone accents or other finish items that make your home unique.

ORDER 24 HOURS!
1-800-521-6797

BLUEPRINT PRICE SCHEDULE

PRICE TIERS	1-SET STUDY PACKAGE	4-SET BUILDING PACKAGE	8-SET BUILDING PACKAGE	1-SET REPRODUCIBLE*
P1	$20	$50	$90	$140
P2	$40	$70	$110	$160
P3	$70	$100	$140	$190
P4	$100	$130	$170	$220
P5	$140	$170	$210	$270
P6	$180	$210	$250	$310
A1	$440	$490	$540	$660
A2	$480	$530	$580	$720
A3	$530	$590	$650	$800
A4	$575	$645	$705	$870
C1	$625	$695	$755	$935
C2	$670	$740	$800	$1000
C3	$715	$790	$855	$1075
C4	$765	$840	$905	$1150
L1	$870	$965	$1050	$1300
L2	$945	$1040	$1125	$1420
L3	$1050	$1150	$1240	$1575
L4	$1155	$1260	$1355	$1735
SQ1				.35/SQ. FT.

PRICES SUBJECT TO CHANGE

* REQUIRES A FAX NUMBER

plan
READY TO ORDER

Once you've found your plan, get your plan number and turn to the following pages to find its price tier. Use the corresponding code and the Blueprint Price Schedule above to determine your price for a variety of blueprint packages.

Keep in mind that you'll need multiple sets to fulfill building requirements, and only reproducible sets may be altered or duplicated.

To the right you'll find prices for additional and reverse blueprint sets. Also note in the following pages whether your home has a corresponding Deck or Landscape Plan, and whether you can order our Quote One® cost-to-build information or a Materials List for your plan.

IT'S EASY TO ORDER JUST VISIT EPLANS.COM OR CALL TOLL-FREE 1-800-521-6797

PRICE SCHEDULE FOR ADDITIONAL OPTIONS

OPTIONS FOR PLANS IN TIERS P1-P6	COSTS
ADDITIONAL IDENTICAL BLUEPRINTS FOR "P1-P6" PLANS	$10 PER SET
REVERSE BLUEPRINTS (MIRROR IMAGE) FOR "P1-P6" PLANS	$10 FEE PER ORDER
1 SET OF DECK CONSTRUCTION DETAILS	$14.95 EACH
DECK CONSTRUCTION PACKAGE (INCLUDES 1 SET OF "P1-P6" PLANS, PLUS 1 SET STANDARD DECK CONSTRUCTION DETAILS)	ADD $10 TO BUILDING PACKAGE PRICE

OPTIONS FOR PLANS IN TIERS A1-SQ1	COSTS
ADDITIONAL IDENTICAL BLUEPRINTS IN SAME ORDER FOR "A1-L4" PLANS	$50 PER SET
REVERSE BLUEPRINTS (MIRROR IMAGE) WITH 4- OR 8-SET ORDER FOR "A1-L4" PLANS	$50 FEE PER ORDER
SPECIFICATION OUTLINES	$10 EACH
MATERIALS LISTS FOR "A1-SQ1" PLANS	$70 EACH

IMPORTANT EXTRAS	COSTS
ELECTRICAL, PLUMBING, CONSTRUCTION, AND MECHANICAL DETAIL SETS	$14.95 EACH; ANY TWO $22.95; ANY THREE $29.95; ALL FOUR $39.95
HOME FURNITURE PLANNER	$15.95 EACH
REAR ELEVATION	$10 EACH
QUOTE ONE® SUMMARY COST REPORT	$29.95
QUOTE ONE® DETAILED COST ESTIMATE (FOR MORE DETAILS ABOUT QUOTE ONE®, SEE STEP 3.)	$60

IMPORTANT NOTE

Source Key

HPK01

■ THE 1-SET STUDY PACKAGE IS MARKED "NOT FOR CONSTRUCTION."

PLAN #	PRICE TIER	PAGE	MATERIALS LIST
HPK0100001	C1	68	
HPK0100002	C2	170	
HPK0100003	C1	49	
HPK0100004	A3	130	
HPK0100005	SQ1	6	
HPK0100006	C2	232	
HPK0100007	C1	114	Y
HPK0100008	A2	66	
HPK0100009	C1	117	
HPK0100010	C2	9	Y
HPK0100011	A4	18	Y
HPK0100012	C3	243	
HPK0100013	L1	209	
HPK0100014	L3	5	
HPK0100015	C1	7	
HPK0100016	SQ1	8	
HPK0100017	SQ1	10	
HPK0100018	C2	11	
HPK0100019	C3	12	
HPK0100020	C3	13	
HPK0100021	C2	14	
HPK0100022	C2	15	
HPK0100023	C3	16	
HPK0100024	C1	17	Y
HPK0100025	C2	19	Y
HPK0100026	A3	20	Y
HPK0100027	A4	21	Y
HPK0100028	A4	22	Y
HPK0100029	A4	22	Y
HPK0100030	A4	23	Y
HPK0100031	C1	24	Y
HPK0100032	A4	24	Y
HPK0100033	C1	25	Y
HPK0100034	A4	26	Y
HPK0100035	A3	26	Y
HPK0100036	C2	27	Y
HPK0100037	C1	28	Y
HPK0100038	C1	29	Y
HPK0100039	C2	30	
HPK0100040	C1	31	
HPK0100041	C3	32	
HPK0100042	C3	32	
HPK0100043	C2	33	
HPK0100044	C3	34	
HPK0100045	C1	35	
HPK0100046	C2	36	
HPK0100047	C2	36	
HPK0100048	C3	37	
HPK0100049	C2	38	
HPK0100050	C2	39	
HPK0100051	A3	40	
HPK0100052	A3	40	
HPK0100053	A3	41	
HPK0100054	A4	42	Y
HPK0100055	A3	42	
HPK0100056	A2	43	Y
HPK0100057	A3	44	
HPK0100058	A4	44	
HPK0100059	A3	45	Y
HPK0100060	A4	46	Y
HPK0100061	A2	46	Y
HPK0100062	C2	47	
HPK0100063	A2	48	
HPK0100064	C1	50	Y
HPK0100065	C1	51	Y
HPK0100066	C1	52	Y
HPK0100067	C1	52	Y
HPK0100068	C1	53	Y
HPK0100069	C1	54	Y
HPK0100070	A3	54	Y
HPK0100071	C1	55	Y
HPK0100072	C1	56	Y
HPK0100073	C1	56	Y
HPK0100074	A4	57	Y
HPK0100075	C1	58	
HPK0100076	C1	58	
HPK0100077	C1	59	
HPK0100078	C3	60	Y
HPK0100079	C2	60	Y
HPK0100080	C3	61	
HPK0100081	C3	62	
HPK0100082	C3	62	
HPK0100083	C1	63	Y
HPK0100084	A2	64	Y
HPK0100085	A3	64	Y
HPK0100086	A2	65	
HPK0100087	C1	67	Y
HPK0100088	C2	69	
HPK0100089	C1	70	Y
HPK0100090	A4	70	Y
HPK0100091	C1	71	Y
HPK0100092	C2	72	Y
HPK0100093	A3	72	Y
HPK0100094	C1	73	Y
HPK0100095	A4	74	Y
HPK0100096	A4	74	Y
HPK0100097	A3	75	Y
HPK0100098	C4	75	Y
HPK0100099	A4	76	Y
HPK0100100	C2	77	Y
HPK0100101	C2	78	Y
HPK0100102	C1	78	Y
HPK0100103	A3	79	Y
HPK0100104	A2	79	Y
HPK0100105	C3	80	
HPK0100106	C3	80	
HPK0100107	C2	81	
HPK0100108	A3	82	Y
HPK0100109	A3	82	
HPK0100110	C1	83	Y
HPK0100111	A4	84	Y
HPK0100112	A1	84	Y
HPK0100113	C2	85	Y
HPK0100114	C1	86	Y
HPK0100115	A4	86	Y
HPK0100116	C2	87	Y
HPK0100117	A4	88	Y
HPK0100118	A2	88	
HPK0100119	C1	89	Y
HPK0100120	C1	90	Y
HPK0100121	A4	90	Y
HPK0100122	A3	91	Y
HPK0100123	A3	92	Y
HPK0100124	A3	92	Y
HPK0100125	A4	93	Y
HPK0100126	A3	93	Y
HPK0100127	A3	94	Y
HPK0100128	A3	94	Y
HPK0100129	A4	95	Y
HPK0100130	A4	95	Y
HPK0100131	C2	96	
HPK0100132	C1	96	Y
HPK0100133	C3	97	Y
HPK0100134	C1	98	
HPK0100135	A2	98	
HPK0100136	C1	99	
HPK0100137	A3	100	
HPK0100138	A3	100	
HPK0100139	C1	101	Y
HPK0100140	A3	102	Y
HPK0100141	A3	102	Y
HPK0100142	L1	103	Y
HPK0100143	A3	104	
HPK0100144	A2	104	
HPK0100145	A4	105	Y
HPK0100146	C1	106	Y
HPK0100147	A4	106	
HPK0100148	C3	107	
HPK0100149	A4	108	Y
HPK0100150	A3	109	Y
HPK0100151	A4	110	
HPK0100152	C3	111	
HPK0100153	C2	112	
HPK0100154	C3	113	
HPK0100155	C2	114	
HPK0100156	C1	115	
HPK0100157	C3	116	
HPK0100158	C2	116	Y
HPK0100159	A3	118	Y
HPK0100160	C4	118	Y
HPK0100161	A4	119	Y
HPK0100162	C2	120	Y
HPK0100163	C2	121	Y
HPK0100164	C1	122	Y
HPK0100165	A3	122	Y

PLAN #	PRICE TIER	PAGE	MATERIALS LIST
HPK0100166	C2	123	Y
HPK0100167	C1	124	
HPK0100168	A2	124	
HPK0100169	C4	125	Y
HPK0100170	C3	126	
HPK0100171	C3	126	
HPK0100172	C2	127	Y
HPK0100173	A4	128	Y
HPK0100174	A3	129	Y
HPK0100175	A3	130	
HPK0100176	C2	131	
HPK0100177	A2	132	Y
HPK0100178	A4	133	
HPK0100179	A3	134	Y
HPK0100180	A3	134	Y
HPK0100181	C2	135	
HPK0100182	C2	136	
HPK0100183	C1	136	
HPK0100184	A4	137	
HPK0100185	A3	138	
HPK0100186	A4	138	
HPK0100187	A4	139	
HPK0100188	C1	140	
HPK0100189	A4	141	
HPK0100190	A4	142	
HPK0100191	C1	142	
HPK0100192	A4	143	
HPK0100193	C2	144	
HPK0100194	C1	145	
HPK0100195	C3	146	
HPK0100196	C3	147	
HPK0100197	A3	148	Y
HPK0100198	A3	148	Y
HPK0100199	A3	149	Y
HPK0100200	A4	150	
HPK0100201	A3	150	
HPK0100202	C4	151	Y
HPK0100203	A3	152	Y
HPK0100204	C1	153	Y
HPK0100205	C1	154	
HPK0100206	C3	155	
HPK0100207	C4	156	
HPK0100208	C4	157	
HPK0100209	C4	158	Y
HPK0100210	C4	159	
HPK0100211	C3	160	
HPK0100212	C1	160	
HPK0100213	C4	161	
HPK0100214	A4	162	Y
HPK0100215	A4	162	Y
HPK0100216	C4	163	
HPK0100217	SQ1	164	
HPK0100218	L1	164	
HPK0100219	C3	165	
HPK0100220	L1	166	

PLAN #	PRICE TIER	PAGE	MATERIALS LIST
HPK0100221	A3	166	
HPK0100222	C2	167	
HPK0100223	C2	168	
HPK0100224	C2	168	
HPK0100225	C4	169	
HPK0100226	L1	170	
HPK0100227	C2	171	
HPK0100228	C2	172	
HPK0100229	C3	173	
HPK0100230	L1	174	Y
HPK0100231	C3	174	Y
HPK0100232	L1	175	
HPK0100233	C2	176	
HPK0100234	C3	176	
HPK0100235	C2	177	
HPK0100236	C4	178	
HPK0100237	C4	179	
HPK0100238	L1	180	
HPK0100239	C2	180	
HPK0100240	L2	181	
HPK0100241	A4	182	
HPK0100242	A3	182	
HPK0100243	C2	183	
HPK0100244	C3	184	Y
HPK0100245	C3	185	
HPK0100246	C2	186	
HPK0100247	C3	186	
HPK0100248	C2	187	
HPK0100249	C2	188	
HPK0100250	C1	188	
HPK0100251	A4	189	Y
HPK0100252	L1	190	
HPK0100253	C3	190	
HPK0100254	C4	191	
HPK0100255	A4	192	
HPK0100256	C1	192	
HPK0100257	C2	193	Y
HPK0100258	C1	194	
HPK0100259	C3	195	
HPK0100260	L1	196	
HPK0100261	C3	197	Y
HPK0100262	C4	198	
HPK0100263	C1	199	Y
HPK0100264	C4	200	
HPK0100265	C2	200	
HPK0100266	C4	201	
HPK0100267	C2	202	
HPK0100268	A3	202	Y
HPK0100269	C3	203	Y
HPK0100270	C2	204	
HPK0100271	C1	204	
HPK0100272	L1	205	
HPK0100273	C1	206	Y
HPK0100274	C4	206	
HPK0100275	C3	207	Y

PLAN #	PRICE TIER	PAGE	MATERIALS LIST
HPK0100276	C2	208	
HPK0100277	L1	208	
HPK0100278	C3	210	
HPK0100279	C2	210	
HPK0100280	C2	211	
HPK0100281	C2	212	
HPK0100282	C1	212	
HPK0100283	C3	213	
HPK0100284	A4	214	Y
HPK0100285	A4	214	Y
HPK0100286	A4	215	Y
HPK0100287	C1	216	Y
HPK0100288	C2	216	
HPK0100289	A4	217	Y
HPK0100290	C1	218	Y
HPK0100291	A3	218	
HPK0100292	C4	219	
HPK0100293	C3	220	
HPK0100294	C3	220	
HPK0100295	A4	221	Y
HPK0100296	C2	222	Y
HPK0100297	C4	223	
HPK0100298	C4	224	
HPK0100299	C4	225	
HPK0100300	C3	226	
HPK0100301	C2	227	
HPK0100302	SQ1	228	
HPK0100303	C3	228	
HPK0100304	C3	229	
HPK0100305	C1	230	
HPK0100306	A4	230	
HPK0100307	C1	231	
HPK0100308	A4	232	
HPK0100309	L1	233	
HPK0100310	A4	234	Y
HPK0100311	C3	234	Y
HPK0100312	C2	235	Y
HPK0100313	C2	236	Y
HPK0100314	A4	236	Y
HPK0100315	C4	237	
HPK0100316	L1	238	
HPK0100317	C4	238	
HPK0100318	C4	239	
HPK0100319	C1	240	
HPK0100320	C1	240	
HPK0100321	C4	241	
HPK0100322	A4	242	Y
HPK0100323	A3	242	Y
HPK0100324	A4	244	
HPK0100325	A2	244	

WE OFFER A VARIETY OF USEFUL TOOLS THAT CAN HELP YOU THROUGH EVERY STEP OF THE home-building process. From our Materials List to our Customization Program, these items let you put our experience to work for you to ensure that you get exactly what you want out of your dream house.

MATERIALS LIST

For many of the designs in our portfolio, we offer a customized list of materials that helps you plan and estimate the cost of your new home. The Materials List outlines the quantity, type, and size of materials needed to build your house (with the exception of mechanical system items). Included are framing lumber, windows and doors, kitchen and bath cabinetry, rough and finished hardware, and much more. This handy list helps you or your builder cost out materials and serves as a reference sheet when you're compiling bids.

SPECIFICATION OUTLINE

This valuable 16-page document can play an important role in the construction of your house. Fill it in with your builder, and you'll have a step-by-step chronicle of 166 stages or items crucial to the building process. It provides a comprehensive review of the construction process and helps you choose materials.

QUOTE ONE®

The Quote One® system, which helps estimate the cost of building select designs in your zip code, is available in two parts: the Summary Cost Report and the Material Cost Report.

The Summary Cost Report, the first element in the package, breaks down the cost of your home into various categories based on building materials, labor, and installation, and includes three grades of construction: Budget, Standard, and Custom. Make even more informed decisions about your project with the second element of our package, the Material Cost Report. The material and installation cost is shown for each of more than 1,000 line items provided in the standard-grade Materials List, which is included with this tool. Additional space is included for estimates from contractors and subcontractors, such as for mechanical materials, which are not included in our packages.

If you are interested in a plan that does not indicate the availability of Quote One®, please call and ask our sales representatives, who can verify the status for you.

CUSTOMIZATION PROGRAM

If the plan you love needs something changed to make it perfect, our customization experts will ensure that you get nothing less than your dream home. Purchase a reproducible set of plans for the home you choose, and we'll send you our easy-to-use customization request form via e-mail or fax. For just $50, our customization experts will provide an estimate for your requested revisions, and once it's approved, that charge will be applied to your changes. You'll receive either five sets or a reproducible master of your modified design and any other options you select.

BUILDING BASICS

If you want to know more about building techniques—and deal more confidently with your subcontractors—we offer four useful detail sheets. These sheets provide non-plan-specific general information, but are excellent tools that will add to your understanding of Plumbing Details, Electrical Details, Construction Details, and Mechanical Details. These fact-filled sheets will help answer many of your building questions, and help you learn what questions to ask your builder and subcontractors.

GETTY IMAGES

HANDS-ON HOME FURNITURE PLANNER

Effectively plan the space in your home using our Hands-On Home Furniture Planner. It's fun and easy—no more moving heavy pieces of furniture to see how the room will go together. The kit includes reusable peel-and-stick furniture templates that fit on a 12"x18" laminated layout board—enough space to lay out every room in your house.

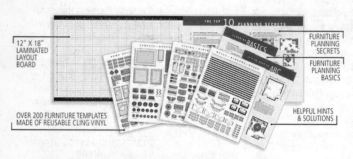

12" X 18" LAMINATED LAYOUT BOARD

THE TOP 10 PLANNING SECRETS

FURNITURE PLANNING SECRETS

FURNITURE PLANNING BASICS

HELPFUL HINTS & SOLUTIONS

OVER 200 FURNITURE TEMPLATES MADE OF REUSABLE CLING VINYL

DECK BLUEPRINT PACKAGE

Many of the homes in this book can be enhanced with a professionally designed Home Planners Deck Plan. Those plans marked with a **D** have a corresponding deck plan, sold separately, which includes a Deck Plan Frontal Sheet, Deck Framing and Floor Plans, Deck Elevations, and a Deck Materials List. A Standard Deck Details Package, also available, provides all the how-to information necessary for building any deck. Get both the Deck Plan and the Standard Deck Details Package for one low price in our Complete Deck Building Package.

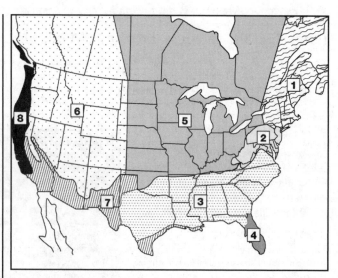

LANDSCAPE BLUEPRINT PACKAGE

Homes marked with an **L** in this book have a front-yard Landscape Plan that is complementary in design to the house plan. These comprehensive Landscape Blueprint Packages include a Frontal Sheet, Plan View, Regionalized Plant & Materials List, a sheet on Planting and Maintaining Your Landscape, Zone Maps, and a Plant Size and Description Guide. Each set of blueprints is a full 18" x 24" with clear, complete instructions in easy-to-read type.

Our Landscape Plans are available with a Plant & Materials List adapted by horticultural experts to eight regions of the country. Please specify from the following regions when ordering your plan:

Region 1: Northeast
Region 2: Mid-Atlantic
Region 3: Deep South
Region 4: Florida & Gulf Coast
Region 5: Midwest
Region 6: Rocky Mountains
Region 7: Southern California & Desert Southwest
Region 8: Northern California & Pacific Northwest

OUR EXCHANGE POLICY

With the exception of reproducible plan orders, we will exchange your entire first order for an equal or greater number of blueprints within our plan collection within **60 days** of the original order. The entire content of your original order must be returned before an exchange will be processed. Please call our customer service department at 1-888-690-1116 for your return authorization number and shipping instructions. If the returned blueprints look used, redlined, or copied, we will not honor your exchange. Fees for exchanging your blueprints are as follows: 20% of the amount of the original order, plus the difference in cost if exchanging for a design in a higher price bracket or less the difference in cost if exchanging for a design in a lower price bracket. (Reproducible blueprints are not exchangeable or refundable.) Please call for current postage and handling prices. Shipping and handling charges are not refundable.

ABOUT REPRODUCIBLES

Reproducibles (often called "vellums") are the most convenient way to order your blueprints. In any building process, you will need multiple copies of your blueprints for your builder, subcontractors, lenders, and the local building department. In addition, you may want or need to make changes to the original design. Such changes should be made only by a licensed architect or engineer. When you purchase reproducibles, you will receive a copyright release letter that allows you to have them altered and copied. You will want to purchase a reproducible plan if you plan to make any changes, whether by using our convenient Customization Program or going to a local architect.

ABOUT REVERSE BLUEPRINTS

Although lettering and dimensions will appear backward, reverses will be a useful aid if you decide to flop the plan. See Price Schedule and Plans Index for pricing.

ARCHITECTURAL AND ENGINEERING SEALS

Some cities and states now require that a licensed architect or engineer review and "seal" a blueprint, or officially approve it, prior to construction. Prior to application for a building permit or the start of actual construction, we strongly advise that you consult your local building official who can tell you if such a review is required.

ABOUT THE DESIGNS

The architects and designers whose work appears in this publication are among America's leading residential designers. Each plan was designed to meet the requirements of a nationally recognized model

building code in effect at the time and place the plan was drawn. Because national building codes change from time to time, plans may not fully comply with any such code at the time they are sold to a customer. In addition, building officials may not accept these plans as final construction documents of record as the plans may need to be modified and additional drawings and details added to suit local conditions and requirements. Purchasers should consult a licensed architect or engineer, and their local building official, before starting any construction related to these plans.

LOCAL BUILDING CODES AND ZONING REQUIREMENTS

At the time of creation, these plans are drawn to specifications published by the Building Officials and Code Administrators (BOCA) International, Inc.; the Southern Building Code Congress International, (SBCCI) Inc.; the International Conference of Building Officials (ICBO); or the Council of American Building Officials (CABO). These plans are designed to meet or exceed national building standards. Because of the great differences in geography and climate throughout the United States and Canada, each state, county, and municipality has its own building codes, zone requirements, ordinances, and building regulations. Your plan may need to be modified to comply with local requirements. In addition, you may need to obtain permits or inspections from local governments before and in the course of construction. We authorize the use of the blueprints on the express condition that you consult a local licensed architect or engineer of your choice prior to beginning construction and strictly comply with all local building codes, zoning requirements, and other applicable laws, regulations, ordinances, and requirements. Notice: Plans for homes to be built in Nevada must be redrawn by a Nevada-registered professional. Consult your building official for more information on this subject.

TERMS AND CONDITIONS

These designs are protected under the terms of United States Copyright Law and may not be copied or reproduced in any way, by any means, unless you have purchased reproducibles which clearly indicate your right to copy or reproduce. We authorize the use of your chosen design as an aid in the construction of one single- or multi-family home only. You may not use this design to build a second or multiple dwellings without purchasing another blueprint or blueprints or paying additional design fees.

HOW MANY BLUEPRINTS DO YOU NEED?

Although a four-set building package may satisfy many states, cities, and counties, some plans may

require certain changes. For your convenience, we have developed a reproducible plan, which allows you to take advantage of our Customization Program, or to have a local professional modify and make up to 10 copies of your revised plan. As our plans are all copyright protected, with your purchase of the reproducible, we will supply you with a copyright release letter. The number of copies you may need: 1 for owner, 3 for builder, 2 for local building department, and 1-3 sets for your mortgage lender.

DISCLAIMER

The designers we work with have put substantial care and effort into the creation of their blueprints. However, because we cannot provide on-site consultation, supervision, and control over actual construction, and because of the great variance in local building requirements, building practices, and soil, seismic, weather, and other conditions, **WE MAKE NO WARRANTY OF ANY KIND, EXPRESS OR IMPLIED, WITH RESPECT TO THE CONTENT OR USE OF THE BLUEPRINTS, INCLUDING BUT NOT LIMITED TO ANY WARRANTY OF MERCHANTABILITY OR OF FITNESS FOR A PARTICULAR PURPOSE. ITEMS, PRICES, TERMS, AND CONDITIONS ARE SUBJECT TO CHANGE WITHOUT NOTICE.**

IT'S EASY TO ORDER JUST VISIT EPLANS.COM OR CALL TOLL-FREE 1-800-521-6797

OPEN 24 HOURS, 7 DAYS A WEEK
If we receive your order by 3:00 p.m. EST, Monday-Friday, we'll process it and ship within two business days. When ordering by phone, please have your credit card or check information ready.

CANADIAN CUSTOMERS
Order Toll Free 1-877-223-6389

ONLINE ORDERING
Go to: www.eplans.com

After you have received your order, call our customer service experts at 1-888-690-1116 if you have any questions.

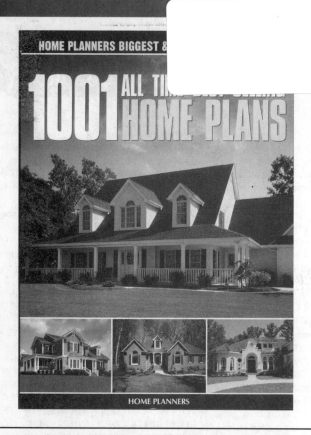
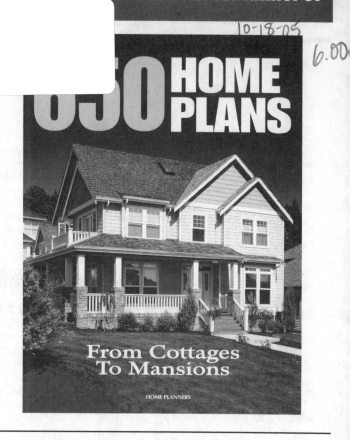
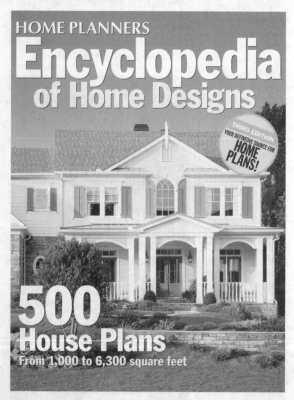